C000007025

BLACKBIRDS BAKED IN A PIE

(Memories of Rozinante)

EUGENE BARTER

With drawings by Mary Jose

BLACKBIRDS BAKED IN A PIE

Copyright © 2013 by Eugene Barter
Cover design and Illustrations © 2013 by Mary Jose

The right of Eugene Barter to be identified as the author of this work
has been asserted by her in accordance with the Copyright, Designs
and Patents Act 1988.

This is a work of memoir. Names and placenames have been changed
as a courtesy.

All Rights reserved. No part of this publication may be reproduced,
stored in a retrieval system, or transmitted, in any form or by any
means without the prior written consent of the publisher and copyright owner, nor be otherwise circulated in any form of binding or
cover other than that in which it is published and without a similar
condition being imposed on the subsequent purchaser.

ISBN # 978-1-907984-16-7

First published in Great Britain in 2013 by Sunpenny Publishing
www.sunpenny.com
(Sunpenny Publishing Group)

MORE BOOKS FROM THE SUNPENNY GROUP:

Dance of Eagles, by JS Holloway
The Mountains Between, by Julie McGowan
Just One More Summer, by Julie McGowan
My Sea is Wide, by Rowland Evans
Going Astray, by Christine Moore
Blue Freedom, by Sandra Peut
Embracing Change, by Debbie Roome
A Flight Delayed, by KC Lemmer
A Little Book of Pleasures, by William Wood
The Skipper's Child, by Valerie Poore
Watery Ways, by Valerie Poore
Far Out: Sailing into a Disappearing World, by Corinna Weyreter
Bridge to Nowhere, by Stephanie Parker McKean
Uncharted Waters, by Sara DuBose
Breaking the Circle, by Althea Barr

*To my family and friends, whose love and support
made the French adventure such fun!
– and to entente cordiale.*

Every man has two countries: his own, and France.

– Thomas Jefferson, America's 3rd President

*J'ai toujours attaché une enorme importance à la
nourriture, à la preparation des aliments. J'y vois
une forme de savoir-vivre, de savoir-aimer.*

– Régine Deforges

Table of Contents

Preface

Running *Rozinante,* my guest house in France, was a progressive experience through a long haul of trial and error seeking refinement and possible perfection. Not that I believe perfection is the ultimate goal, since personal taste is reflected in the ultimate choice of recipe and *Rozinante* was a special experience of catering for many different nationalities, although principally French and British. There was the added incentive of trying to prove to the French that British cooking was not as bad as they feared and every French compliment after a meal was music to my ears.

"Where do you get your recipes from?" a friend, a former opera singer with a life-time of exotic meals behind her, asked me after a party recently and without hesitation I replied, "From seven years of running a guest house in the French Pyrenees." But lying in bed that night, when one's thoughts circulate around the day's events, I realised that my response was only partly true and what I should have said quite simply was, *From my mother,* because it is there that an interest and love of food and cooking commences and continues throughout one's life and my dear mother not only loved cooking but enjoyed the fruits of her labours – as her weight testified.

Where to begin?

Well, at the beginning of course, and growing up in Wales in the 1930s there was hardship due to economic recession, just as the War, later in the 1940s, dictated the circumstances of what there was to eat. When I was young

1

most families had allotments and grew their own fruit and vegetables, and my earliest memory of really enjoying food was a plateful of freshly picked and cooked garden peas with a knob of butter and a thick wedge of my mother's own brown, home-baked bread. Equally delicious was a plate of mashed swede, served in the same way. Breakfast often consisted of the crust of the loaf smothered in 'dripping', the solidified fat from the Sunday meat roast.

From the War years and rationing came the enduring experience of eating offal, which, unlike meat, was not rationed. Hearts, livers, kidneys, sweetbreads, brains, tripe, sheep's head, and pigs' trotters and ears – all appeared regularly and were much enjoyed. It grieved me that I could never serve such dishes at *Rozinante,* since modern tastes are geared towards convenience and fast foods, palates often having been neutralised to reject all strong tasting food. Nevertheless, guests thoroughly enjoyed eating a first course of *charcuterie* and *pâté de campagne,* which relied heavily on the offal I have just described! Fortunately, in many parts of France traditional regional cooking prevails and menu boards outside restaurants will often offer offal dishes of kidneys, liver, pigs' feet and tripe, which are delicious.

Apart from offal, during the War it was 'corned beef hash' that made repeated and welcome appearances. This consisted of a tin of corned beef mixed with mashed potatoes and fried onions, baked in the oven with cheese and slices of tomatoes on top. Along with rabbit pie it was a great favourite, only replaced by tins of Spam once the Americans arrived on British shores, since slices of Spam could be fried, dipped in batter, chopped up on rice or just served cold with salad. We had never tasted anything quite like it, and I still enjoy it.

Once the War was over there was the long, slow decline of the individual grocer, butcher and baker, as the growth of the supermarket industry introduced us to a far wider range of food than we had ever had before. Simultaneously there was a tremendous expansion of world commerce, and the influx of immigrants into Great Britain accounted for much of the international content of stores today. With the increasing number of women going out to work there has also been an acceleration in 'fast food', with microwave ovens and other kitchen aids such as mixers, pulverisers and bread-making machines, to name but a few, which have all brought culinary change in their train.

To try and write a cookery book today is to compete in one of the most difficult publishing fields and, whatever one's criticism of the 'fast food' syndrome, for the person who genuinely enjoys food the choice of recipes is limitless – as a glance at the culinary section in any bookshop will confirm. Foreign travel is so commonplace that dishes such as *paella, moussaka* and *coq au vin* are recognisable anywhere, and there are specialist books on almost every food culture conceivable.

There are growing numbers who reject meat and animal fats and look for vegetarian dishes, quite apart from those on diets who want wholesome but light-weight foods. Tastes have simplified and there is a far greater use of fruit and vegetables and much less fat in food these days, as people are aware of 'healthy' eating. We are also more familiar with people who suffer allergies and illness relating to certain foodstuffs.

I welcome the diversity of information now available. All I can hope is to offer a lifetime's interest in cookery, and how I was forced to hone whatever talents I have to suit the taste of my guests at *Rozinante*. If there is an emphasis on stews, casseroles, pies, sauces, cakes, and camouflage for left-overs, then this is, too, the result of catering for guests who would arrive and want to talk to me! I could not be locked up in the kitchen but would have to have prepared as much as possible in advance, and thus be free to socialise and help my clients to enjoy their holidays. The recipes are essentially French and Catalan in flavour because one uses local ingredients, refined to suit different tastes and, as I have discovered, it is not necessary to mix too many flavours or to try and prepare too rich or too exotic a dish.

The culmination of my cooking experience has been expressed in my *Rozinante* recipes. I hope that in using them the reader will understand, from this anecdotal account of our life in the Pyrenees Orientales, how integral to the joy of living in France was the dining table!

Bon appétit!

"... round and round in circles."

Chapter 1

Le Début

W here's the restaurant?" asked my sister, pushing her way impatiently through the swing-doors of the hotel we had booked for a week's intensive house hunting in France, but her progress towards food was unceremoniously overruled by the male members of our party, who steered us purposefully towards the bar! Drink, not food, was required after a fraught drive through the tortuously narrow streets of Perpignan's centre, where French direction arrows proved deliberately ambiguous, often indicating right when they meant straight ahead! Driving on the right hand side of the road in a left hand drive car frequently involved much turning on of windscreen wipers instead of indication signals, thus causing havoc to traffic behind us.

There was also conflicting and often acrimonious advice from passengers to driver as to which lane he should be in when there were four to choose from – all this hampered by the fact that the French are notoriously impatient drivers and the slightest hesitation on a driver's part produces not only a chorus of protest from a dozen car horns but verbal abuse and shaking fists from car windows. Modern-day psychiatric investigations have produced conclusive evidence of distinct character changes in both men and women once they sit behind the wheels of their cars.

The French are no exception, often admitting – when challenged as to why they prefer to overtake on dangerous bends instead of safe stretches of road – that they do suffer from suicidal tendencies. Stopping for advice or directions also produces such conflicting instructions in rapid-fire

French that we soon regretted stopping at all.

"Tout droit," said a gendarme dismissing us brusquely with a wave of his white-gloved hand.

"Non, non," protested an onlooker (the French are always interested bystanders), *"c'est toujours à gauche!"* Which meant that we went around in circles, only to return like homing pigeons to the same vantage point.

Consequently it was a distinctly dishevelled and irritable foursome that finally unearthed the small hotel in the cul-de-sac we had passed constantly in our travels. Only the drinks and an eventual evening meal restored our British *esprit-de-corps.*

It had long been my ambition to live in France, although an incredulous friend could not believe the news when I told him I planned to retire there. When I asked why he was so surprised, he raised a mocking eyebrow and said, "But, the French, my dear, the French!"

"What about *entente cordiale?*" I countered.

"And what about perfidious Albion?" he replied darkly.

It is hard to explain one's motivation to people, although having a French sister-in-law helped, since her devotion to her country of origin had never been in doubt, despite 30 years of living mainly in London. It was largely her advice that directed us to the Rousillon which was, we discovered, a natural, unspoilt region of France, little-known and only tentatively explored, with a lush vine-growing plain extending from the snow-capped Pyrenees to the dark, red coastline of the Mediterranean.

"There's skiing in winter," I defended my choice of location to friends, "and swimming and surfing in the summer." What more could you ask for – and with property prices at a fraction of their counterpart on the more sophisticated Côte d'Azur, yet with a comparable climate?

In any event, the exploits of Don Quixote, the elderly Spanish knight who set off late in life for new adventures, sparked a reciprocal feeling, so that to me it did not seem at all strange at the age of sixty to find a house to use as an *auberge* and prepare to tilt at whatever obstacles came our way.

The very first of these obstacles appeared in the form of successive estate agents whose 'wide knowledge and expertise in helping clients to find the home of their dreams' soon expanded into several nightmarish days of being shown property which looked as if nothing had been done to it since the sackings and lootings of the 18th Century French Revolution.

Opening the front doors proved impossible in some houses where every known kind of rot and worm had tortured the frame beyond endurance. We discovered marble sinks, but no electricity or running water. We had been warned that water was a scarce resource in the south of France and consequently we should always verify its whereabouts. To my amazement, 'a source' often meant a stream at the bottom of the garden which ran in the winter but dried up in the summer!

Time and time again, in one ramshackle house after another, having been told that *'tout est impeccable'*, my brother-in-law would ask what 'impeccable' really meant, while drawing my attention to a particularly large hole in the roof. Our initial disappointment with the properties we were shown owed nothing to language difficulties, since I had chosen English agents (fearing my inability to cope with the problem of house buying in the French language). So one listened sympathetically to the explanations of agents, but after three fruitless days chasing around the countryside we wondered whether the English agents had been left with those pieces of property the French had either failed or did not wish to sell!

On the other hand, one English agent said that most of the English who came prospecting frequently arrived with a long list of 'priorities' in their hand, such as *near the sea, cheap price, house of character* etc, and then ended up with a house that was miles inland, of very little character and quite expensive.

"The result is," she said wearily, "we now largely ignore what the client says he wants, show him a cross-section of everything available and just hope to find something he can afford."

"... we now largely ignore what the client says he wants."

This somewhat cynical response was, we found, typical of the agent – Mrs Cadwallader, a formidable figure of great girth and weight who, despite her ungainly appearance, was prone to wearing brilliant yellow or red tracksuits. Don't hide it, flaunt it, seemed to be her motto.

Driving a van with reckless ease, she explained that on the death of her husband she had started to transport English antiques (mainly paintings, china and glass) from their original premises in Bath to market towns in Provence, where she had set up a stall and sold her wares. From these modest beginnings she had branched out into the buying and selling of property and it quickly became obvious that her driving skills were matched by an equally ruthless and determined approach to the property market.

Mrs Cadwallader had taken us in charge. It was she who introduced us to the Prades area of the Roussillon which proved to be a small market town nestling in the foothills of the Pyrenees, with a firm reputation as the cultural centre of the region. The world-renowned Pablo Casals

"... nestling in the foothills of the Pyrenees."

music festival took place every year at the local Abbey of St Michel de Cuxa to commemorate this musician's stay in the town after his flight from Franco's Spain during the Civil War.

The first house she showed us was a converted mill, but the route to the village in question was so steep, with sheer drops on either side, that I could imagine myself nervously checking the car brakes every time I ventured out. Consequently we decided to rule out mountain retreats, and returned to the depths of the valley with a sense of disbelief, as our week's house hunting was now nearly over with no sign of our dream property in view. I began to regret the many newspaper and magazine articles I had read extolling the beauties and reasonable prices of French property, without realising that a country as large as France has many regional variations and architectural designs.

The Dordogne, I discovered later, had in the 18th Century been a wealthy part of France from where the rich sent their sons to be educated in Paris. Once influenced by the capital's splendid buildings, they returned to embellish their own homes. Perpignan, on the other hand, had been the centre of Catalonia – a poor, often struggling part of France, without rich soil or wealthy landlords, despite the mountain loveliness and beautiful climate. The Industrial Revolution had also passed it by, both an advantage and a disadvantage in as much as the natural beauty of the countryside prevailed, but the poor subsistence-style farming precluded the creation of fine houses and landscaped grounds.

On the very last morning of our week's stay, there was just one more house to view at a village called St Eulalie, and this tiny village burst upon our startled gaze with what may only be described as a vision from another world, since the magnificent landscape was dominated by the majestic and mysterious mountain of Canigou. There was inevitably another steep climb and another hairpin bend to be negotiated, so I closed my eyes and groaned, only to be told, "We've arrived!"

"... modern, but mellow and honey-coloured."

The house was modern but mellow and honey-coloured with steps around the side that led to a full and uninhibited view of the whole face of the mountain that still leaves me with a sense of awe every time I gaze at it. To our delight the house had a balcony, and although contemporary in design sported some rustic, solid-looking beams, both inside and out, that lent it a time-worn appearance. There was also – joy of joys! – a full-sized swimming pool, in need of minor repair and which the owner, should I agree his price, was willing to put in order. The price, incidentally, was just within our range.

My sister fell in love with the house instantly. "How happy the dogs would be here!" was her oft-repeated opening remark, which proved both prophetic and true.

Fortunately the purchase of a house in France is simple, with no possibility of gazumping. It took only a brief meeting at the Notaire's office in Prades, where a young solicitor spoke fluent English, to ease us into the first phase of property owning in France: an agreement to pay ten per cent of the purchase price immediately, and the remainder within three months. Any change of mind on my part and I would forfeit the ten per cent.

Once these brief formalities were over we all relaxed, ready to fly home and face the removal process, and it was the furniture removal that was to give us our first real taste of French bureaucracy, along with all the other formalities insisted upon by the French Consul in London before our departure. There were medicals by French doctors, attestations of character, declarations of financial solvency, and other references from eminent people.

But the furniture posed the biggest problem, since every item had to be declared together with estimated values and agonisingly difficult decisions had to be made about whether or not we really needed half the things we had been living with and cherishing for most of our lives. There were endless discussions on the relative merits of great grandmother's potpourri pot and, more to the point, her solid mahogany bedside commode (might be both useful and valuable one day). Harsh decisions were taken – and often later regretted – while the amount of rubbish that continued to accompany us resides to this day in the cellar below. Old cookery books, school exercise books and drawings, broken cricket bats, a half-worn croquet set, a parrot cage without the parrot (a much-loved bird whose famous phrase, "Christ, we've hit the bloody rocks again!" was clear witness to the family's obviously chequered maritime past) ...

"... what could be considered useful?"

However, by the end of March three of us were sitting in the garden of our beautiful villa in St Eulalie waiting for the furniture removal van to arrive, and it is just at such a moment in time, with the sun shining out of a cloudless blue sky, and when you feel that God is in his Heaven and all is well with the world, that something inevitably nasty rears its ugly head.

"I say," said my brother-in-law who, being deaf, generally speaks in a very quiet non-committal way, "someone's got a good fire going over there."

My son and I snoozed on regardless, and it was some quarter-of-an-hour later that we noticed a slight increase of concern in the tone of Ray's voice. Now standing apart from us, he said, "By Jove, it's gone up the hill and is now going down the other side!"

With the distinct smell of smoke in the air we leapt to our feet, to discover the long strip of forest on the other side of the valley blazing away and well into the process of leaping over the skyline towards the village of Corneille.

I could not believe my eyes, and my first thought was one of betrayal, since the previous owner had assured me that this part of France never suffered from forest fires. Yet here we were, on our very first week in the Pyrenees Orientales, with a blatant example of a forest fire blazing away, and there was still no water in our swimming pool to counter any insurgent approach. To confirm our worst fears, the air was soon filled with the sound of helicopters and aircraft spraying water, while fire engines and police cars raced along the narrow mountain tracks, now almost obliterated by large clouds of thick, black smoke.

What have I done? I agonised. Had I really bought a house only to see it reduced to cinders before we'd actually moved in!?

Needless to say, I did not sleep that night and spent the next three days harassing every Frenchman I met to ask in fractured French, *"Y-a-t'il des incendies ici?"* Since the bulk of those I met in the village spoke Catalan only, I did not get much in the way of a satisfactory response. With time, we learned that it was an isolated experience so far as St Eulalie was concerned and simply amounted to gross carelessness on the part of one of the oldest inhabitants when trying to burn too large a pile of rubbish at the bottom of his garden. Negligent in his supervision, he had ignored a sudden wind change, which had shot sparks over the garden fence with the dramatic consequence of igniting the dry scrub between the fir trees. It had been a very warm, dry spring, and fanned by the wind the fire had spread with alarming rapidity to the adjoining valley.

The experience was to prove helpful, as we learned from it the strict rules that apply in France to the lighting of domestic garden fires. Most are forbidden by the end of May, especially after dry spring seasons, and the penalty for provoking a major fire may be imprisonment. The memory of that fire licking and eating its way up the fir slopes was to have an unhappy and dramatic sequel some months later at *Rozinante*.

However, it was during the turmoil of the forest fire that our removal men arrived and the next two days were consumed with the feverish activity of trying to arrange furniture that had been collected from three different homes. Carpets proved to be too big or too small, while case after case of china and glass refused to be accommodated in the limited kitchen cupboard space. Electrical equipment, with British plugs, could not function in the French sockets, while tables and chairs that had looked perfectly at home in an English country setting now looked sadly out of place in the south of France.

We decided reluctantly that we did not need chintz, cretonne or lamps with lace frills, let alone English hunting and sporting prints. What I could imagine in their place was dark Catalan style settles and chests that would match the high-beamed ceiling and Spanish style tiled floors. But just as life is a series of compromises, we reached some kind of order eventually.

The days were lengthening, along with the hours of sunshine, and if the nights were cold because of our altitude we could close the shutters, light the log fire and, with full central heating, snuggle into bed and drop into deep and dreamless sleep.

Once again, it is precisely at this soft, unsuspecting moment, when you seem to be sliding into unaccustomed ease, that fate has a surprise in store.

Chapter 2

Un Resource Minimal

It was late one night, when my brother-in-law Ray and I were alone in the house, that I was jolted suddenly into wakefulness by the insistent throbbing from the garage of the pump that was responsible for distributing water around the house. Having suffered from deafness for most of his life, Ray was forced to wear a hearing aid, which he removed at night. The problem was that once asleep no sound would rouse him. On rare occasions, in emergencies when his wife had been forced to wake him, he had been known to mutter threateningly as he reapplied his hearing aid, "This had better be good!" In other words, fire, flood or other natural disaster, but not something trivial like, "I think I can hear a mouse in the room!"

But after standing at the top of the cellar steps for some time listening to the insistent throb of the motor in the darkness below, I made up my mind and shook Ray awake. Without hesitation, once he had heard my complaint, he ran down the stairs to disengage the pump which was, he discovered, on the point of blowing up! The reason for the pump's aberrant behaviour was not hard to see when the huge plastic tank holding our water supply in the garage was found to be bone dry – thus no water in the tank for the pump to circulate, and so panic had been justified.

The next and most obvious question was – had I committed the ultimate folly of buying a house in the south of France, not with a forest fire problem, but an insufficient supply of water in the well problem? My French sister-in-law's injunction to always verify my water source was ringing in my ears. Hurried questions on the phone to the previous owner produced reassuring noises about how well the system had worked during his tenure, but the Notaire was not so reassuring as he advised gloomily that in the event of this proving to be a real and enduring difficulty, there would be no recourse in French law to sue the previous owner for misrepresentation, as it seems once you buy a house in France, you buy it warts and all.

Eh alors, que faire?

The Water Board said the matter could only be dealt with at a local level, which meant a visit to the office of the mayor. In this respect the system in France is a great deal more efficient, since every small hamlet has a local mayor who is the fountainhead of local administrative knowledge and expertise. I had intended visiting M. Cazenova to introduce myself and pay my respects, and had envisaged a delightful meeting full of *entente cordial.* The reality was somewhat different, as I now appeared at his door grey with lack of sleep, demanding fretfully what had happened to my water supply. (I was tempted to mention how that morning I had been forced to spend several pennies in the garden behind our one and only hedge, but since many Frenchmen enjoy doing that sort of thing, I realised it would not carry much weight!)

The mayor, once he grasped the situation, launched quickly into a defence of his territory's watering facilities, including the local canal system, which was used for watering crops and gardens. The canal, he explained, had been built by the Romans and operated on a system of sluices and channels which would release water into our property for one hour every week, with a calendar giving us our particular watering hour. These watering hours, he emphasised, had to be observed in the strictest sense, otherwise... The mayor spread his hands out and I had a vision of angry local farmers marching up my drive, pitchforks at the ready.

Noting my apprehension, he warmed to this theme and pointed to the necessity for us to understand local customs and traditions, which prompted me to say that my own native land of Wales had its own brand of rituals concerning foreigners. When I mentioned that certain groups of politically motivated Welsh Nationalists had been known to set fire to or bomb holiday homes owned by the English, M. Cazenova rose to his feet in horror, and throwing his hands in the air said, "We are not barbarians and such things do not happen in France, Madame."

Thus reassured, attention was once more focussed on a solution to our problem, which evidenced itself eventually in the person of M. Arabia, *le responsable* for the local water supply. He explained that due to the height at which our house had been built, any lowering in the local reservoir meant pressure problems on my supply. However, he quickly produced two local council men, who arrived to tackle the problem with a triumphant squeal of brakes and a flourish of tyres in an old battered council lorry.

In halting, bad French I gave explanations while they climbed ladders and peered gravely into waterless depths, with accompanying clicking and clucking noises and the inevitable French habit of raising their hands above their heads and rolling their eyes expressively as if to say, "The cure, Madame, is in the lap of the Gods!" It was with enormous relief that we saw them remove a rusty filter from an outlet pipe and within two seconds the blissful sound of running water filled our ears.

"Pas de problème," they assured us with a casual wave of their hands as they prepared to leave.

"That's all it was?" I asked incredulously.

"Seems so," they replied in a deliberately off-hand way, although they confessed reluctantly there had been some works in the water supply down below in the valley, and, of course, given the height of the house and pressure problems... their voices trailed away significantly. The sky seemed to darken imperceptibly above my head.

"A pressure problem?" I quavered. "You mean there really is a water problem in St Eulalie?"

"Ah, Madame," the taller of the two said, "it is always a miracle when water arrives at St Eulalie."

Was the ground giving way beneath my feet, or was there a glimmer of humorous delight in their eyes? It took me some time and several catastrophies later to realise what a couple of well-meaning comedians these two council boys were – and why not? The sight of an elderly English lady having a *crise de nerfs* over her water supply was an irresistible temptation.

"Bonne chance," they waved happily as their tyres churned the gravel on the drive. "We'll be back tomorrow."

"What for?" I queried fretfully, wondering if this crisis was going to prove a daily one.

"We accidentally knocked the float off in the tank, but don't worry we'll get another one, unless you like fishing and can hook it up from the bottom!"

True to their word, they returned the next day to replace the float in the tank that was now, thankfully, brimming with clear mountain water, and from that fraught beginning was born a friendship and back-up service for all the minor irritations that living in an isolated community can present.

Unlike some council workmen I have known, these two men were exceptionally skilled in many basic trades such as plumbing, carpentry, electricity and general building repairs. Between them they ran the community along well-oiled lines and could be seen on almost a daily basis, collecting refuse, putting up lights for festivals and fête days and sustaining with an endearing sang-froid every eventuality and contingency a hamlet of some six hundred souls could devise. We discovered that Bernard, the taller, more grave-faced of the two, was a well-known and respected wood carver, able to hold occasional exhibitions of his work. The funny little float he designed for my water tank is a constant and happy reminder of his casual, humorous style, which I much appreciated – a tiny but aggressive French cockerel holding over its head a very British umbrella!

Having survived the domestic water problem it was time now to turn our attention to the garden. Following up on the mayor's explanation of the system, we walked to the top of the hill at the back of the house to inspect the canal with its succession of sluices, which we had the right to open once a week throughout the summer watering season. It was M. Terrades who belched up the drive one day in his Deux-Chevaux waving a calendar at me and who, with thick Catalan overtones, pointed to the fact that, as the latest arrivals to the district, we were more likely to find our watering hour at 2 o'clock in the night rather than 10 o'clock in the morning!

Needless to say, this information was given with a cackle of delight at our obvious dismay, while Ray was quite stunned at the news and on the appointed day and time had to be bribed with several whiskeys before setting out with a hurricane lamp to climb the hill and open the appropriate sluice.

This, however, proved catastrophic, since most of the irrigation ditches leading to the garden had not been cleared out for some time – with the result that the water, when finally released, rushed triumphantly down the hill, missed the target intended, and escaped through unexpected channels to sweep down our drive and along the road, ending up in the farm yard below. Worse was to come with morning's early light, when most of our cellar was revealed to be under water, with some earth shelves collapsing, while Jean-Bertrand, our French neighbour, erupted over the horizon to point to a small pond that had accumulated outside his kitchen door and which, he yelled, was now undermining the foundations of his house. The French words for 'I'll sue you!' were repeated so vigorously we had little need for our French dictionary to comprehend his intentions. A spirited run up the hill was organised to check the flood and close the sluices.

Much debate ensued over this problem, until the two men of the family rolled up their sleeves and dug a large hole in a natural hollow of ground which, in the course of time, was sanded, covered with a plastic sheet and filled with a permanent supply of water so that watering could take place whenever we required it and not when the sacred calendar decreed. As to the clearing of the ditches bordering our two properties, there was little debate but considerable dispute with our neighbour over who was responsible for what and the atmosphere was tense with ill feeling.

But if we thought our watering problems were over, we had discounted changing weather patterns, with disastrous consequences.

Like many British settlers in the region, we assumed the sun was a permanent fixture in the sky, taking into account the proud boast of the Roussillon that the area enjoyed no less than three hundred days of sunshine a year. This is true when times are 'normal' but otherwise can change dramatically. Without warning, at the end of a very sultry, hot September afternoon, the sky darkened and the worst torrential rain I had ever seen poured down from an angry swollen heaven, to the point where the river at the bottom of the valley became a raging torrent, overflowed its banks, and changed course entirely, tearing like a rampaging beast across the countryside, destroying everything in its path. Whole swathes of trees on either side of the banks were tossed like matchsticks in a foaming tide of debris and destruction.

As for *Rozinante*, the sudden violent surge of water cascading down the mountain behind the house rapidly flooded the garage, thus putting at risk our electric boiler and other installations. The deluge continued until midnight with each member of the family taking it in turns to man the pump to keep the water level down, while the next morning revealed the extent of things lost such as boxes full of books and papers, quite apart from apples, vegetables and other stored produce. But the damage suffered at *Rozinante* was nothing compared to houses situated near the river in the valley below, where walls and garages had been swept away. Inevitably, once the river subsided it left a filthy residue of sludge and mud, stones and rubble that took weeks to clear away, while in the long run it took the local council four years to complete a new road building programme to replace destroyed routes to isolated farmhouses. Our own reaction was to dig more drains and listen attentively to the French weather forecasts for warning signs of storms in future.

The scarce resource, it seemed, could sometimes be anything but scarce!

Chapter 3

Manjana

One of the most attractive features of the house when we first saw it had been the sight of a full-sized swimming pool, protected from the wind and elements by a sheltering bank of sturdy laurel bushes, while the backdrop of the mountains lent the whole scene a picture post-card kind of surrealism. The pool, however, despite the previous owner's attempts to repair it, remained uninviting, as the water, which had been filled from the local canal, was a turgid grey colour. Repeated calls to the firm concerned with the repair to come and improve the quality of the water met with promises, but no action.

By the end of April, the 'promise to return' syndrome was something we had yet to come to terms with since it is strongly related to the local Catalan, *'façon de vivre'*. Several telephone calls to the company always produced the comforting response of, *"Oui, Madame, on arrive."* But when you asked for more specific details of the actual day of their arrival, then a cautious vagueness appeared. Perhaps tomorrow, or next week... they were very busy... they would be in touch. At first we believed the promises made, but as time went on we became uneasy, doubting and perplexed, while the colour of the water in the pool turned from grey to slimy green, and the smell was far from reassuring.

Watching my handwringing amusedly from the scaffolding he had erected in our living room was Claude, the young half-English, half-French painter and decorator. He had arrived at my urgent request to remove the ludicrous black and gold rose wallpaper, which the original Belgian owner of the house had plastered between the wooden beams of the salon and mezzanine. Just to gaze upwards was to shudder. "That will have to come off, for starters," had been the unanimous verdict of us all, and Claude had been recruited quickly to do the job. However, having lived in the area for over twelve years and mixing by virtue of his profession with other craftsmen, all engaged in the renovation of houses, he was well aware of the Catalan attitude to work and their sense of priority. Happily stripping off roses, he would glance with wry amusement at my anguish around the pool.

Unable to stand this one morning, he swung down from his perch under the ceiling to deliver a well-intentioned lecture. "You will never be happy here," he said kindly, "unless you learn to take things far more calmly than you do at present. Remember," he added by way of explanation, "we are very near Spain where *manjana* is the order of the day.

"*Manjana*. 'Tomorrow'," he continued. "Here, people have very little sense of urgency when it comes to getting things done. Even offices and business hours are different. It is largely to do with the climate, since the farther south you travel the hotter it gets and the more relaxed life is. Shops and offices open at eight o'clock and close from midday until three or even four o'clock, as lunch is the main and most serious meal the French eat and is followed by a siesta. In fact, a man frequently refuses to work far from home, as his two- to three-hour lunch is sacred to him. But although business does not start again until three in the afternoon, it often does not close down until seven or eight at night."

All this advice, however kindly delivered, did little to relieve our anxieties at the time, although later we did learn to have a more relaxed attitude to the locals and were grateful for Claude's insights.

Once May arrived and the real summer weather began to scorch the grass, the men from the swimming pool company soon came out to treat the pool, and within five days the water was sparklingly clear. It warmed up quickly, and by the end of the month we were all swimming happily every day.

It was the sudden and unexpected storm that changed

the situation dramatically so far as the grass surrounding the house was concerned. Having first seen the property in January, when the grounds had been severely tailored to winter fineness, it hadn't been very obvious just how much grass cutting would be required. But the real peak of concern was not reached until Claude, looking out on the garden from his scaffolding, remarked one day in a deliberately off-hand way, "You'll have to keep the grass down if you are going to avoid snakes here." We leapt out of our deckchairs as if we had received electric shocks.

"Snakes!" I shouted. "You mean venomous ones?"

"Oh, yes," said Claude calmly, savouring every moment of our dismay. "Plenty of snakes here. Nasty they can be, too – I've known many a bite prove fatal, especially if you cannot get to a doctor within twenty minutes." And to enjoy the effect he was having he embarked upon a long horror story of an elderly Englishwoman, living alone half-an-hour from the local hospital in Prades, who being carried in one minute past cut-off time was, quite naturally, pronounced dead on arrival!

"... waiting to strike the unsuspecting."

In a flash the garden assumed a sinister air, and whereas before we had marvelled at a cloud of blue butterflies hovering over long, silky grasses, now we wondered whether within the depths vicious and deadly fangs lurked, waiting to strike the unsuspecting. The prospect was daunting to say the least.

"Of course," continued Claude with relish (how was I to know in those early days that he loved to tease and provoke people?), "you can always go to your doctor and ask for serum to inject yourself as an antidote after a bite, but there have been adverse reactions to the serum. In other words, the remedy might prove more lethal than the bite!"

The problem, we reasoned that evening over supper, must have a solution, and the first and most obvious thing that sprang to mind was the acquisition of a large, powerful grass cutter. Ray had been trundling around the garden with a small but ancient machine we had brought with us, but its blades were worn and the engine had taken to coughing like a chronic asthmatic, so there was no hope of it coping with the field alongside the house where waist-high grass and weeds wound upwards, triffid-like.

A day or two later I spied the Spanish worker who came regularly to spray the apple orchard at the back of the house. Knowing that he had lived in St Eulalie for some thirty-odd years, I struck up a conversation in the hope he would refute Claude's warning about snakes, but not a bit – M. Ribeira was only too quick to point to his hob-nailed boots which, he said, he always wore in long grass as a protection against vipers, the most vicious of local snakes. The grass, he agreed emphatically, was dangerous, but if Madame wished to buy a machine he would be happy to escort her to a suitable supplier and demonstrate its use.

True to his word, at the appointed hour his van thumped its way up the drive and, in a wild series of kangaroo style leaps, we set off for Prades.

Inevitably, he drove his van in much the same way he drove his tractor – that is, with a total contempt for everything else on the road. Whistling his own version of *Carmen,* shouting imprecations to anyone who hooted at us (and most Frenchmen do), I realised quickly that French and Catalans alike much prefer a loud horn to their brakes.

We finally screeched to a halt in a yard full of lethal-looking cutting machines, all of which I discovered cost thousands of francs. The discussions that followed were held entirely in Catalan, which excluded my participation completely, but I was never left in any doubt that M. Ribeira was driving as hard a bargain as he could from the diminutive old man who hopped like a bird from one machine to another with a trapezists's disregard for the hazards of the blades he was demonstrating. To my dismay, in the end it dawned upon me that we were about to leave without buying anything.

"What's the matter?" I asked anxiously as we walked away towards the car.

"WE DO NOT BUY!" M. Ribeira was beside himself with Spanish rage, emphasising the seriousness of his feelings by vigorous stamps to the ground of his outsized hobnailed boots. He accompanied this with what seemed to me a particularly unpleasant series of short, sharp prods to the little salesman's very insufficient shoulder; he was now keeping pace with us in a pleading, servile manner that I found personally quite upsetting.

"AND WHY NOT?" I decided to bellow back.

"Because this cretin will not give us a free replacement blade in case the original one gets broken."

"But why," I asked with incredible naïveté, "should the blade break on a new machine?"

But M. Ribeira, with a lifetime of broken blades behind him, since he drove mowing machines just like his car or tractor (that is to say over stones, boulders and any other obstacles in his path), was not to be moved.

A torrent of Catalan ensued, with the poor salesman now becoming, quite naturally, sulkier and sulkier, often flashing me appealing glances, which M. Ribeira scornfully intercepted and dismissed with contemptuous gestures. No free blade, then no sale.

Just at the point where I felt I had to intervene, the collapse came and within two minutes we were walking out with a monster of a machine with such a powerful motor that it almost took Ray's arms out of their sockets each time he used it. Indeed, its rocket-like thrust sent him whooshing around the field like a Sputnik, with an accompanying roar to awaken the dead.

"...la machine infernale ... capable of cutting a swathe through the tallest grass."

But all these distractions aside, *la machine infernale* was capable of cutting a swathe through the tallest grass with consummate ease, and slicing one or two vipers in half *en route!*

In retrospect, the incident was an object lesson on the need to bargain when buying anything. In terms something like that of the Middle Eastern Souk, the would-be seller is disappointed if there is no struggle, and any purchase of whatever commodity, if paid for in cash, is worthy of some discount or other. There was one interesting sequel: later, when shopping in Prades market, I saw an Arab trader with Eastern carpets, and spotting one in red and blue colours that I *must* have immediately, I started – with encouragement from my sister, Margaret, who had spent most of her life in the Middle East – to bargain for it.

"Laugh contemptuously when he tells you the price," she commanded, and I duly laughed contemptuously. "Tell him," she continued, warming to her task, "that the carpet is worn and faded in several places and that he must have been trying to sell it for more years than he can remember."

Since I had no idea what the French words were for 'worn' and 'faded' and my sister kept nudging me in the ribs to keep going, I have no idea what garbled version of her instructions came out. In the event, a small crowd of interested onlookers had appeared at this stage, which had a strongly inhibiting effect upon my doubtful bargaining powers.

My sister began to lose patience with me. "Tell him," she said, "that I have lived most of my life in the Persian Gulf and I know a cheap carpet when I see it. In fact," she added extravagantly, though it subsequently proved true, "it's probably a fake."

"C'est pas une vraie," I managed to squeeze out somehow in desperation and it was at this point the Arab exploded in wrath.

"I don't give a **** where you or your sister lived," he shouted at me, red with indignation, "she is a fake, you are the fake, this is a bloody good carpet!"

His knowledge of the English vernacular was as impressive as it was unexpected. I grabbed my sister's arm and we ran away as fast as our legs could carry us.

Some weeks later, at the same market but a different Arab trader, I saw the same carpet, but on this occasion it was placed under a sign that said, '50% off original price'. When I enquired, the reduced amount proved to be exactly the same price the original trader had demanded, but this time I paid up without a murmur, because I wanted that carpet – and that, according to my sister was the nub of the matter.

"Never," she said, speaking slowly for great emphasis, "ever show, by even the faintest gleam in your eye that you are INTERESTED in something..."

I decided it was time she started to learn French and do her own bargaining, since gleams in the eye must be very hard to eliminate.

Chapter 4

Shades of the Prison House

With a new gleaming monster of a mowing machine, the next problem was the disposal of a mountainous pile of grass cuttings. Some illegal tipping might be carried out, but then June turned both hot and unexpectedly wet, which only encouraged the grass to grow more vigorously than ever. While we all realised the cuttings would have to be disposed of we were also wary of starting forest fires, thus no-one was willing to strike the first match.

The days went by until one evening a great cloud of smoke billowed up from our neighbour's garden and pointing to it I said something to the effect of, "If he is burning his cuttings, why can't we?" Fatal question, for after lunch the next day Ray nonchalantly approached the first pile of cuttings, lit a cigarette, tossed the match onto the pile, and within seconds it had exploded into flame. A mischievous whisper of a wind swiftly fanned it into a roaring blaze, sending terrifying tentacles of fire travelling with lightening rapidity across the field in several different directions at once.

Where after-lunch somnolence usually prevailed, a horrified cry of "Fire, fire!" soon sent everyone crashing about for buckets, water hoses, shovels, anything we could lay our hands on; but without any real experience of fire in these circumstances it was quickly apparent that everything we did only worsened the situation. We gazed on, stricken, while the blaze rapidly gained momentum and before our agonised eyes seemed ready to devour the whole field, spreading into the neighbour's prize apple orchard before roaring up the hill and on to heaven knows where! For an eternity, it seemed, we stood frozen before the enormity of our ignorance and stupidity, while the prospect of prison bars closed about our heads.

It was at this precise moment of chaos that the small, cocky figure of our neighbour appeared. To our amazement, he crossed the intervening ground between his house and ours, slowly and deliberately, the inevitable Gauloise stuck to his lower lip – which only served to accentuate the normal sneer with which he greeted all our British efforts to do anything that impinged upon his consciousness. In his hand he carried the longest-handled shovel I had ever seen. He proceeded systematically and carefully to run the flat back of the tool along the ribbons of fire until they were extinguished. Once the red streamers had been reduced to black scorching earth, he began to beat out, with practiced and efficient strokes, the ring of flames around the main fire, while we dragged out every utensil we could find to imitate his movements.

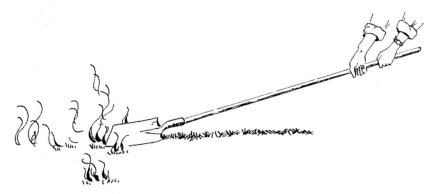

" ... the longest handled shovel I had ever seen. "

Eventually, with sweat streaming down our smoke-blackened faces, we succeeded in controlling the fire into one gigantic blaze which, according to our neighbour, we could now continue adding to until all the cuttings had been burnt. To keep this under control a chain-gang of water carriers kept the ground around the fire soaking wet.

In direct contrast to our neighbour's deliberate calm, his wife, Rosanne, kept shouting, *"Est-ce-que, j'appèlle les pompiers* (should I call the fire brigade)?"

But her husband was quite clear on this point since calling out the fire brigade cost money. *"Certainment pas,"* he told her, *"mais cognac, oui!* (Certainly not, but cognac, yes!)"

It was several hours before the whole field had been raked and burned and once completed, the neighbours' cognac long since having been consumed, my son found another bottle and we all lay on the ground and giggled drunkenly, savouring the kind of relief that comes when disaster has been narrowly averted.

It was a hard lesson to learn, but enormously effective, since all subsequent fires were rigorously controlled on ground previously soaked with water from the reservoir-pool we had dug in the garden. Needless to say, we were extremely grateful to our neighbour, Jean-Bertrand – the only one we had, as we lived in some isolation from the main village – and because of this euphoria there was, for a short time, a truce between us, since normal relations had been precarious. From our very first days, people in the village had never been tired of commiserating with us on having to live next door to someone who was variously described as *'très difficile'* or not so politely as *'un cas special'*.

Most of Jean-Bertrand's problems seemed to stem from his initial deviation from a planning application on the kind of construction he intended to build on the land he had acquired right next to us. From what we had heard from the locals (and there were several versions) his original request to the council had been for planning permission to build a barn. This had been allowed on the grounds that the land he had bought was considered 'agricultural', and thus a barn came within the category of potential rural use. However, what Jean-Bertrand proceeded to build was a house – in direct contravention of his original request – and it is universally accepted that if you build without correct planning permission, the authorities have the right to demolish it.

That this had not happened to our neighbour was entirely due to the forbearance of the local mayor, who, incidentally, did not want the expense of having to hire a bulldozer to carry out the demolition! Tempers had been strained on all sides, and to punish his intransigent behaviour (because the inhabitants of the village demanded it, Jean-Bertrand not being a 'local' but a 'foreigner' from Bezier) the mayor had denied him access to the village water supply. Thus every day the stocky little figure of our neighbour could be seen setting off in his van, piled high with plastic containers to be filled with drinking water from the local source. In addition to this daily labour, he had dug an enormous pond at the end of his property which somehow mysteriously filled with filthy water on which several noisy ducks squabbled all day and which, we presumed, piped into the house, solving some of his more basic needs.

On our arrival at *Rozinante* Jean-Bertrand had made a point of walking across to shake our hands and welcome us, and I found his presence next door comforting and helpful. He translated letters from the electricity boards, gave advice on where to get the best insurance, and where to buy wood at a competitive price. With our very modest ability to speak French, these attentions were more than welcome. However, it soon became clear that he was a man of variable mood, sometimes smiling and expansive, but on other days – when unshaven and morose – he was belligerent and deliberately rude in criticising the way we had trimmed a hedge or tried to put up some outside lights to the house.

"Not like that – stupid British!" he would say, while we smiled uneasily and watched while he, with considerable French flair, raced up and down ladders. True, he was single-handedly building his own home, but from only a cursory view it was obviously in a state of crisis. Occasionally an enormous tractor would arrive, pulling a monster excavator to scoop out fresh mounds of mud from the bottom of his pond or, in one bravura display, to remove vast quantities of earth from what, we were told, would be an underground garage and swimming pool. The mounds of earth increased daily and it was with an equally increasing sense of dismay that we looked across our dividing hedge at the gaunt, unfinished building, the whole surrounded by a no-man's land of concrete mixers, piles of rubble, sand, bricks, empty paint pots and ladders. It was not long before the hole filled with rainwater, so that the excavated mounds of earth ran rivulets of mud amidst the general chaos.

"... a no-man's land of concrete mixers, piles of rubble ... bricks ... and ladders ..."

To compound these problems, Jean-Bertrand was endeavouring to establish himself as an agriculturalist, thus complying with local laws that the land he bought should continue to be used just for these purposes. All manner of experiments had been tried, such as goats, guinea fowl, ducks, and geese, to prove his professional status. But when at the end of the day profit and loss were taken into account, many of his ventures came to abrupt ends, since he was unable to compete with the generally accepted form of factory-style farming.

Since we were forced to endure both the noise and the smells, we waited each time with some trepidation for the next experimental undertaking.

"Chickens," he announced one bright spring day, having just returned from Toulouse with two hundred and fifty baby chicks. These he bedded down in the loft of his house to keep them warm and presumably alive until they were big enough to go into the hastily erected sheds outside.

Our involvement in this latest enterprise only came to light when he arrived one morning to ask for the loan of our lengthy electricity cable, which we used for the pump to water the garden. We handed it over and he promised to return it within two to three days. As a month passed, then two, with no sign of the cable, I gave in to temptation one day when passing him on the road and suggested he return it, but a black look accompanied by an exaggerated roar from his exhaust left me in no doubt that my tentative reminder had not been a welcome one.

Later that afternoon the solid thump of his boots on our patio alerted us to his presence, but before words could be exchanged the cable was flung to the ground, and our neighbour's back was the last we saw of him.

We had hardly finished breakfast the following morning when the same boots appeared on the patio, but this time accompanied by a roar of rage and a flood of French from which we salvaged eventually a demand for fifty francs to pay for the loss of five small chicks who had, apparently, died in the night because of the lack of cable and subsequent loss of heat.

"I told you," he yelled, "you stupid British, that I needed twenty-four hours' notice before I returned the cable, and now look at the result... five dead chicks for lack of heat and it's all your bloody fault!" He held out his hand threateningly with the demand for compensation.

There are times when one is almost at a complete loss for words and this was just such an occasion, although I recovered rapidly.

"Over my dead body you'll get fifty francs, you ungrateful wretch," I told him firmly, once my anger allowed me to speak, but when he advanced suddenly towards me, the 'dead body' bit suddenly seemed something of a mistake on my part. However, the family closed ranks behind me, and the fact that he had managed to provoke my anger, rather than our usual meek acceptance, had the effect of calming him somewhat. The normally polite and phlegmatic British were this time fighting back! So he turned on his heel and stamped away, muttering imprecations to himself, no doubt all connected with perfidious Albion.

It was a couple of months later that we decided to have

a barbecue party. We felt the time had come to bury the hatchet, and so sent over a formal invitation for our neighbours to join us. His wife, Rosanne, and their daughter, Claudine, arrived dressed impeccably to mingle unobtrusively with our guests, but not so Jean-Bertrand, who had neither bothered to wash or to comb his hair, nor change his normal mud-streaked, filthy working clothes. To dramatise his appearance he had stuck on his head a large floppy straw hat that had at one time been a typical Spanish sombrero, with little red woollen balls around the rim which jerked up and down spasmodically as he walked. He savoured my shocked reaction to his appearance and a mocking smile split his face to reveal tobacco-stained teeth and foul breath. He might just as well have made the obscene gesture with his fingers of 'up yours!'

Silently I handed him a large gin and tonic and after several more he lay down in the shrubbery and to everyone's relief fell fast asleep.

"How do you put up with it?" an English friend asked as she was leaving.

All I could say was, "He's my Cross of Lorraine!"

" ... to everyone's relief, fell fast asleep. "

Chapter 5

Chambres d'Hôte

When we first opened our doors to summer visitors (for we had long decided to try our hands at bed and breakfast), our earliest visitors were serious-minded French men and women who had deliberately chosen the Pyrenees Orientales for their climbing and 'back to nature' holidays. The French, I believe, no matter what their social status, have an annual longing to get back to their roots and 'mother nature' and the countryside for city dwellers has an irresistible appeal. This is not hard to understand when you realise that just prior to the Second World War, sixty per cent of French people were working the land in some capacity or other.

Typically, they would arrive with cars packed to the gills with all the appropriate gear, knapsacks, sticks, hobnailed boots, thick socks, maps, compasses, and an accompanying Scouting sense of being prepared for all eventualities written all over their faces. It was an earnest operation for being at grips with nature; 'red in tooth and claw' is a serious, if not at times dangerous, experience.

Early morning calls were asked for as the Jeeps they had organised would be leaving villages at the foot of Mount Canigou at 8 o'clock sharp – for climbing Canigou, the sacred mountain of the Catalan people, is the main object of their visit. Canigou is the second highest mountain in our range of the Pyrenees. It is a test of climbing ability, so I was always ready, especially for city-dwellers, to make the appropriate congratulations when they returned, exhausted but triumphant, at the end of the day. However, just how much of an achievement it is was not apparent to me until the Baxter family arrived and invited my sister and I to join them in a trek up the mountain. It was shortly after Midsummer's Night, when we had watched from the garden the torch-light processions of both young and old climbing Canigou to celebrate the summer's solstice.

It was a particularly beautiful morning when we set off up the mountain track in an open Jeep that lurched and bumped its way along a road which, so far as I could see, consisted mainly of stones and holes. The views however were breathtaking, although my stomach grew queasier and queasier the higher we climbed, and just glancing over the side at the sheer drop below was enough to make me close my eyes with a shudder.

"... glancing over the side at the sheer drop below."

To exacerbate matters, the driver kept turning around (always a tricky manoeuvre, I thought, especially on blind bends) to point out some landmark or other – which, as he spoke mainly Catalan and was always accompanied by a grinding and gnashing of gears, made most of his explanations quite unintelligible.

Sitting alongside him was a tough, soldierly-looking man who had an enormous pack on his lap which, he informed us, was a parachute, since he was about to climb Canigou in order to parachute down again – favourable winds willing, of course. We enquired if he'd done it before. Several times, he assured us, so we all wished him *bonne chance* as we climbed out at the *auberge* where we had booked lunch for 2 o'clock, having been assured that the climb to the top would take no more than one and a half to two hours.

People were milling about everywhere. To our surprise two young men had very small babies strapped to their backs, and this seemed to give the whole scene an air of a Sunday School Treat – which proved to be the case for the first half-hour's gentle stroll past the lake and through the trees, until the path began to wind steadily upwards. From then on the twists and turns became so severe that we were forced to stand aside at times, to give way to those younger and more eager to reach the top before anyone else.

Observing them as they passed I was amazed at the motley nature of the people climbing that day. There were earnest-looking Scandinavians with muscular bare legs and purposeful feet, clad in very thick boots, alongside square-shaped, red-faced Germans, who looked with some disdain at the babies and children in sunhats often accompanied by voluble Spaniards sporting even larger straw hats. Bringing up the rear were two young Englishmen, puffing and panting, hotly pursued by two Danes, with whom they were in obvious competition.

Indeed, the whole atmosphere seemed charged with this sense of competition, as if someone had fired a starter's pistol and the race was on to see who could be first up Canigou.

"... who could be first up Canigou."

Even I, unconsciously, quickened my step, which proved to be disastrous as I began to feel dizzy and had to be escorted to an outcrop of rock to rest and recover. The French family who took pity on me at this stage proved to be loaded with rucksacks and picnic baskets, full of food and bottles of Roussillon *vin de pays*. They had quite rightly decided that the climb was much too strenuous for them and had found a grassy ledge. Since it was now nearing midday they were prepared to settle down to the far more important business of the daily extended French lunch.

To my delight a cloth was produced, along with plates, knives and bowls of delicious radishes, cheeses, tomatoes, eggs in mayonnaise, salamis and cold meats. Would I join them? they asked politely. Guiltily looking around for the rest of my companions, I found with immense relief that they had long disappeared over the brow of the hill, so I fastened a napkin under my chin and shared the feast.

The valley below shimmered in the heat, and cowbells tolled as radishes and salami went happily down with the wine, to be followed eventually by a blissful after-lunch snooze. Vaguely, from time to time I was aware of the steps of those returning from the summit. Noticeably, much of the chatter and conversation had been replaced by grunts and groans, if not irritable slaps and admonishments to tired children who had to be goaded on to complete the descent. Reluctantly, I left my now replete and happy French friends to their siestas and walked slowly back to the *auberge* to await the arrival of the others as one by one they trickled back, tired but triumphant at having made it to the top.

The ride back home was a very happy one, with a real sense of achievement, and the ability later on to boast of having climbed the second highest mountain in the Pyrenees.

As the holiday season advanced, more and more guests intent on walking and climbing holidays arrived. Most were sensible and stayed well within the limits of their knowledge and abilities when setting out on climbing expeditions. If ever there were problems they always came from people who were over-confident. One such guest brushed aside my cautionary tales by telling me he had been a member of an Alpine climbing club and had travelled the world on climbing expeditions. Ignoring my advice that autumnal mist might make late afternoon climbing dangerous, he missed a vital turning coming down a steep incline and in poor visibility fell badly, smashing his glasses, and so arrived back eventually with a badly cut face which needed hospital treatment. He was angry at first at this misadventure because his self-esteem had taken a beating, but we were attentive in a very discreet way and when we asked for his help in writing down clear climbing instructions for other guests to follow we swung his mood around, and parted eventually on very good terms.

Another misadventure concerned a Scots tax inspector who informed us on arrival that there wasn't a mountain in Scotland he hadn't climbed! He stayed a week and went out every day, but failed finally to appear for dinner the last evening before he was due to return home. By nightfall we were really alarmed, and rang the local mountain rescue team, but could not indicate the precise area he had set out to climb.

"Perhaps he's gone off for a spot of *ooh la la*," the officer at the other end of the line suggested, to which I replied indignantly, "Good heaven's no, he's British not French!" The officer laughed and promised to come out and see me the following morning.

He duly arrived at ten o'clock – at the same time as my weary guest, who had mistimed his return and, caught by nightfall, had had to take refuge in a ditch, covering himself with leaves and branches to ward off the cold. He had not been able to continue his descent until early morning light. He was cold, wet, bedraggled and hungry, so we provided a traditional English Breakfast of bacon, eggs and sausages, which the rescue officer also enjoyed after promising me that no mention whatsoever would be made of *ooh, la la*!

Chapter 6

Head Cook and Bottle Washer

Our spring-time trickle of visitors had now become a steady stream. By the end of May we had adjusted to making up beds, washing and ironing sheets, putting fresh flowers in rooms, setting out chairs and parasols in the garden and checking fridges for supplies in case evening meals were required. For English guests we tended to experiment with French dishes, such as local rabbit cooked with prunes, quails with mushrooms, and Catalan spiced meatballs in a fresh tomato sauce. There were so many different varieties of salad that we could always improvise and present attractive cold dishes and many kinds of open fruit tarts. We soon discovered that English guests tended to eat their food very quickly and expected course after course in rapid succession, whereas the French would take hours over their meals, quite prepared to eat yards of baguettes and savour their food and wine, always asking how a dish had been prepared if it was new to them.

One very warm summer evening we had two French couples from Vichy staying. We laid the table alongside the pool, helped by English friends who were in a celebratory mood, having finally found 'the house of their dreams' near Codalet. They produced champagne and the mood became quite boisterous, so that it was with quite a flourish that I served the main dish of the meal – a very English-looking pie.

The Frenchman on my left leaned forward and, savouring the aroma from the crust, asked, "What is it, Madame?"

To which I replied, "A pie, an English pie."

Seeing his incomprehension, and having had a little too much champagne, I proceeded to sing aloud:

Sing a song of sixpence, a pocket full of rye,
Four and twenty Blackbirds baked in a pie;
When the pie was opened the birds began to sing –
Wasn't that a dainty dish to set before a King?

The poor Frenchman looked absolutely appalled. "Blackbirds?" he asked incredulously.

"Mais oui," I confirmed rashly, and rapidly served the pie, giving generous portions, especially to the French.

It was amusing to see the caution with which our guests approached their food, first tackling the pastry, and then gradually gaining confidence when they agreed amongst themselves that, blackbirds or not, it was quite delicious. Once this stage was reached, I explained the true contents – steak and kidney with mushrooms – and the rest of the evening was devoted to describing, in detail, other recipes for English pies, a method of presentation not generally known in France.

It was when we were clearing the table by the light of the moon that I asked the Frenchman's wife, "Your husband, Madame, he is very interested in food?"

"Why yes, of course," she replied laughing, "in our part of the world he's quite a famous Master Chef!"

I vowed to be more cautious in future with my tale of blackbirds but pies became a firm favourite of the French from then on.

We were, of course, extremely fortunate to have a weekly market at Prades, which provided us with a magnificent source of fresh fruit and vegetables. There were huge mobile vans of *charcuterie,* game patés and sausages, which vied with a dozen different stalls piled high with every kind of olive, fresh herbs and spices, together with fish, fresh sardines, local river trout (still alive and swimming in tanks), and dozens of other smaller colourful fish for soups and stews. We were always pleased to present a choice of vegetables to our guests, because we found this was not always the case when we dined out. Generally we found that *nouvelle cuisine* prevailed, resulting in microscopic spoonfuls of purées of spinach with two miniscule potatoes, accompanied by transparent slithers of meat and sauce.

Everyone assumes there must be a little French bistro just around the corner from wherever one happens to be, with red and white check tablecloths, candles in bottles and a fat patron behind the bar wiping glasses. There would be an equally plump *patronne* presiding over the cash desk, since traditionally Madame controlled the finances, while the delicious smells emanating from the kitchen testified to the *plat de jour's* gastronomic ingenuity, at the incredibly reasonable price of fifty to sixty francs per head.

Such bistros do exist, but not necessarily just around the corner, and between the basic and 'good' restaurants can be found dozens of inferior, indifferent, and downright bad, eating places. Unfortunately the fast-food syndrome, the multi-chain hamburger variety, the pizza parlour, and the *crêperie* (pancakes), are now universal. The Roussillon is no exception and good restaurants, where they can be found, are very good indeed, although not cheap, and where consecrated to *nouvelle cuisine* the portions can be so small you often leave the table as hungry as when you sat down.

Cheap Catalan food can also be disastrous since lentils, fat sausages, black pudding, and other fatty meats, can form the substance of their own version of the *cassoulet,* which is excellent if you are a labourer in need of replenishment at the end of a hard day in the fields, but likely to send you home clutching your stomach if not.

The best meal we had ever experienced was discovered when we ventured one day into the Cerdagne. In the corner of the old farmhouse was a roaring wood fire where a Chef was busy grilling steaks, chops, and fish while young waiters dashed to and from the kitchen with a dazzling array of dishes for delivery to diners at long wooden tables, where the expressions on faces verged from the satisfied and replete to the downright euphoric. It proved to be, as often is the case in France, a family-run business, and on this particular day three generations of the Bardinets were involved in their task of satisfying their customers. Grandparents were cutting up fruit and vegetables, parents stirred pots over the stove, whilst youngsters were shelling nuts, whipping cream, and occasionally slapping down a rag-tag, bob-tailed lot of dogs and cats who were salvaging the crumbs from above.

The meal started with a substantial soup from an elaborately decorated soup tureen, of the kind not seen since my Victorian grandmother's day. The soup had a distinctly gamey taste to it, and large chunks of carrot, leek and onion – almost a meal in itself. A game paté followed, made by the patron, who came himself to ask if we enjoyed it and which, we found, was interspersed liberally with peppercorns and tasted miraculous. The main course was a choice of venison, hare, rabbit, salmon, or trout (from their own tank in the courtyard outside), fresh crayfish with cucumber sauce, or kidneys stewed in wine with mushrooms.

We took a one hour breather before the cheeses, which arrived in a beautiful basket lined with vine leaves and proved to be the largest collection of soft cheeses I had ever seen. All six varieties were served with small bowls of their fruit preserves – blackberry, raspberry, strawberry, gooseberry, blueberry and crabapple – it being the custom of the house to eat cheese in this way. It was simply the most delightful combination I had ever tasted, since most of the cheeses had a delicious creamy texture which reminded me of days in my childhood when an aunt used to send us clotted cream from Devon.

The puddings, too, were based on the family's own fruit preserves, with a superb vacherin of peaches and profiteroles, with spun caramelised sugar. By the time we had our coffee, and their own homemade chocolate mints, we had been sitting down for four hours, an unprecedented time for us to take over a meal. The bill worked out at just under 90 francs per head, with three bottles of a good, fruity red wine.

We tottered out and walked down the road to a small stream where we crossed a small bridge and, climbing unsteadily, made our way up the hill to reach the brow and look across at the rolling hills and countryside of the majestically calm Cerdagne – it proved, in memory, to have been a perfect day.

But there were other days when we drove home regretting the money we had spent on indifferent food, and working out what we could have bought with the money in the local market instead of squandering it. These mixed experiences made us all the more cautious about what we served our guests, and especially the French, who do not have a high opinion of English cuisine, although many have never visited the British Isles!

Most of the recipes we used at *Rozinante* were the result of a French cookery course, based near Sarlat in the Dordogne, which I had attended some years previously. I had answered an advertisement in the English magazine, *The Lady*, and it was only when I was actually *en route* by plane from London to Bordeaux that I began to wonder what I had let myself in for.

However the school, when we reached it on a hot August afternoon, was in a beautifully converted farm house constructed around a central courtyard, where a fountain gave relief to the sun blazing down on walls festooned with vivid red geraniums. Georges Pestourie, our Chef and instructor, turned out to be French to his fingertips. Small, bustling, with a neat little Gaelic moustache, he served our first supper with considerable panache, avocado with sea food, followed by duck with a raspberry sauce, cheese, cherry *clafoutis* and coffee. I remember staggering off to bed saying to fellow students that I doubted, at this rate, if I would be able to stay the course. But it is extraordinary how one's capacity extends and, as day after day of gastronomic feast followed, we all found our appetites increasing and meeting the challenge. Georges, needless to say, was delighted.

He had impressed us with his life-long devotion to cooking on the very first morning when he announced, "I do not like the *nouvelle cuisine*." This, he believed, had been invented to titillate the palates of wealthy people who, being bored with traditional cuisine, enjoyed change for change's sake. "I am from the Perigord, and proud of it," he declared, waving his wooden spoon in the air, "and I will teach you the cookery of the region, which I am sure you will appreciate."

And we did, along with all his accompanying explanations and demonstrations and, since we ate all that we cooked, there was plenty of time for sampling, comparing, and above all, enjoying.

Georges, it transpired, had trained at the Ritz, both in London and Paris, and before the War had been Head Chef at a fashionable hotel for the British at Deauville. "That was the thirties," he would recall with nostalgia, "when English ladies were thin like my finger, and wore long gowns to dinner, drank their aperitifs and touched their glasses, toasting each other with, "Chin, chin, old dear."

When it was time to leave, Georges' parting present to me proved to be a pot of goose fat to see me through my culinary efforts. "Don't put it on your chest when you have a cold or a cough," he stipulated, "but spread it on your cabbage leaves, *pour le bon goût*." He had noticed how much I enjoyed his stuffed cabbage leaves with tomato sauce.

When I reached London I returned the compliment by sending him a packet of English Tea and a pot of Cooper's Marmalade – the only things, it seemed, he had appreciated from his stay in our capital city. He had also, he told me, loved our fish and chip shops, but I baulked at the idea of sending him a sample of that, no matter how many wrappings of the essential newspaper!

He wrote back, "God bless you, keep cooking!" And I am, Georges, believe me, and God bless you.

Chapter 7

Pablo Casals

With the end of July came a new influx of visitors for the main cultural event of the year, so far as Prades is concerned – the Pablo Casals music festival, when chamber music lovers gather from all over the world at the beautiful venue of St Michel de Cuxa, a monastery with Arabic and Romanesque features of a stark and moving simplicity. The festival is held in honour of the famous Spanish cellist, Pablo Casals, who fled France's Civil War in Spain in the thirties and settled, like many Spanish refugees, in the small town of Prades.

" The Abbey of St. Michel de Cuxa. "

A museum at the rear of the syndicat d'Inititiative in the town holds a splendid collection of memorabilia, photographs, and other souvenirs of his life. Every year devotees of this kind of music spend considerable time, effort, and money to ensure the high standard of the orchestras, while internationally renowned musicians and singers play to appreciative audiences, and honour the great cellist's memory. Many of the famous musicians spend part of their time giving lessons to students, and those showing the greatest promise are invited on the final Sunday night of the concert season to play at the festival.

During our first year at *Rozinante* we were delighted to welcome Gerard and Josette during the festival, two young music students from Paris who had come to study under their respective maestros, who had been engaged for the festival. Both were in their mid-twenties and half-way through their formal training, Gerard occupied with the French Horn and Josette with the violin, having recently completed two weeks' work study at the Yehudi Menuhin school at St Emillion.

They settled in quickly and, while Gerard went off to Prades every morning for lessons, Josette spent her time practising in front of a large mirror in the bathroom. Since the house was not that large, the noise seemed to permeate every room. For those of you who are familiar with music practice of any kind, you will understand that, far from enjoying a given and varied repertoire, the player merely performs the same piece over and over again until the various scrapes and squeaks of mistaken notes lowers one's tolerance to breaking point!

At lunch time Gerard would reappear and there was a blissful hour of silence while they swam and ate, picnic-style, in the garden. But promptly at 2 o'clock, when most guests were seeking the shelter of their rooms for shade and siesta, Gerard would march purposefully into the lounge and attack, with the same kind of fervour with which a soldier embarks on target practice, a particular piece for the French Horn, while Josette returned to her own brand of excruciating noises from the bathroom.

Our other guests, both doctors, who had also come for the festival, quickly set about decamping their families for car excursions as far away from *Rozinante* as possible. Fortunately both families were passionate chamber-music lovers and, during interludes, when the youngsters were not practising, there were long and much appreciated discussions of the various pieces played at the Abbey. Everyone was delighted and celebrated the occasion when Gerard appeared triumphantly one evening to say that his Music Master had asked him to play in the *Concert des Etudients*. Champagne corks popped, and we all sat in a circle on the lawn while Gerard played his heart out. He confessed afterwards he had not played so well on the actual night, and I suggested he should have taken some champagne with him!

The first of our doctors to reach us that year for the festival came from Lyons, with a very attractive wife but an absolute dragon of a mother-in-law, whose chief function in life seemed to be that of expert wrecker of peace and harmony. Whenever I suggested tentatively that they might like an aperitif before supper she would scowl and say, "Certainly not, we do not drink!" Not surprisingly, we discovered the doctor had a secret hoard in the filtration plant of the swimming pool, where every evening at sundowner time he would hide behind the hedge and consume as much as he liked of his favourite tipple. How else, we sympathised, could he possibly endure the dragon?

Contrary, however, to his copious drinking, the doctor to begin with ate sparingly, but gradually improved his intake as the week went by. It was only after five days, and on the point of leaving, that he confessed how worried he had been about staying in an English-run guest house. Apparently his two brief visits to the United Kingdom had left him with nothing but the most bitter memories of English cuisine.

Was I familiar, he asked, with dumplings, Irish stew, sausage and mash, not to mention overcooked vegetables, and Brussels sprouts in particular? I wondered privately where he had stayed, and only remarked that English food could be delicious but potentially disastrous when badly prepared. Warming to the subject, I said that I felt much the same way about Catalan *cassoulet*.

"Ah well," he replied quickly, "you must go to Toulouse for a true *cassoulet.*"

Catalans, I thought, take note, although his response confirmed my belief that the French react instinctively to criticism, and will invariably attribute any failure of appreciation to not being in the right place at the right time. It seems you have to be in Perigord in the Dordogne to understand and appreciate *pâté de foie gras* and truffles; Marseilles for *bouillabaisse,* and Normandy for anything cooked in cider. Outside these strictures you would suffer *pastiches* and not 'the real thing'.

As for our second doctor, Remé Bouchard and his wife Marie, they came from Paris and, apart from the festival, were on holiday to walk up in the mountains. In fact he had made a point of telling all his patients of his intentions to walk in the Pyrenees, and to those who were grossly overweight he had recommended the same kind of holiday. True to French style, they both appeared on their first morning dressed to the hilt in walking gear, which was all the more exotic for having been purchased in France's capital and most chic city.

Much to our delight, they sported special hats to keep the sun out of their eyes, special shoes with special soles for getting to grips with rough mountain tracks, and special gloves which left fingers free but protected the palm of the hand from the handles of special walking sticks. Everything was explained in great detail (prices just hinted at) and was much admired as being *très elegant et à la mode.* However, by far the most beguiling aspect of the handsome doctor's outfit was a delightful Tyrollean-style hat, with a brave little green feather on the side. We were all utterly enchanted.

On the stroke of ten they strode away purposefully towards the summit of the nearest hill, map in hand, hope in their hearts, and a spirit of adventure that made us call out, "Your patients will be proud of you!" So it was with considerable surprise that one hour later we heard them return. Their appearance was deplorable. The doctor's Tyrollean feather hat had collapsed, while the face beneath was streaked with dust and perspiration. Knapsacks, once bulging, were now empty of water bottles and provisions, and bobbed like pricked balloons on bent backs.

"It was too hot!" they gasped as the fumbled their way through the doorway – they should have taken our advice and left earlier, at dawn, before the sun had risen; tomorrow, God-willing, they would try again.

But tomorrow dawned bright and clear, and the day proved even hotter than the one before, thus making the pool an even greater temptation. They swam and lazed the days away, eating lunch out of doors, and talking through the afternoon about music, art, and English literature. Marie proved to love the English Metaphysical Poets, Donne and Herbert among others, together with the mystic, Blake. Apart from her busy life as wife and mother, she taught yoga and believed strongly that it should not just be a physical exercise but a mental experience as well. She told me she read Blake aloud to her classes and found that the language and the forms blended perfectly.

I went and rummaged for some of my favourite poems, Edward Thomas's *The Owl* and, of course, Dylan Thomas, after which we sat under the wide-striped canopy while the afternoon sun blazed and scorched the grass, and read *Fern Hill, Do Not Go Gentle Into That Good Night*, and finally, *In My Craft or Sullen Art*:

In my craft or sullen art
Exercised in the still night
When only the moon rages
And the lovers lie abed
With all their griefs in their arms,
I labour by singing light
Not for ambition or bread
Or the strut and trade of charms
On the ivory stages
But for the common wages
Of their most secret heart

… while we ate bowl after bowl of dark red cherries, which my sister spent her time picking from the trees loaded with fruit at the top of the field.

In the evening the Bouchards changed into evening dress to attend the concerts. Marie loved combinations of black and white and often, in her slender, pale perfection, seemed to float into the evening air as they walked down the drive. They later described the concerts as 'magical', and it was at one of these that they met the artist from Prades, François Branger who, on learning that they were staying at *Rozinante*, asked after me, calling me by his own nickname of 'Madame Don Quixote'. He had been responsible for the beautiful painting of the Don's mule, *Rozinante*, which hangs in the salon of the house and is much admired. Branger was a close associate of Pablo Casals and much involved in the establishment of the now famous music festival.

We were sorry when the festival ended that year, for it meant the Bouchards leaving us which we much regretted, and he kindly left us his hat with the little green feather as a momento of all his good intentions.

Chapter 8

A Shepherd's Tale

Closely following upon the Pablo Casals music festival is a film festival, and the 40th coincided with a celebration of David Lean films. *Passage to India* and *Lawrence of Arabia* drew crowds to an outdoor showing, at which the English contingent was much in evidence.

The British Consul and his wife took the opportunity to spend a few days in the area, meeting us all and dispensing much wit and charm in the process. Since his parish covered Marseilles to Biaritz, and he was at that time deeply involved in a murder case of two British businessmen, it occurred to me he had his work cut out! No tension showed, however, and we had a pleasant evening finding out what all the other British families were doing in the Roussillon, and getting quite a few surprises at some of the varied and enterprising businesses in relation to our own modest bed and breakfast efforts. None of the British I met on that evening complained of their choice of location, and all expressed their happiness at living in such a beautiful, unspoilt part of France. *Un coin perdu* (a lost treasure), the French called it, and 'long may it continue' we all echoed as, full glasses in hand, we gazed at the golden glow of the sunset over the mountains.

It was while I was contemplating the view that a very attractive young English girl introduced herself to me. Emma was tall and willowy, a natural blonde with what at first sight appeared to be a slight fragility. But how deceiving first appearances can be, we discovered when we visited her cottage later and found that, single-handed, she had transformed an old shepherd's barn into a spacious and delightful home. In fact, it was one of the most attractive conversions I had ever seen; most of the plumbing, electrical repairs, stone masonry and carpentry had been done by Emma, with occasional help from local craftsmen. Bringing in the timbers from the forest, she admitted, had been one of the trickiest jobs, and then hoisting them up as beams in the ceilings.

We were speechless, and to our paeans she turned a deaf ear. Perhaps, she admitted, the cold had been the worst aspect initially when, without a bedroom, she had spent the nights in a sleeping bag in front of an open fire, which quickly went out when not replenished from a wood-pile outside the back door. This had endured for three months; then, with the coming of spring, the shepherds had come down from the mountains, the fields filled with flowers, the sun reappeared over the horizon and she could stop the constant tending of the fire.

One of the shepherds, Armand, had sold his barn to Emma and, while he had been helpful with some of the heaviest tasks, he now proved to be a mixed blessing since he continued to behave as if the cottage still belonged to him, whilst his curiosity at the changes wrought by Emma knew no bounds, particularly the installation of an indoor lavatory and constant hot water. Emma deduced that, with only cold water in his time, he had rarely, if ever, washed.

Because she scarcely had time to cook proper meals on her rather rustic cooking equipment, Armand took it upon himself to bring her part of his lunch every day, which usually consisted of a sloppy mess in a greasy bowl, with his black thumb imprint deep inside it. Emma, whose appetite was normally quite good, rapidly found herself wondering what the fame of French cuisine was all about, since Armand's messes grew daily more revolting, and were obviously fabricated from those parts of a sheep's anatomy that were unwanted by the local *boucherie*. However his kind intentions were unmistakeable and his knowledge of the house and the area were invaluable in getting the basic necessities of life installed, so almost daily Emma's relationship with him seemed to increase.

Since transport was a problem, she began to consider the possibility of buying a little *motorcyclette*, similar to the

75cc that Armand popped around on, so one day, in simple French, she asked the question and was astonished at his surprised and then ecstatic response.

To her amazement he rushed away to get – she imagined – his motorbike, but instead to her horror, when he did reappear, he was accompanied by 75 sheep, which promptly invaded her living room, so pleased were they to be back home again!

"Seventy-five *moutons* (sheep)!" Armand bawled out the price, his wolfish grin revealing all his blackened teeth, and demanding instant payment.

"No, no," protested Emma, "I meant 75 *moto*, not 75 *moutons!*"

" I meant 75 moto, not 75 moutons!"

But the shepherd was not to be dissuaded; having successfully rid himself of his home, he was now quite happy to divest himself of his flock as well. Thus it took several neighbours and a visit from the mayor of the village to restore order and remove sheep and owner from her home. Armand, naturally, retired in great dudgeon and no bowls of sloppy mush appeared thereafter, much to

Emma's relief. She began to relax and look forward to the annual village fête, as all her neighbours regaled her with stories of the music, the dancing, and the fun to be had in store.

The night dawned clear and beautiful, with one of the most wondrous moons that Emma had ever seen. Undecided what to wear, she chose finally a soft, voile dress that matched her dreamy mood at the sheer, magic beauty of her surroundings. From afar the music sounded very Spanish and a considerable amount of handclapping was going on as she walked down the road, little suspecting the ordeal in store.

The central *Place* (Square), when she entered it, was heaving with people. Many smiled shyly and one or two made way for her to find a place to sit on one of the wooden benches under the trees, which were festooned with coloured fairy lights. Dancing was desultory at first, but grew more energetic when a group of boys from another village roared up on powerful motorbikes with their girlfriends, having obviously visited a few bars *en route*. The handclapping now reached a new intensity and the Place was a whirl of bodies that dipped and swayed in a sea of motion. Emma watched, entranced, and shyly joined in the handclapping as no one seemed to be taking any notice of her and only the mayor had made a show of shaking her hand and inviting her to dance, which she declined graciously, as the dance in question had been the *Sardane*, which she did not know and preferred to watch.

Then, suddenly, while she was swaying to the music, out of the shadows at the side of the church lurched a vaguely familiar figure. From his walk it was obvious he had had too much to drink, and when he struggled through the crowd people shrugged their shoulders away from him as they allowed him through. It was only when he lurched into the lights from the bandstand that Emma felt her real misgivings, for it was Armand, an Armand with a leer on his face that was distinctly worrying, added to the fact that he had only one purpose in mind – to reach Emma.

Petrified to move, let alone run away, Emma realised for the first time in her life what it was to feel like a lamb about to be slaughtered.

"Dance," Armand commanded, rocking back on his heels and, without waiting for a reply, he lifted the fragile Emma completely off her feet and up in the air before crashing her down and pushing her purposefully through the mêlée. His breath stank, his boots were hob-nailed and, as he made no attempt at co-ordinating his steps to the beat of the music, her feet in open-toed sandals soon felt like raw plates of meat.

"*Arrêt,* stop!" she called feebly as she realised that, quite apart from propelling her around with one hand, he was now lasciviously groping her behind with the other. Horror of horrors, her dress, flimsy at best, seemed to be creeping up to her waist!

She started to struggle, twisting and turning in his grasp, trying desperately to break away from his fetid breath and sweaty torso, not to mention the smell of sheep that hung about him permanently. She felt on the point of fainting when the music stopped, but, as if by providence, they found themselves in front of the mayor who, after at first giving her an amused glance, then realised her dilemma and gallantly stepped forward to extract her from the shepherd's embrace.

But Armand was not to be so easily deterred and, when a slight push from the mayor had no effect, he made as if to pick up Emma and, as she described it later, "Carry me off King Kong-style to heaven knows what destination..."

But the mayor was not going to have his sole English resident abducted in this way and, with a word or two to friends, Emma was finally, if not somewhat brutally, detached from the hairy monster who suddenly collapsed in a heap and was thus easily removed to the churchyard nearby, where he was dumped behind the first available headstone to sleep for some hours.

Naturally this story, in time, took on an apocryphal tone, and was oft repeated with embellishments to many visiting friends and clients.

Chapter 9

Le Droit de Seigneur

During our daily walks with the dogs we frequently encountered the *Seigneur* (lord) of our local *Petit Château* (manor house) which, in itself, represented on a microscopic scale the social divide of those who once ruled as opposed to those who obeyed. M. Henri de Sauvignon, we discovered, was 96 years old, and every afternoon between two and three o'clock, even in winter, he could be found with his hounds taking his daily 'constitution' along the small promenade just below his ancestral home – a modest enough *château* by any standards, but entitled, in any case, to be called a castle.

It was during our third year at *Rozinante* that I noticed M. Henri began to take our meetings for granted, not only for the exercise, but to *bavarder* (chat) a little. I grew to respect and like the old gentleman enormously, not only for his olde worlde courtesy and charm, but for the slow and precise way in which he spoke French, which was so much easier for me to understand than the local farming community's mixture of French and Catalan.

He was just as interested in talking about the past as he was about the present, and did not fall into the trap of so many elderly by comparing the past unfavourably with the present. His powers of discrimination and judgement, I discovered, were quite unimpaired despite his considerable age. Much of our earlier discussions centred on his four years of experiences in the trenches in the First World War. One afternoon he invited me back to the *château* to talk in the comfort of his study, where I was amazed at his scrupulously kept collection of diaries, giving day-by-day accounts of his own and other men's sufferings from 1914-18. His personal writings were augmented by cuttings from newspapers and magazines of the day, and were not dramatic in their presentation, but infinitely moving on account of their simplicity and sincerity. He had not attempted to hide the often mutinous feelings of ordinary men, who after the first euphoria of fighting for their country and the defence of their homes and families had begun to wonder at the *raison d'être* for such endless and senseless slaughter.

"It was like that," the old gentleman would say, without bitterness, and what remained with him always was the smell and stench that came from a wasteland of mud, human excrement and rotting corpses on which the rat population fed.

From the War, he moved on to describe his civilian life in the consular service of his country, finally ending his days as Consul in Morocco, which he had left upon retirement with his family to return to his origins in the Roussillon. Frenchmen, he informed me, invariably returned to their roots and it was natural for him to come back to the 'family seat' which had been theirs for over four hundred years.

On his small estate there were three farms, which were leased to local farmers and if the ties had been feudal in origin, there were, he told me, very definite changes in these relationships once the Socialist Party came to power in France and held the majority of seats in Parliament. For the first time in his life, the farmers had failed to doff their caps in his presence and one of them had said by way of explanation, "We are all equal now."

I was much amused when he told me of an incident which had arisen during the marriage celebration of one of his five daughters, who had brought home a suitable suitor for her hand in the shape of a young naval officer from a well-known Toulon family, who boasted the proud name of Jean-Marie Cyr de Tourraine. The addition of 'de' in any French name signifies an aristocratic connection, but no one in the Sauvignon family paid much attention to this and so it was with no premonition of trouble that the intending groom set off with his future brother-in-law one evening to meet the local mayor and complete the formal documentation for the civil ceremony, which always precedes the religious occasion in France. Unknown to the groom, the local mayor was an ardent Communist and although all went well initially, when it came to the actual signing of the relevant documents, the mayor's face darkened when he saw the offending 'de' in the groom's name and demanded he delete this aristocratic convention *tout de suite* (with all haste)!

But he reckoned without the long naval tradition and pride behind the groom's family and drawing himself erect, Jean-Marie Cyr de Tourraine announced calmly but emphatically, "That is my name and that is the signature I shall sign on this document."

"Over my dead body," cried the mayor dramatically, leaping to his feet and striking a pose that Robespierre or Danton would have appreciated.

"Then no wedding," said the young man, turning on his heel and walking firmly out through the door.

It was M. Henri's wife who, seeing the men return in a sombre mood, sensed the need for quick and positive action.

"When in doubt," she explained later, "I always descend to the *cave* (cellar) and look for an appropriate bottle" – in this case a much treasured Napoleon brandy.

"Tell the mayor it is a gift from me," she informed her son. Having been a very handsome woman in her day, and knowing the effect that had had on the local mayor from time to time, the son duly turned around and went back to the lion's den.

Some time later, much of the fine liqueur having been drunk and with the mayor in a far more conciliatory mood, the little quartet returned. The register had been signed under the nose of the mayor, whose breath was now redolent of the very finest French brandy!

After this conversation M. Henri invited us to a formal reception at his home, which allowed us to explore the *château's* interior. Situated in the middle of the village of St Eulalie, it resembled from the outside a Scottish forti-

fied manor house, and only the park and land surrounding it marked it out from the many houses adjoining it.
Inside proved to be a rabbit warren of rooms, all small and
dark, since the original trees around the house had grown
to monstrous proportions and cast their shadows as high
as the attic windows. The great hall was the most impressive, with a magnificent staircase that led to a minstrel's
gallery above.

Typically, thick swathes of dust lay everywhere but
which failed to conceal the moulded banister and intricate
woodcarvings on library doors and handrails. Significantly,
we noted there was only one bathroom and toilet upstairs to
serve some eight or nine bedrooms, and like the rest of the
house the bath was immensely old and travel-stained and
could only be reached by mounting three steps. M. Henri
admitted that guests always queued for bathing facilities,
but such were the enormous dimensions of the bath that
with a totally inadequate hot water supply, only the first
could ever be served adequately! The amusing addition of
a spanner and pliers at the side of the bath was simply, he
explained, to facilitate the turning of the taps which, worn
out over the years, were reluctant to perform any function
whatsoever – rather like himself, he admitted.

But whatever the privations of washing, the house
revealed a number of rich tapestries and a very fine library
– a real treasure trove of beautifully bound volumes covering both French and foreign literature. M. Henri sensed
my enthusiasm and suggested I returned whenever I
wished to browse and enjoy, a facility which I took up with
considerable enthusiasm, especially as no inventory of the
contents had ever been made. I came to the conclusion
after several visits that whatever the merits of the house,
the book collection was of immense value, while the decoration of the library with its superb panelling and beautifully wrought doors was testimony to the superb crafts-
manship of the 16th and 17th centuries.

I became so preoccupied with my study of the library,
and the compilation of the inventory, it was with complete
disbelief that I learned one morning from a distraught
member of the de Sauvignon family that there had been
a disastrous robbery and that most of the furniture and

books had been removed. Police investigations proved subsequently that a pantechnicon must have arrived in the middle of the night and parked outside the *château* while the robbery took place, and since the house was situated in the middle of the village, the gendarmes were at a loss to understand why no one (the family being away at the time) in the village had seen or heard anything of the disturbance.

The family, naturally, was devastated, as nothing like this had ever happened in their four hundred year occupancy. Worst news of all was to discover that no adequate insurance had ever been taken out to cover the contents of the house, so secure had the family felt in their ancient possession. M. Henri took to his bed, one of the few remaining, and it was obvious to us all that it was a blow too many for his 96 years to sustain. In the cold and frosty weeks that followed he grew daily more feeble, finally dying quietly in the middle of the night, having carefully arranged his papers and his last Will and Testament on his bedside table before closing his eyes on a world he felt had betrayed his trust.

It was thus incumbent upon his son and heir, who arrived hot and flustered from Paris, to continue the endless discussions with the police on what exactly had been stolen. Since no proper inventory of the house's contents had ever been made and my own catalogue of the library had never been completed, the task proved insurmountable. From the blank spaces on the wall it was easy to estimate how many paintings had been removed and similarly how many chests, wardrobes and beds – the total was staggering, to the point where the police suggested there were several pantechnicons rather than just one!

There was an almost daily stream of villagers pouring in and out of the front hall, agog with curiosity. Some expressed their concern and condolences but others were barely able to conceal their satisfaction that it was the *Seigneur* who had suffered such losses while their own possessions remained untouched. There was eventually and inevitably some acrimony and dispute with the new head of the household, who ordered the daily processions to cease, which caused much shaking of heads and mutterings in the local bar.

Some six months went by with no result at all from police enquiries and the villagers still maintaining a stubborn silence. Patience was strained on all sides and there was much ill feeling, to the point where I gave up buying bread in the local grocery or drinking my usual round in the accompanying bar.

My own relation with the new younger *Seigneur* (55) had got off to a bad start as a result of my attempt at using English humour to defuse a fraught situation. For many years the entry hall of the *château* had been dominated by a painting of the Virgin Mary which stood on an easel beside the library door. It had been executed by a great-grandmother of the family and as such was respected, though not necessarily loved as it was generally acknowledged to be the most hideous daub imaginable. Even the thieves had ignored it, and upon being told that it was still in its accustomed place, I tried to comfort the new owner with the thought, "If you still have the Virgin Mary, all is not lost!"

But this light-hearted attempt on my part was greeted with blank incomprehension and I realised, not for the first time, the great divide between one nation's sense of humour and another's. A Britisher, I felt, would surely have replied, "We just wish they *had* taken the bloody thing!"

To our amazement, some six months later, we awoke to hear that yet another robbery had taken place at the *château* and that this time the floor boards, shelving and library doors had been removed. The house, it seemed was little more than an empty shell. However, there was a deviation from the original burglary as this time the removal van used by the burglars had been bold enough to arrive in daylight hours. Furthermore, just before leaving the village, and obviously in full sight of the inhabitants, they had the enormous effrontery to stop at a small cottage on the perimeter, where some cases of champagne had been delivered to an old couple about to celebrate their 60th wedding anniversary. One of the gang had jumped off and picked up the crates before taking off again. But this time, a villager was quick off the mark and ran down the road to take the number of the van so that before it could reach safe harbour, the police had caught up with it and arrested them all. The excitement in the village was intense; morning, noon and night, groups of people could be seen on corners discussing the events and adding their own embellishments.

It was a tremendous occasion when the floor boards, shelving and library doors were returned and re-installed. But, as we discovered, it was a full six months later before we had news of the other contents, when a police report revealed that a large warehouse in Marseilles had been discovered full of stolen property, ready for shipment to other parts of the world. The family were contacted to go and investigate to see if any of the items could be verified and retrieved. It was René, a young cousin, who later told me of the impossible task facing the family, who on entering the warehouse had found a veritable Aladdin's cave of treasures, which offered an impossible task without the benefit of an inventory or photographs of any kind. The two family members had wandered down one alleyway after another, gazing in mounting frustration at tables, chairs and cupboards piled high on either side with clocks, china, and *objets d'art* of every conceivable period and style. They grew weary, until one of them stopped at a clock and, seizing it triumphantly, bore it off to the clerk sitting at a table at the end of the warehouse. But before she could even begin to stake a claim, a firm hand descended on her shoulder and a man behind her said, "That's my clock you're stealing!" – and so it proved to be.

They were forced to return to the village empty handed and face the fact that the *château* would have to be refurbished by their own efforts. The work of renovation is continuing to this day, but much of the original charm and substance has been lost forever, though a new bathroom suite had gained a loyal and grateful following.

When the dust had settled I regretted the passing of my friend, M. Henri, and our afternoon walks together. We had often discussed politics, for while both France and Britain had experienced the vicissitudes of Left and Right political parties, he often reminded me that England had been spared what he called the 'Bolshevik threat' – which I knew from many conversations with other French people had so influenced attitudes during the Second World War. As it was, Communism had been a potent force in France and particularly in the French Resistance Movement during the last War, since they hoped for political power once the War was terminated. M. Henri explained that the Allied armies had been forced to detour from their main thrust into Germany in order to liberate Paris so that General de Gaulle could make a triumphant return and secure the capital city from the threat of a Communist take-over.

"If I say I have no sympathy with Communism's political aims and economic systems, since I think it works contrary to human nature, then I shall be accused of *'le droit de seigneur'*," M. Henri explained; "but in my opinion, it does more harm to the ordinary man and woman than ever Capitalism has to answer for."

I regretted later that he had died before the collapse of the Berlin wall and the eventual revelation of the weaknesses of the Russian system which he had so long deplored.

Quite apart from my conversations with *le seigneur*, I enjoyed talking to the farmers, who never failed, like all their compatriots, to complain about the weather, the markets and all the other forces, as they saw it, marshalled against their wellbeing. And it always astonished me how freely the French, especially the agricultural section of the population, would take to the streets in protest, sometimes violently, against whatever circumstances they believed infringed their liberties. If the price of peaches fell because of a glut one year, then lorry loads of this fruit would be strewn across access roadways all over the Roussillon. The wanton wastage of this delicious fruit astounded me but farmers insisted on their rights to demonstrate, stemming from rights arising from the French Revolution. This bloody period in French history was frequently invoked and the differing perceptions of this event was never more marked than when Mrs Thatcher attended in Paris the 200th anniversary and told the President, in no uncertain terms, that she could not understand why the French were celebrating such a blood-stained event!

All we could say was, *"Vive la difference!"*

Chapter 10

The Language and the French

It was just after the music festival, and I became impatient with my lack of progress with the French language. I had studied it off and on for many years and had assumed once I lived in France that some sort of fluency would simply descend, as it were, from heaven above, but no such luck. For some very gifted and possibly much younger person this might have proved to be the case, but three elderly English people living together and speaking English all day long is not conducive to learning a foreign language.

To exacerbate the problem many of the locals spoke only Catalan, while others, although speaking French, had such strong accents, it was like listening to yet another language. Visitors to *Rozinante*, that is the Dutch, German and Scandinavians, were only too happy to use the occasion to speak our language as well.

A daily sortie to the nearest grocery shop had frequently become our solution to local problems. In this instance Juliette, mother of four and still suckling the youngest while happily slicing cheese or bacon, was delighted to give me the name and address of a local retired school teacher, Catherine Duselles, who readily agreed to give me lessons in French, provided I gave her English ones in return.

On the day appointed I set off for our first encounter with a certain degree of confidence, but had hardly managed, *"Bonjour, comment-allez-vous?"* when she announced firmly that she regarded herself as a 'purist' so far as language was concerned and consequently I should expect to be corrected whenever she felt I had transgressed a French grammatical law. Just how complicated these laws are only devotees of language learning will appreciate, but the net result was that every five seconds of my fractured efforts she exploded into a flood of grammatical niceties that shortly reduced me to complete and somewhat resentful silence. I was greatly relieved when the hour was up and she announced, "Now we speaks h'inglish and I dos ze teas."

"Great balls of fire," I thought, as a purist, "where do I start with that?"

The rest of the afternoon was a nightmare, as the addition of an 'h' where not required and its omission when vital was a personal peculiarity of Catherine's comprehension of the English language. When we parted and she realised how exhausted I was, she waved her hand in explanation and said, "Nevaair minds, your French bad, you work 'ard and h'it appreciates. My h'inglish verray good – it give you no troubles."

Thus my weekly sessions with Catherine soon made me fear for my sanity, such was her confident abuse of my native tongue, and my mind became so accustomed to her eccentricities that to my horror I often found myself repeating them. The climax came at our Christmas party, when having told the Duselles that 'Bottoms Up' was an alternative to 'Cheers' when drinking, I introduced them to a young artist who was staying with us at the time, only to hear them say cheerfully as they raised their glasses to him, "Up your bottom!" While he choked on his drink, I relegated English lessons to the background of my life, if not for ever.

Language as you get older is more difficult, as one's memory deteriorates, while words and phrases, no matter how well-learnt, will simply disappear if not used. In our early days at *Rozinante*, often with plumbing and domestic problems, I had to search the dictionary for words like ball-cock and valve, gasket and fuse, though frequently, as a last resort, I found you could always use the universally accepted *kaput* for anything not in working order.

Misunderstandings are however inevitable, and one dramatic confrontation with a local solicitor who later claimed I had not understood his 'English' made me more aware than ever of the minefield language can present. When I requested an explanation of the solicitor's unfounded accusation against me (the matter in the end proved to be one of mistaken identity) the *Maître de l'étude* (senior partner) explained expansively and forbearingly, "Ah, Madame, you must understand my colleague is young, impulsive and Catalan!"

He was also, I later discovered, engaged to be married to the *Maître's* daughter!

While I had been warned I would have to learn to understand the French, I realised quickly that quite apart from the French it was more the Catalan attitudes I would have to come to terms with. In our own village many of the inhabitants only spoke Catalan, although quite able to speak French as well. Street names were in Catalan, such as *Cami de Serdinya,* and on fête days and other national holidays the Catalan flag would take precedence over the French.

At one time the whole area had been part of what was both French and Spanish Catalonia with Perpignan, the capital of the short-lived Kingdom of Majorca (13th and 14th Centuries) and the second largest town in Catalonia, after Barcelona. It had all reverted to France in 1659 and explains why Perpignan, in character, is both Spanish and French, with a centre of alley-ways and narrow streets full of markets and small shops, while the outer parts of the city are dominated by wide-styled French boulevards and gardens.

Traditionally the region had been poor economically, especially in relation to other parts of France, while the coast had never been developed in the same way as the Côte d'Azur, despite its wonderful climate. Unlike the rich architectural heritage of the Dordogne and Perigord regions, farmers in Catalonia had been preoccupied with survival and built houses that were solid and practical, four walls and a roof, with the animals quartered below in order to heat the rooms for the family living above.

But if the domestic architecture was austere and functional, the great abbeys of St Michel de Cuxa, St Martin de Canigou and Serrabone were wonderful examples of Romanesque architecture in stunning locations.

"Romanesque architecture in stunning settings."

Quite apart from being special tourist attractions, they were also working monasteries with monks and nuns, affording regular Masses for all who chose to attend.

As a Protestant and regular church-goer, I had always imagined France as an essentially Catholic and devout country, but found to my surprise that our local village church was poorly attended and sometimes closed for want of a parish priest, as young men were not so easily attracted to the ministry. It was with a particular sense of loss we mourned the lack of choral services in France, and one Christmas we decided to seek help. We visited the church of St Peter of Villefranche de Conflent where, with difficulty, we unearthed the priest from a dimly lit sacristy. We found him suffering from a heavy cold, and he was consequently so wrapped up in woollens it was hard to identify him!

He advised us in lugubrious tones to try the church at Corneille de Conflent, and so one Sunday morning we set off in search of a service where, we hoped, we could sing our hearts out. Upon arrival we found a modest collection of about twenty people assembled in one close group at the front of the church, in an atmosphere that was truly glacial. In desperation, we searched for any sign of a heater before realising that the small congregation had sensibly already gathered around the only form of heating in the place, with positively no room for extras to judge by the instinctive closing of ranks once we appeared. However, even as we watched the faint blue glow of the gas burners, a final expiring popping sound signalled its demise, so that the cold and iron could now enter our souls unimpaired.

At a quarter-of-an-hour past the appointed time, while we were blowing on our hands and stamping our feet, the same little gnome-like priest from Villefranche entered and began the Mass. As he was alone we searched vainly for signs of choral support, only to be rudely awakened by the sound of an amplifier high up on the wall alongside us, which began laboriously to regale us with piped music. And so it went on, with unseen hands wielding unseen cassettes, and on and on went the appalling recordings, accompanied by the crackling distortions often associated with outdated mechanical devices.

After living in Wales for most of our lives, where choral singing is an integral part of life, the experience could not have been more painful. It was with enormous relief that we found the pale sunlight outside and flexed our numb fingers and toes – so much for the choral Mass at Corneille.

Shortly after this experience we had the first of many visits by a young Englishman, David Freeman, who had been captivated by the mystery of Rennes le Château. One of the BBC Chronicle programmes had inspired his interest, and he arrived clutching a copy of *The Holy Blood and the Holy Grail* written by Henry Lincoln, one of the producers of the same programme. It revealed how, when trying to restore his church at Rennes le Château at the end of the 19th Century, a priest named Saumièr had discovered something which, when he had taken it to higher authorities in Paris, transformed him from a poor parish priest into an extremely wealthy man. He was able to return to his village as a great benefactor to build new roads to enable his parishioners to take their goods to wider markets, while his own personal indulgence had been to build a magnificent home and library for himself which he could stock with rare books and manuscripts. To the great chagrin of all who followed after him, he died without ever revealing the secret nature of what it was he had found. Was it some long-lost Catalan treasure or documentation of some kind? Whatever it was, the mystery remains. David's obsession was infectious and we talked about nothing else during his stay.

One conclusion we came to about declining church observance was to appreciate the French love of drama so that feast days, or *jours de fête,* were great religious festivals. The highlight of such manifestations in the Roussillon is the Good Friday Procession, known as the *Sanche,* which reproduces a medieval file of men and women who walk in bare feet and carry replicas of Christ's cross through the streets of Perpignan, in total silence except for a solemn drum beat. One cannot fail to be impressed.

At a local level, for Christmas, the same love of drama makes the *Pesébre,* or Nativity play, a deeply moving experience, since the entire community takes part. A mother nurses a real baby for the roles of Mary and the infant Jesus, while local shepherds arrive with their sheep and farmers with their oxen. It may be the local baker who plays the role of Joseph, and the village postmistress the role of Mary, which certainly gives authenticity to the two thousand year story of the birth of Christianity. Discussing the service later we agreed that while we bemoaned the lack of choral singing at church services, the *Pesébre* performed at Molitg had an emotional impact that would long be remembered.

Chapter 11

Certified Catalans

It was an announcement on a board outside the village Post Office that made us aware of a Pentathlon tournament to be held in Vernet-les-Bains the following Sunday. My son, Mark, had also heard about it from the main buzz of conversation in the local bar, but since his French was little better than mine he failed to understand the full implications of what he was letting himself in for when he agreed with another couple of local lads to join in the proceedings.

Bundled unceremoniously into a car before he could change his mind, he was driven at speed to the spa town where, to his surprise, he found himself in a Roman style arena. To complicate matters loudspeakers were announcing, in totally incomprehensible French, a series of instructions to competitors, whose appearance had been greeted with a gladiatorial roar from the extremely enthusiastic and doubtless inebriated audience of several thousand spectators. It was, so we discovered later, the highlight of the Catalan sporting calendar.

The crowd of supporters from our own village were delighted to have a representative, even *un étranger* (a foreigner), representing them, and six of them enthusiastically bore Mark off in triumph to the refreshment tent, where several drinks were encouraged down his throat. While all this was going on unknown hands pinned a large number eight on his back and chest to the accompaniment of much back slapping and the French equivalent of *For He's a Jolly Good Fellow*.

By this time my son was distinctly uneasy, and after

three or four more drinks had great difficulty in grasping the fact that the urgent voice on the loudspeaker calling for *'Numero Huit'* actually referred to him, and that it was his turn to perform in the Arena. But those around him fully aware of his plight promptly escorted him to the sawdust-strewn space, in much the same way (as he said later) Inca priests must have carried their victims to the sacrificial alter.

Once he managed to focus reasonably well, he discovered several other stalwarts in the ring, all of whom, he saw with dismay, were armed with vicious looking axes and standing braced in front of massive piles of logs. All the warmth, bonhomie and euphoria of the refreshment tent were soon dissipated when, axe in hand, Mark quickly realised that if the honour of the village, not to mention his family, were to be upheld, then the sooner he chopped up logs the better. Easier said than done, especially when competing against expert woodsmen who had been demolishing logs since they had been weaned from their mothers' breasts.

" Numéro Huit !"

A whistle blasted and several pairs of arms brandishing axes went up in the air and cracked down fiercely on the inoffensive wood. Up, down, crash, wallop! The very first contact sent a shudder up my son's arms, which only ceased when it passed out through the top of his skull. Up, down, crash, wallop! More pain, more stress. Casting an eye around as the din increased, he realised quickly that while his pile of wood was as high as ever, all the others had nearly finished.

It was at this point that St Eulalie supporters started to shout, *"Allez Mark, allez!"* (at least, that's what he thought they were shouting), so that he started threshing madly with chips of wood and sawdust spraying in all directions. When the final blow fell, he lay on the ground unable to release the axe from his hand; it seemed to have become a natural extension of his arm. But the same willing hands once more bore him back to the refreshment tent.

"Thank God that's all over", my son thought privately, and happily consumed another pint of locally brewed firewater – but then could hardly believe his ears when a voice over the loudspeaker again urged the appearance of *"Numero Huit, s'il vous plait, Numero Huit!"*

"It isn't fair!" my son wanted to cry to the world at large, "all these chaps are farmers, foresters, lumber-jacks and supermen!"

By now the sun was beating down and the crowd, souped up to exaggerated proportions, were all urging Mark – alias *'le rosbif de l'Angleterre* (the roast beef of England)' – to 'get his finger out', or the French equivalent.

Back to the arena, this time to a task involving hammers and nails with yet more monstrous piles of wood. A hasty look around confirmed Mark's fears that all the other competitors were no doubt expert hammerers, blacksmiths, carpenters and heaven knows what, but any further reflections ceased when the whistle blew and, more by luck than good judgement, his first nail hit the right target, then the second and the third, until with a mighty roar the St Eulalie supporters went up in the air as one and screamed, *"Magnifique, rosbif!* (Magnificent, roast beef!)". This time he was picked up off the ground and raced to the refreshment tent as a real hero. To his surprise it felt good, very good indeed. In fact it seemed he had actually won Round Two, so what matter that he had been last in the other one? What matter, indeed! He was feeling so good; two more beers went down without any trouble at all.

All over, he thought to himself with the kind of beatific smile that only comes with inebriation, but *"Numero Huit, Numero Huit..."* came over the loudspeaker again and it was back to the arena for the third event.

This time it proved to be more complicated than chopping, slicing and hammering wood. There were ropes hanging in all directions, so that Mark wondered if there were final lynching parties. Daylight dawned however, when with a pantomime of demonstration it was explained that the rope, the pulley and the bale of hay simply meant that all the fodder had to be drawn up to a platform above the competitors' heads. Each time a bale reached the platform there was a roar of approval from the crowd.

To the delight of those present, one of the very small contestants, having with considerable difficulty heaved his bale up to the platform, accidentally loosened his grip on the rope, thus forcing the bale to descend at great speed. Unfortunately this whipped the contestant half-way up to the platform, where he stayed suspended, legs flaying in all directions, shouting imprecations to all and sundry and quite unable to get down again until, taking pity upon him, one of the timekeepers reached up for a leg and hauled him down, awarding him penalties as he did so.

It concentrated the mind wonderfully, so that Mark's first attempt was reasonably successful, as was the second and the third... and it was then that disaster struck, when slightly over-confident he, too, slipped and let the rope spin out of his hands, discovering to his horror that in the process most of the skin had been ripped from both palms; thus each subsequent hauling session was a searing agony.

When the final bale was lodged, with blood streaming down his arms the same willing hands bore him, not to the refreshment centre, but to the First Aid tent, where to add to his misery pure iodine was poured liberally onto open wounds.

Determined now to resist any further calls for *'Numero Huit'*, he had to be manhandled into the arena for the final event exclaiming, "I cannot go back, look at my hands!" But apparently he did not need his hands for the final event – just his feet, since the last sequence consisted of several laps around the arena, not in shoes, but in clogs. In Mark's case *'les sabots'* proved to be several sizes too big, so that he lost a clog every time he put on a spurt. In desperation he stopped at a wastepaper bin and stuffed bits of whatever he could find into the clogs just to keep them on. When he staggered eventually off the road into the arena and the final tape at the foot of the mayoral stand, people were swaying to the music of the local band and roaring their approbation every time a contestant reached the finishing post.

A quick brush-down, his shoes restored to his blistered and aching feet, more bandages wrapped around his hands, and Mark's surviving remains were pushed back for the Award Ceremony. To his surprise, he was told that out of forty contestants he had come tenth, at which time he submitted to the ordeal of being kissed by the mayor's wife and accepted his certificate confirming his position.

Perhaps the final and most endearing memory of the day came when the mayor, in turn, kissed him warmly and, after discovering that Mark was Welsh, declared firmly that he was now to all intents and purposes a certified Catalan!

Chapter 12

L'Épicerie

We had always considered ourselves fortunate that our village was blessed with an all-purpose shop. True, when we passed through the first time, the appearance of the premises was so dilapidated we assumed it had closed down. We discovered subsequently, however, that the owner, Juliette, had just had her fifth child and her preoccupation with the running of the shop, her home and family meant a certain amount of general disorder. In fact, the first time my rather shy brother-in-law went down to buy bread, he was totally unprepared for the sight of Juliette breast-feeding her baby while attending the check-out till! In those early days of French village life, first impressions could be traumatic.

When I met Juliette I realised how five pregnancies and an extremely hard life had taken its toll, with loss of teeth and lank, dispirited hair which, in accordance with French women's passion for dyes, changed its colour from bright red to black depending on her mood. Despite this, her personality was sparkling and vivacious and her instinctive discretion was something I appreciated immediately, and in the first few months of moving into *Rozinante* we did not know what we would have done without her advice. Our queries came thick and fast: To whom did we complain about our water supply? Where can we buy wood for the fire? Can you recommend a plumber or an electrician? Is there a reliable local garage? To all these questions there were instant replies, often in the form of little notes with precise instructions, correct addresses and telephone numbers.

When not in the shop, Juliette served frequently behind the counter in the *Piano Bar*. No one knew the derivation of the name, since no piano had ever been seen there, and it was a small snooker table that dominated the room, with a noisy gang of youngsters from the village milling around it in their uniform style of jeans and black leather jackets. Artificial flowers and plants, all dusty and decrepit, hung despondently from bar shelves, where high-coloured bottles of exotic fermentation glistened and shone with constant use.

It was in this atmosphere that Juliette's personality found its proper outlet, and we watched fascinated as she teased and flattered, rebuked and cajoled the endless procession of drinkers at the bar. We were sitting there one evening when a middle-aged farmer arrived, panting for refreshment and exhibiting on the shoulder line of his shirt a large and jagged tear.

"Hah, hah," said Juliette, delightedly poking an insinuating finger into the gap revealed, "what have we here?" All accompanied with such a lewd and exaggerated leer that the audience collapsed in laughter, especially when the farmer, responding to the unaccustomed attention, puffed out his chest and flushed with delight.

Bernard, her husband, a local rugby player, would shrug his shoulders at these shenanigans and look on bemusedly. Not only did he help run the shop and bar, but also worked on seasonal jobs when business was quiet.

The French tourist season is concentrated within the narrow bands of July and August, when the entire population takes to the roads in search of sun, sea, mountain or general change of venue. Roads are choked with traffic, cars steam and break down, hotels are full, there are queues everywhere, and while pundits on radio and television say "This is madness," the rest simply brush it aside and enjoy the chaos.

Despite its small size, St Eulalie is *'plein de monde'* (crowded) during these months and Bernard would be up at six a.m. and rarely in bed before three p.m., having decorated a cellar under the shop to act as a disco, a crude form of 'night life' for the benefit of the hundreds of campers who filled the local sites. For those living near the shop, these two months became a nightmare of blaring music each evening, punctuated by drunken youths, roaring motorbikes and cars, all blasting up and down a narrow roadway in pursuit of happiness in the *Piano Bar*. Pianissimo it definitely was not, and we avoided it like the plague, only suffering from the noise when the wind changed direction.

The highlight of the holiday season was the annual fête, when the village *Place* would be festooned with fairy lights, with a rough platform for the band and musicians hired for the occasion. At another period in time the music would have depended upon a piano accordion, the odd drum perhaps, and violin, but now all this had been replaced with electronics and other 20th Century equipment, so that the sound was amplified to the point where the entire countryside was ravaged with the beat of *Viva Espana,* or the more popular dance of the year, the *Lambada.*

On market days, I would pass Juliette and Bernard in their battered van, hastily stocking up with supplies to feed the hundreds now besieging their doors, and from their drawn and haggard appearance I wondered if they would survive the season. *"Ce sont les vacances,"* they would shout as they passed, *"Ce sont les affaires."* In other words holiday for some, but business for them. Their children were, of necessity, packed off to stay with grandparents while customers poured in, drinks flowed, the plastic flowers would be taken as souvenirs and pinball machines overused to the point of blowing their fuses.

Strangely enough, during the two months without the children, while Bernard grew more bleary-eyed through lack of sleep Juliette thrived and changed the colour of her hair almost as often as she changed her clothes, and could be seen pirouetting to the *Lambada* at every opportunity. Alternatively she busied herself replacing barrels and bottles, mopping out the bar, cooking mountains of steak and chips, rabbit casserole and seafood special, in addition to draping bunting over the outside of the shop to hide its shabbiness, while singing Catalan songs in a cracked Edith Piaf kind of way and generally being adored by everyone.

It was with much sadness we heard at the end of one

summer that they had decided to move on, as the business, despite the 'high season', could not sustain the needs of their burgeoning family. Bernard was keenly missed in the local rugby side, as was Juliette in the shop and bar, and business plummeted to new depths when their eventual replacement turned out to be two new clean-sweepers who, by their sheer antiseptic niceness, successfully drove any 'characters' away from the premises forever.

Despite this change no-one in the village could have anticipated the dramatic sequence of events that was to eventually close the shop down entirely.

It was towards Christmas of that year when the new owner, René, decided because of declining business to call in all the outstanding debts owed by the locals for purchases or drinks that had been allowed negligently to rest 'on the slate' by Bernard and Juliette, whose *laissez-faire* attitude had contributed so much to their popularity. Reluctantly, the bulk of people complied and paid up, but threatening in the process to go and drink elsewhere, which in view of their past poor record of payment did not seem to worry René unduly.

Eventually there was only one young man of a somewhat 'simple' mentality who refused to comply with the new bar rules, and after a violent confrontation one Saturday night René succeeded in throwing him out, much to the disgust of others in the bar who sympathised with the young man's mental condition. René was to regret his action; the young man concerned returned that night with a rifle and fired systematically at every window in the shop, bar and house premises, so that the terrifying effect of gun shots and shattering glass sent René and his family, plus two dogs, scurrying to the cellar for safety. Not content with the devastation of the shop, the young man turned his attention to René's parked van in the central *Place,* which he doused with petrol and set alight.

By now the local *gendarmerie* had been alerted, while the whole village was awake and reeling from the shock of a blazing van in the *Place,* which had now ignited two of the majestic plane trees, not to mention the entire set of Christmas decorations wishing everyone peace and goodwill and which were exploding violently in all directions.

Nothing like it had been seen in St Eulalie since the end of World War Two!

But most tragic of all was the sequel to this horrifying night, when the young man, realising that escape from his actions was futile, returned home and shot himself not once but twice, since the first shot simply took off his right ear! There was no sparing of gory details from interested though shocked locals.

The young man's funeral had the largest attendance of any funeral ever held locally. As the mayor explained to me, the man may have been 'simple-minded' but the village tended always to protect its own. As for René and his family, they left the following morning and were never seen in the area again, while the village shop remained closed for an indefinite period.

The loss of the shop worried us considerably, since all over France small businesses were being forced to close by hard competition from super- and hyper-markets. We had grown to depend upon the local shop for bread, which was delivered daily from a baker in a nearby village, and we had always tried to buy other items there too, in order to give local support to the one and only shop in the village. We were only too well aware that the baker's son in the adjoining village had no wish to follow in his father's footsteps, since it entailed getting up at four in the morning to light the ovens to bake the bread!

It was a great relief for St Eulalie when one year later an enthusiastic young couple with local family connections came to re-open the shop, bar and restaurant, with excellent meals, so that the *Piano Bar* came into its own again.

Chapter 13

Occupational Therapy

Many people have asked me why so late in life I had taken up *Chambres d'Hôte* (guest housing), but in coming to France to retire I knew it was important to have some idea of what I was going to do with this newly-won time on my hands.

If you have led a busy life at a chosen career, the breaking-off point for retirement can be traumatic unless you have made some plans. I am a social person, enjoy peoples' company and am very interested in cooking. Nothing pleases me more than to put on a good meal with wine and have a circle of people around the table enjoying the food and conversing on as wide a range of topics as possible with enthusiasm and interest.

Certainly as far as coming to France is concerned, it is important to find something to do that the French *do not* like doing, and *Chambres d'Hôte* is a case in point. Although there are parts of the country in the north where this form of catering is quite popular, it is not so well known in the south and certainly not as widespread as in the United Kingdom. The French seem to regard their homes as essentially private places, and the worst thing that can happen to them is for people to call upon them unexpectedly. It takes a long time for you to be invited to dine in a French home, although you may often be invited to eat out in a restaurant, but for the French, the thought of strangers using their homes as their own is anathema.

For me it was the happy nature of the people who came to stay that lay behind the pleasure we derived from the frequently hard work in catering for and entertaining them.

The most appreciated remark for us was when guests would say as we welcomed them at the door, "It's like coming home," while the worst was, "Oh, what a lovely view, but what on earth do you find to do here?"

It is the latter remark that causes most problems, since you realise that not only will you have to accommodate your guests but organise their holiday as well. This may involve hours pouring over maps, plotting routes for walks, making phone calls for train times and other information, and generally shepherding them around, which is very tiring and time consuming. From our experience the British were the worst offenders, and the least likely to have prepared their holiday before arriving, while other nationalities gave their vacation meticulous research and care.

Among our first guests was a German doctor with an American wife from the well-known spa town of Baden-Baden. We discovered immediately that their holiday was based on a tour of the Cathar fortresses of the region and the doctor, with typical Germanic thoroughness, had researched the subject extremely well and was pleased to show me the books and references he had brought with him. His English was excellent and we began to look forward to the evening, as they made it clear they wished to talk to us. However, it took several meetings and drinks around the log fire before the doctor confessed one night to having been stationed in Northern France during the last War, and it was only when we prompted him that he admitted reluctantly to having been a Luftwaffe pilot engaged on several bombing missions of ports, airfields and other installations in Great Britain when Hitler's tactic was to isolate us from our supply lines and starve us into submission.

The doctor went on to say that the British at that time had a totally mistaken impression (in his view) of German air superiority, since many German planes were not well-built, especially those he had experienced with severe undercarriage problems. In his own case, on a return flight to France, his undercarriage failed, and with the inevitable crash landing and the injuries he sustained, he had been invalided out of the Air Force and allowed to resume his medical studies in Berlin (much to his relief). It also saved his life, since his entire bomb crew were killed when their plane crash-landed in a minefield during the North African campaign later in the War.

He explained that his family in Bremen had a long history of trading links with the cotton industry of Liverpool. Every generation had sent at least one member of the family to that great English port to learn English. He remembered his mother, before the War, holding a weekly tea party with like-minded friends, when only English was spoken in order to retain fluency in the language. He regretted the War deeply and admitted that people like his father and grandfather should never have countenanced the rise to political power of a madman like Hitler, but by the time they realised how manic and dangerous he was, it was all too late.

Our next clients proved to be rather an odd couple, who arrived late one evening hot and tired, having already climbed Canigou. With very few words they retired to bed, having asked for breakfast to be served at seven the following morning.

I set the alarm for six-thirty and dropped into deep and dreamless sleep, only to be shaken awake by my sister at five a.m.,who had witnessed from her bedroom window our guest's car creeping down the drive as silently as possible.

"The silver!" I said, and we both galloped down the stairs to check the one or two family heirlooms on the dining room sideboard, only to find to our relief that all seemed present and correct.

What else could they have stolen? – For thieves we decided they must be, since people would never leave in that fashion without having committed some indiscretion or other. Another quick canter down the passageway and we burst into the bedroom to check the linen and towels, only to find, to our surprise, the wife sitting up in bed clutching the curlers in her hair and looking very apprehensive at our sudden entry. The husband's bed was, of course, empty.

"Your husband, *Madame*?" I asked "How has he left the house with all the doors locked?"

Sheepishly she explained that her man, unfortunately, was an insomniac, and frequently felt the need either to walk somewhere at night or simply drive the car around for an hour or two. As to how he had left the house, he had climbed down the drainpipe outside the bedroom window!

I muttered something about not being insured for drainpipe climbing and returned to my room in some disarray, thinking to myself what a rum old world it was once you opened your house to total strangers.

At about seven o'clock, just as sheepishly, the husband drove his car back into the drive, but this time I was ready with the front door held wide open for him to enter. They left quickly after breakfast and have not been back, and I often wonder what part of France he is driving around in the middle of the night and how many miles of drainpipe he has climbed down over the years.

" ... and climbed down the drainpipe in his pyjamas. "

It was great fun a few days later when we welcomed Tex and his wife, Rose, from Dallas, who arrived in a brand new Citroen car with a notice prominently displayed in the back window saying, "We are spending our children's inheritance!" – and why not, indeed! It was the kind of humour they specialised in and Tex, it transpired, had volunteered to fight in World War Two at the age of 29 because his forebears had a long-standing business connection with France and the wine industry, and every generation had sent some member of the family to France to learn the language and the cultivation of *les vignes* (vines).

"Yeah," Tex would say in a wonderful Southern drawl, "I fought World War Two from Cirencester..." Which made us fall about, as Cirencester must be one of the sleepiest and quietest of English towns, far, far, removed from violence and war of any kind.

In turn, once he had expounded on his exploits in defeating the Germans almost single-handedly, we described how excited we had been at the coming of the 'Yanks' to the UK before the D-Day invasion and how every Saturday night a truck from the nearest American camp, G40 at Barry in South Wales, would wait at the town centre for about 30 young girls to take them down to the Saturday night camp 'hop'.

"Hah, hah!" said Tex delightedly, "so you were one of those camp followers we had so much trouble with!"

"Not quite," I said quickly, "not quite," and pointed out that apart from the jitterbugging that went on upon the dance floor, it was the free access to the kitchen and the delights of American army food that most appealed to me, aged 16 and still growing! The age of Permissiveness and the Pill were yet to come.

One morning at breakfast, Rose looked startled when she saw our huge golden retriever, Buster, ambling by the window with what seemed to be one of her brassieres in his mouth. But when a moment later Buster passed by again with nothing in his mouth, she thought she must have imagined it. However, a few minutes later the dog once again passed the window and this time there was no mistaking the pair of lace panties he had trailing from his jaw. She leapt to her feet and rushed out just in time to stop him dropping it in the hole he had dug with her bra in it.

Explanations followed and we were forced to admit that as a retriever, this is precisely what he was expert at, and his predilection for underwear was something we could do nothing about. Like a thief in the night, he would slip into bedrooms via the French windows, snuffle around the floor until he found something unwashed, and then trot off to bury it.

Time and time again I had had to extract underwear from his large soft mouth and wave it in the air to clients sunning themselves in the garden to ask, *"A qui les sales culottes?"* which roughly translated into, "Whose dirty knickers are these?"

Tex and the family were unanimous that if ever I wrote a book about *Rozinante*, the title should be *Who's dirty knickers, etc...* but I am afraid I chickened out on that one, as the book might have been regarded as salacious and sexy and ended up in bookshops frequented by a certain clientele.

"And why not?" Tex would ask – and why not, indeed!

After Tex and Rose left, our next visitor was a *Mijnheer* (Mr) van de Hoorn, who looked harmless enough until we saw the welter of plastic bags that surrounded his arrival. His initial booking had come from Belgium. Refusing to join us at meal times and watching his frequent sorties to the local grocery, we assumed he was feeding himself in his bedroom and, fearful for the fate of the room, I ventured in one morning and fell back aghast at the piled mountain of bags from which emerged nauseating smells of rotting food.

On his return from another shopping expedition I challenged him on his behaviour, at which he collapsed on the floor like a pricked balloon and began a sustained paroxysm of crying and wailing that soon seemed to be developing into some kind of a fit. With real anxiety, I ran downstairs to find the original telephone number I had taken from the initial enquiry, hoping to speak to some responsible member of the poor man's family, only to find myself talking to the director of a small mental hospital near Bruges.

Yes, the director assured me, *Mijnheer* van de Hoorn was a patient, a model one. He seemed surprised at my complaint. Of course, if there was a problem then please do return the gentleman to them, as apparently he had been a patient there for six long years.

Later, seeing his pathetic tear-stained face pressed to the window when his flight eventually took off left us feeling very inadequate, but somewhat relieved.

But worse was to come when this time we were the victims of a superbly played 'con' by an English family of five, plus their nanny. The Roylances (if that was their real name) arrived late one wet afternoon after travelling by Land Rover (brand new) from their holiday home (so they said) in Portugal.

The father, handsome in a rakish sort of way, and prone to wearing a silk scarf knotted at the throat, asked me as soon as he arrived where he could get hold of a copy of the Financial Times. We assumed, gradually, that he was 'someone' in the City of London's financial world.

His wife, Jackie, was small, blonde, lively and full of fun, always devising interesting games for her twins, Jack and Jill, and son Roland, and encouraging us to join them in Trivial Pursuit sessions, which proved hilarious and kept us all up late at night. The nanny was middle-aged and Swiss, and incredibly willing to help us – to the point where after one or two days we left the bedroom and bathroom severely alone for her to look after, since she insisted she had nothing to do, disliked the sun, and preferred 'to be busy'.

Coming to the end of their fortnight's stay with us they said that instead of lounging around the pool, they were going to visit Carcassonne in order to provide a history lesson for the children, who rushed around excitedly collecting sketching pads and pencils.

Unsuspecting, we packed a huge picnic for them and since they did not expect to return until late, we promised to leave outside lights on and would provide an early breakfast for their departure the following day.

True to our word, my sister and I were down early the following morning to prepare breakfast, and it was not until my sister noticed the absence of the Land Rover that we realised with alarm they had not returned from their expedition.

Our first reaction was to worry that they had had an accident, but my sister suspected otherwise and investigated their rooms, only to discover empty wardrobes, despite a prominent display of slippers peeping out from under beds and the odd pyjama jacket folded neatly on the pillows.

The bill for hundreds of pounds, which I had carefully compiled the night before, was relegated to the ashbin along with some of our illusions about running a guest house.

Later we sat dissecting the incident and I recalled a long conversation I had once had with a top London hotelier, who told me the most efficient 'con' clients who never paid their bills (or 'bilkers') were those with excellent acting ability and who frequently came with sporting titles such as Lt, Col, Arch-Bishop or Lady So-and-so. It seems they invariably asked for the most expensive suites and tipped lavishly during their stay, thus building up confidence everywhere, and then leaving silently like the thieves they were.

Our real anger and frustration centred on the fact that we had been betrayed by our own countrymen!

But many years later, when our days at *Rozinante* were over, we took comfort from the fact that we only suffered one or two unpleasant incidents, which were greatly outweighed by the pleasure we had had from the hundreds of other guests who passed through our doors.

Chapter 14

Les Pommes

We were always more aware of the fruit growing around us when M. Ribeira arrived to prune the apple trees in the extensive orchard at the side of *Rozinante*. Many of the trees were old and leaned precariously close to the ground, making it difficult for the tractor to manoeuvre, with the result that a great deal of the work had to be done manually.

The economy of our particular part of the Roussillon depended entirely upon fruit trees, and around St Eulalie this consisted of five different varieties of mountain apples with a very distinct and delicious flavour, a far cry from the universal golden delicious so beloved by wholesalers for their long conservation. Our own apples in the course of time grew wrinkled and withered looking, but still retained their flavour and gave a much enjoyed cidery smell to the cellar where they were stored.

M. Ribeira had been tending this orchard, along with many others, for over thirty years for his Catalan employer, M. Bartholemol. Like many Spaniards, he had drifted over the border looking for work and had settled eventually in our village, and while his French was fluent it was so overlaid with a strong Spanish accent that we managed only to converse with a pantomime of gestures.

However, his knowledge of the soil, the sudden changes in temperature, the arrival of frosts, and the extent and nature of fertilisers, was invaluable, and his squat, solid stance in the orchard became a familiar and reassuring sight to us. Sadly, he told us, the apple industry was diminishing each year as young people left the farms to look for work in towns and cities. M. Ribeira's only son, for example, had left to work in a local garage which afforded him a much better life, according to M. Ribeira, much easier than his own, which he felt had been too hard, the hours too long and the pay too little.

I wondered about his reasoning, since he so obviously enjoyed his life in the open air. He had learned over the years through meticulous experience where the hazelnuts were thickest, where the much prized mushroom, the *Cèpe*, could be found, along with luscious black figs and the most abundant cherries. I would pass him on the hill occasionally and see him filling his pockets with the local mushroom, known as *les Roses des Près* (nearly-roses), and I would always shout and wave, *Viva Espana!* – the music he always sang when his large tribe of relatives turned up from Puigcerda to pick the autumn harvest.

It saddened us to see the orchards declining, for higher up the hill on our daily walks with the dogs we would pass by those that had been abandoned, where brambles covered the blackened remains of once fruitful trees.

When I asked the reasons from local farmers for the decline, the general response was one of apathy and indifference. They were a forgotten part of France, they told me, too few people lived in the Roussillon for the politicians to take account and there was not enough wealth or financial influence to change, modernise or update the economy.

Privately, and this was a selfish view shared by many foreigners who had settled here, I hoped the Roussillon would stay as wild and untouched as it was, having seen parts of Spain destroyed by too great an exploitation of concrete and glass developments.

But change was inevitable according to Pierre Brune, a local carpenter from Codalet, doing a five week stint converting a small room upstairs to another bedroom. He was proud to tell me his father had been a miner until the local iron-ore mines had closed and that he, in turn, had opted to train as a carpenter, while his son, now studying law at Perpignan University, would once qualified be the first family member ever to practise as a solicitor.

It was my French teacher, who had been born in the neighbourhood, who also explained, with many illustrations, the nature of the country people living around us. They had endured hard times, she said, and were, in consequence, perhaps narrow in their outlook. But it had always been and would continue to be a question of self-preservation and survival at the end of the day.

One of her stories concerned the building of their own house on land they had bought from a Catalan farmer. In the course of time they persuaded him to part with another field so that they could extend their garden and retain their privacy. They had decided to leave untouched the orchard at the end of the field, and were quite willing for the farmer to go on helping himself to the rich crop of apples, pears and peaches.

Some years passed and one day the Duselles suggested that as one or two of the trees were old and rotten, the farmer should cut them down and, as they were about to leave for their annual holiday, the time seemed appropriate for this work to be done.

It was upon their return to the house three weeks later, that the Duselles discovered to their horror that the entire orchard had been decimated, leaving rows of ugly stumps, still awaiting removal. A hurried investigation revealed that the farmer concerned was obdurate: he had been told to cut down *all* the trees.

"No!" wailed the Duselles, "only the two that were rotten and why, in heaven's name, leave all the stumps?"

"It's your field," the farmer replied, "you'll have to clear that yourself!"

The field was cleared eventually, for quite a considerable sum of money. In the meantime, the Duselles felt at liberty to enquire what had happened to the wood that had been cut down, since wood in France is a valuable commodity, as most open hearths and stoves are wood burning.

"Oh, the trees were rotten, I had to burn all that," the rogue of a neighbour explained, but discreet enquiries revealed that he had in fact sold all the wood and made himself a handsome profit.

"You see," Madame Duselles explained, "although he sold us the field and got the price he asked for, he went on believing that the ground was his to do what he liked with – and let's face it, he succeeded in doing so!"

I took this as a cautionary tale, but having lived for some time in a rather remote and very rural part of Wales I could imagine similar histories of people who, having farmed land for generations, always resented the intrusion of outsiders in their lives, even when making capital out of their presence.

Trees, we discovered, figured largely on the horizon, not only because of the fruit economy but also because wood is such an important source of fuel, and it was wood-cutting that provided us with another insight into local perceptions.

"Trees figured largely ..."

Trees often marked boundary lines between properties, as my neighbour Jean-Bertrand discovered to his cost when he decided one day to cut down some old ones at the back of his top field for fuel. No sooner had the wood been cut and stored when a farmer living quite some distance away appeared as if by magic to lay claim to the newly sawn-up supply of logs, since the trees, he maintained, were his and not my neighbour's. (The allocation of land among the local farmers was reminiscent of the medieval strip-farm system).

A hot dispute ensued, during which time, mysteriously out of the undergrowth, several supporters or detractors appeared, and so it was a total of eight by the time the descent was made to the local mayor's office to demand attestations and other official manoeuvres to prove one claim against another.

It turned out to be a black day for Jean-Bertrand, since the official verdict was not in his favour. Worse was to ensue, since offers to pay for the wood, even to cut it up into smaller pieces, were all spurned. Not only was the wood to be returned but my neighbour was to be summonsed as well!

The court hearing hung over his head for several weeks and occasioned many visits to our house for endless speculation as to what the verdict might be – transportation to Devil's Island was our most popular contribution – all accompanied by rounds of gin and tonic, for which Jean-Bertrand was acquiring a passion and which, we felt, was one way of groping towards *entente cordiale*.

In the end, the fine was exactly the same sum that Jean-Bertrand had offered his accuser in the first place but, while one Frenchman felt persecuted and aggrieved, the other felt vindicated and elated. Such are the trials of country folk.

When the autumn nights began to draw in and the early morning frosts became severe, we began our first hunt for logs, as we had quite a substantial hearth to heat the large salon of the house.

Every house we passed had great piles of logs stacked everywhere, in barns and outhouses, not to mention the cavity between ground floor and eaves. Then where, we wondered, did all the wood come from – were there secret little forays into the woods to cut down supplies as required?

The modest pile I managed finally to extract from a local farmer was dumped unceremoniously from his tractor in the middle of the yard. As it consisted almost entirely of one hundred centimetre pieces, which were far too big for the hearth to take comfortably, a considerable amount of sweating and swearing had to be endured, as our one and only saw was old and very rusty. It was a long time before I lived down the error of not asking for fifty centimetre pieces. All part of life's learning curve, I reflected.

The following year saw the same problem, with people

promising to deliver but failing to do so, and I came to the reluctant conclusion that when faced with a direct question, no self-respecting Catalan will admit defeat and say "No". He compromises with half-truths and half-promises, with the result that we were never certain what to expect.

A similar situation arose over the boiler for the central heating system which needed a complete overhaul and clean at least once a year. It took several phone calls and just as many weeks before an extremely young man appeared, so young-looking in fact that I was prompted to ask, somewhat suspiciously, if he was familiar with boilers, and Franco-Belge ones in particular.

My fears as to his competence were confirmed when two hours after he left the thickest black smoke we had ever seen belched forth from the boiler chimney, expertly depositing a thick layer of soot on a clothes-line of freshly washed linen.

Urgent phone calls to the offending company revealed it was closed for annual holidays, and it was several weeks later when an elderly plumber came to tell us that the boiler was in terminal decline and desperate for some vital new parts. Needless to say the order for the parts could not be completed for several weeks!

Rozinante became colder and colder and was renamed 'Ice Station Zebra'. We all took to wearing several layers of clothes and eating thick vegetable soups, peppers and curry. It was only when an early spring brought the sun out again that we all thawed out.

As for boiler inspection and wood supplies, orders were placed in June the following year and so much wood was delivered we had to have a special shed built to house it all. The family decided I was fast turning into a real Catalan!

Chapter 15

Back to Nature

We had not been in the Roussillon long before hearing of another English family running a Walking Holiday Centre from the site of an old iron works, complete with original sheds and railway sidings. The Newcombe family, we discovered, had been renovating these works for over 20 years and, in the course of time, had built dormitory style accommodation and a restaurant to cater for up to 40 people. The beauty of the centre proved its accessibility to many different valleys where the soil, rock formation, flora and fauna varied considerably.

Early clients of theirs had consisted mainly of school parties on Geography trips, but over the years the behaviour of the young, not to mention the staff, had deteriorated to the point where too much wine and too many amorous experiments had led to teenage disasters. Accordingly, the Newcombes had quickly and sensibly shifted allegiance from the young to the elderly nature enthusiasts, whose interests concentrated on the countryside and not on their drinking capacities or sexual prowess.

Each spring a bus bearing some twenty or more mixed clients arrived at *Mas Floriana,* ranging in age from 65 to 85 years. These 'old dears' it was hoped were far less likely to get drunk and certainly not pregnant!

Wishing to share in one of these organised excursions, my sister and I arranged one bright, sunny morning in June to meet the bus from *Mas Floriana,* which duly took us north of Prades on the road to the lovely thermal spa-town of Molitg-les-Bains and thence up to the Col de Jau, famous for its gentians.

From there we went on to explore the nearby water-meadows and the many varieties of wild orchid, among other things. Although I had once studied Latin, the fluency of these ladies with the Latin names for all the flowers soon earned my respect.

"Ladies, do come and see this magnificent example of *Galega Officinalis...*" ("Goat's Rue," was my sister's whispered clarification in my ear). Professor Peter Beaton, eminent botanist, the leader of the group, would encourage us and immediately one of the entourage would say, after consulting her nature book, "But Professor, don't you think it might be *Myrica Gale?*" ("Bog Myrtle," translated my sister). At which an extremely tolerant professor would reply, "I am sure you are right Dr Saunders, but I do believe this is one of the few places in the world where you will find examples of this kind," which led us all to press even closer around him to view, with an attendant sense of awe, the leaf or flower in question.

"... but Professor, don't you think it might be Myrica gale?"

Personally I found it hard to concentrate on the specimens studied, but the ardent group of botanists and amateur enthusiasts were enchanted with their journey.

Clad in climbing boots, thick socks, floppy hats (as a precaution against the sun), and with water bottles at their hips, it was staggering to see their endurance; long into the day, no matter where the professor led us, we followed, often into the thickest undergrowth imaginable. They were, I decided, a typical group of British nature lovers, predominantly female, all looking a little bit like Margaret Rutherford, with binoculars at the ready and notebooks to hand, in which excited references were written.

The only male in the group stood aloof and abstracted in his own thoughts, so it seemed to me, and it was only when one of the ladies rather spitefully remarked that his confusion related to the amount of wine he had drunk each day that I realised the poor chap was trying most of the time to remember exactly where he was!

It was while I was musing on the beauty of the land-scape that a voice suddenly said very sharply beside me, "I do hope you are not thinking of picking it?"

"Picking what?" I asked stupidly.

"Why," she replied, pointing her finger to the ground in front of us, "that rare specimen down there."

Since I could not identify anything at all, I said rather feebly, "Oh good heavens, I wouldn't dream of it."

"Good," continued the formidable voice. "You see," she added, "I have discovered two members of our group in the very act. Sabotage, sheer sabotage!" She was livid at the memory. But worse was to come: "Tonight," she warned, her tone now full of menace, "when we get back to base, I intend to hold a thorough investigation, after which, I assure you, heads will roll!"

I was flabbergasted at the thought and looked around quickly for an escape route, which I found in the presence of Harvey Newcombe who, bored with the trip he had done many times before, was happily reading behind a bush the latest copy of the Daily Mail. We chatted away and, moving eventually towards the bus, he said, "Do come and have a drink with us when we get back."

To his surprised, I said most emphatically, "No thank you, Harvey, I have no wish to find myself hanging from the yardarm tomorrow morning!"

By the end of the day though, we agreed we had enjoyed

ourselves enormously but were grateful that our own transport had avoided the inquisition at the Forge and the possible sound of tumbrels thereafter.

Shortly after this nature trip, we learned from an English friend of the existence of local walking groups that met in Prades on a weekly basis to explore the surrounding countryside. Checking, first of all, that we were eligible to join, we found ourselves meeting the Caminem group, as they called themselves, one Thursday morning outside the Prades railway station. Like the others, we wore stout shoes and carried walking sticks with packed rucksacks on our backs, ready for a full day's walk either on the coast or, more likely, in the foothills of the Cerdagne or the range of the Albères.

The bulk of the group were French and we congratulated ourselves on having found a means of making French friends, speaking their language and learning the geography of the area. What I had not taken into account were the actual rigours of the walk.

The route as we descended from our cars at the village of Castlenou, near Thuir, seemed deceptively easy until we left the main road and started down a rough track to a small dried-up river bed, after which we began to climb sharply upwards, on and on and ever upwards. The crude path soon gave way to shale and slippery patches of heather and rock and while others, to my astonishment, continued to laugh and talk to one another, my breathing became so laboured, I felt as if I was sucking air up from my feet and expelling it, with great difficulty, out through the top of my head.

An English couple, the Olivers, were quick to spot my distress and while Henry offered me his stick to hang on to, his wife Roberta kept shoving her hand forcefully against my backside to give me the necessary boost to keep me upwardly mobile and stop me descending to the depths again. These push and shove operations were extremely painful!

When we finally scrambled up the last couple of yards to the top I was speechless and puce, and it was no help to my morale when Roberta appeared at my side to whisper in my ear, "See if you can spot the man in the group who has artificial legs!"

I leapt to my feet, for if this was the case how could I possibly complain, leave alone let the British side down in front of all the French!? Roberta's remark had, as usual, hit the nail on the appropriate head. Worse was to come however, as the respite proved brief and even rougher, tougher tracks awaited us.

To my everlasting shame, I brought up the rear and while others, once we arrived, admired the stunning view of the castle and talked about the epic struggle of the French resisting the marauding Spaniards of the past, all I could do was fan my brow and fortify my dwindling reserves by thinking that if this was the final peak, then it must be downhill the rest of the way.

And so, thank heavens, it proved, although downhill was often as tricky and precarious as climbing up since no pathway, as such, existed and one simply had to watch carefully where you placed your feet between rough shale, sharp brambles and other hazards in order not to break some vital part of one's anatomy.

As for the chap with artificial legs, I was beginning to wish I had a spare pair too!

The village of St Colomb de Vennes, when we reached it, turned out to have a *cave* whose dark, damp recesses and glistening rows of bottles were a rewarding retreat from the noonday sun. There was also a stream nearby where a halt for lunch was called, and I took advantage of the break to prise off boots and socks, and to stick what was left of my feet in the cool water and watch the steam rise.

The main conversation during the break centred around a June trip to the Cerdagne of some two days duration, and which would involve spending the night in a Refuge. It was, the leader informed us, a trip for the courageous, training a keen eye on me as he said it – he knew a weak link when he saw it.

Roberta, once we returned to Prades, was much more direct and suggested I join a Monday group of walkers, whose efforts could be classified, she said, "as more strolling than walking."

"I have been judged and found wanting," I explained once I returned to the safe haven of home, where the halls seemed to receive me like an old friend and I surrendered my aching bones to the pleasures of a very hot bath.

And so it turned out that my sister and her husband qualified for the Thursday Caminem group, while I joined the Monday strolling players. My sister became familiar with the high ground and I the low, but our knowledge of the countryside around us grew extensively as there was a fund of knowledge to be gleaned from dozens of subsequent walks, and the mountains always had some secret or other to be revealed.

"... he knew a weak link when he saw it ..."

Meanwhile, the Monday group turned out to be a very jolly crowd indeed, several of them bringing dogs with them, one of which, a little Jack Russell terrier called Rosalie, was fourteen years old and had never missed a walk in her life.

As fourteen in canine terms means about ninety in

human years, I took strength and courage from this fact and followed her as a yardstick. When she stopped to pant a bit, I did the same, and if she hugged the wall for shade, I followed suit. When every now and then she flopped down for a rest, I copied her. *'Rosalie Numero Deux* (Number Two)' I was nicknamed, and whenever I disappeared from view and the party forged ahead without us, they only had to stop and call, *"Rosalie, viens ici!"* and we popped up our heads and everyone mooched on again.

Dogs really are man's best friend and Rosalie soon realised that, like herself, I was a genuine 'old soldier'. Quite quickly, through trial and error, I discovered what she liked to eat – Smarties and chocolate of all kinds she adored, along with sausages of every shape and hue. Bread and cake she scorned, but raw carrot and apple were firm favourites and as we tottered into base camp together, we knew to the last step and the last gasp exactly where we would settle.

If water was within striking distance she would find it, and often before eating she would sit down in the stream with a blissful expression on her face, while I envied her simple ability to cool down her derrière and had to content myself with putting my feet in the water, just hoping the swelling would go down and enable me to put my shoes back on again.

It was near Campone one day that, sitting idly on the bank of a stream, I felt suddenly a violent stinging sensation in my rear and leapt to my feet, horrified to find that I had been sitting on an ant's nest. The pain became excruciating and so, in agony and with complete disregard, I tore off my pants and collapsed in the water alongside Rosalie, who took my aberrant behaviour with all the calm splendour of her 90 years.

The group, after their initial shock, put it all down to eccentric British behaviour and discreetly turned their backs when I rose finally to dress again. My rear end, however, took several weeks to recover and in the history of the walking club, the day was remembered for the Geronimo-style yell I gave as I took off from the ant's nest.

One other impression I made on the group was my introduction of Irish Whisky to the annual end of walking year *grillade* (barbeque), when we all sat down in fields overlooking stupendous views to eat and drink in a manner only the French can assume: champagne with hors d'oeuvres, wild game pâté, Pyrenean cheeses, exotic puddings, accompanied by sweet Muscat wines – very French-style indeed.

I regretted my whisky contribution momentarily later when, on visiting the supermarket to replenish my stock, I found the shelves bare – the Walking Group had got there before me!

" *Immortelles* "

Chapter 16

Les Immortelles et la Fête de Pommes

Throughout the summer, my sister and her husband worked hard in the garden, although most of the time was spent cutting grass. Nevertheless, a most successful *potager* (vegetable patch) provided an excellent crop of onions, leeks, peppers, courgettes and a large bed of potatoes. Accompanying this was a bed of parsley, basil, chives and other herbs, which we used extensively in our cooking. At the end of one of the rows, half-a-dozen sunflowers reared their heads to a height of twelve feet, and as one plant alone had several great heads there were many references to the Van Gogh of the Roussillon.

On the whole though, we discovered the soil was poor in quality and were glad to take some chicken manure from our neighbour and dig it in to encourage fertility. The first time Ray did this, however, he spread it evenly over his newly dug beds without warning us what the resultant odour would be. My first intimation of disaster was when one of my guests came to ask me if I thought something had died in the garden.

"Something dead?" I repeated incredulously to the guest, a homeopathic doctor from Lyons. "What on earth do you mean?"

"Well, Madame," he replied, "if you come to the side of the pool, you will appreciate that something is putrefying somewhere."

It sounded like the opening of an Agatha Christie novel.

A brief glance over the hedge at the new *potager* quickly solved the puzzle, and from then on the foul excrement was dug in rather than left to dry on the surface in the sun.

Lower down the garden, my sister busied herself with her cultivation of dried flowers or *les immortelles,* as the French call them. They are naturally grown flowers that could be picked and dried, after which Margaret arranged them in baskets or other receptacles for sale.

We realised quickly that a marvellous outlet at St Eulalie would be the annual *Fête de Pommes* (Apple Festival), and formal application was made to the mayor's office for a suitable stall at this annual village fair. The main purpose of the Fête is to sell apples, and the local farms turn out in force to set up their tables and pile them high with their beautiful rosy mounds of fruit. There are always six or seven varieties, and it's a marvellous opportunity for banter and exchange of news among the farmers and their families.

The French, when they are *en fête,* are always out to have as wonderful a time as possible, and locally the Catalan flag is much in evidence, as is bunting, fairy lights and lanterns, all strung lopsidedly from one end of the field to the other, often ending in total confusion above a small stage, where the combined bands of three villages play in active and vigorous competition with one another.

It never ceases to astound us how casual the French are when it comes to strewing lights and cables willy-nilly up and down streets, around chimney pots, in fact, any convenient vantage point that presents itself! While the general tidiness and cleanliness of village streets is never in any doubt, the whole effect is often ruined by the haphazard – and in our view, dangerous – way the cables are bunched together. At Christmas time, when the lights and decorations are added to the general confusion, it is horrifying to see the cables swaying in the winter wind, and one is at a loss to understand how safety and security standards are met.

The *Fête de Pommes* is no exception to this total disregard for safety, leave alone aesthetics, and in the evening when a wind whips up the perilous dipping and swaying of the lights matches and accompanies the movements of the dancers who, being Catalan, revel in the rumba, tango, samba and anything else that requires vigorous handclapping and indiscriminate *Olé*s!

It is only towards the end of the evening that the mood changes and everyone joins in the national dance, the *Sardane*. Hand in hand we circle the village *Place* to point our toes and sway languorously and luxuriously this way and that to the rhythm of the music. It is always a happy and satisfying end to a lovely day.

" ... the Sardane, when hand in hand we pointed our toes ... "

The day of our first Fête dawned dull and cold, with the top of Canigou unhappily shrouded in menacing low cloud. A chill and unaccustomed wind ruffled our table-cloths while we struggled to anchor them down with pins before arranging the flowers as attractively as possible: large bouquets at the back and small baskets to the front.

All around us the apple-growers, many of whom sported cheeks as red as their apples, were busy piling up box upon box of produce and casting an experienced eye both at the weather and the arrival of the first bus load of visitors, all armed with baskets to collect their winter supply of *pommes*.

111

"Colder than last year, but it won't rain until four," they would forecast cheerily (which it did not), and "Hello, Madame Guichard, back again I see, how many can you carry this time? Let's have your basket then."

All morning two bands of young girls, with drum majorettes throwing their batons into the air with consummate ease, had marched to and fro to an ear-splitting and often inaccurate rendering of *Viva Espana*. Several competitions involving bowls and bottles were in progress and there was some satisfaction on our part when Ray threw a single bowl to win the first bottle of wine of the day.

Apple selling was brisk, though there were complaints about the cold with accompanying foot stamping and arm waving. The French, especially in the south of France because of the generally warm weather there, cannot stand the cold, leave alone wind and rain, and I was accused constantly when I met locals of bringing the bad weather with me from Wales – an observation that tended to wear a little thin after a time.

At one point in the morning the mayor, together with the local president of the Chamber of Commerce, weaved his way through the crowds from stall to stall.

"This is a Welsh family," the mayor explained to the dignitaries when he reached us. "They run a *Chambres d'Hôte* here and also grow dried flowers for sale."

"Quelle initiative!" The president seemed duly impressed, wished us luck, but passed on without buying anything.

Having completed his round of duty, the mayor climbed onto the stage in the centre of the field and asked for a fanfare of trumpets before making a short introductory speech to welcome the guest of honour.

Once this functionary seized the microphone, it soon became clear he was using the occasion for political purposes. There was a stream of promises of government aid for new roads, improved water supply, grants for this and grants for that – small wonder that with typical French cynicism the locals, who had heard it all before, began yawning and shuffling their feet. Soon there were several mutterings of discontent as the president, carried away by his own rhetoric, began to exhort his listeners not to leave the land but to work harder than ever!

Farmers all over the world are notoriously never very happy with their lot (understandable at times) and the longer the speech continued in this vein, the more restless grew the crowd, until the odd obscene gesture could be seen. The natives, I decided, were definitely growing restless. It was also midday, a time for food and drink, and it was with a general sigh of relief that the crowd responded to the president's final words of "I now declare the refreshment tent well and truly open."

He might just as well have fired a starter's pistol, for before he could descend from the podium there was an accompanying roar of approval from the crowd and a mass stampede ensued, the object of which, so far as we could see, was to discover who could reach the refreshment tent first. How difficult this was to prove could only be appreciated when we realised that several farmers and their families had placed themselves strategically in front of the refreshment tent, so that immediately there was a massive congestion of bodies all fighting to get through the restrictive entry point.

To add to the confusion, those who had ignored the rules (and the French are very good at this) and slipped in beforehand were now being manhandled out of the way by the next successive wave of impatient and thirsty bodies.

"Order, order," shouted the mayor who along with the president was also fighting to reach the drink counter, but he might as well have saved his breath for it was well past midday, the sacred hour when the whole of France turns its rapt attention to the enjoyable but serious task of eating their principal meal of the day. The frustration on this occasion of waiting beyond the appointed hour had sent appetites and thirsts soaring to unprecedented heights.

Two of the largest farmers I had ever seen took it upon themselves at this juncture to gather the tent flaps at the entrance and endeavour to close them, but this dangerous move only had the effect of incensing the crowd even further, resulting in a concerted renewed charge, which sent one fat farmer one way and the other several yards in the opposite direction.

There was complete chaos within the tent now as chairs

and tables were overturned, and those manning the bar were soon fighting for their lives to save the counter and the hundreds of bottles and glasses upon it.

To his credit the band-master, realising the approaching crisis point, picked up his baton and burst into a lively rendering of the *Marseillaise*. Unfortunately it failed in its unifying purpose and only added fuel to the fire that was burning out of control in people's hearts and bellies. Total disaster was at hand, for now village rivalry had taken a hard hold of the struggling mob, and just as the Scottish clans of old would rally their clansmen to their sides, so the cry of *"Casteille to me"* or *"Sahorre to me"* brought out the worst in everyone.

"It's rugby that starts it all," the mayor was to explain to me later, which, in his opinion, lay at the root of all inter-village rivalry. But rugby or not, this day there was a sudden gust of very high wind at the precise moment when the tent pole supporting the whole makeshift structure decided to give up its uneasy role and, with a terrifying tearing and rendering, the whole tent capsized with hundreds of folk buried beneath it.

The blast from the collapse blew our table over, and with it the last two baskets yet to be sold. We decided cowardly that retreat would be discreet and, leaving the men folk to join in the rescue operations, we made our escape. Later we were relieved to learn that aside from minor cuts and bruises, no one had been hurt seriously and, more importantly, most of the wine had been saved!

The mayor's post-mortem revealed that some drinking by stallholders had gone on long before the official opening of the refreshment tent and it was decided that severe restrictions would be enforced in future.

The one and only serious casualty apparently had been a drum majorette who had lost her baton.

Chapter 17

The Sporting Life

Like a lot of Frenchmen, our neighbour, Jean-Bertrand, was devoted to the sport of hunting. The preparation for this must, we thought, take infinitely longer than *la chasse* itself since it required, first of all, acquiring the gear. Dressing up for the role to be played is very important in France and accounts locally for the large number of stalls in the Prades market which are devoted entirely to the sale of surplus army jackets, combat gear, boots, stalking hats, camouflage suits and so on. One could be forgiven for thinking that World War Three was about to break out but, in reality, it is all associated with the Notice on the door of every *Mairie* in October of each year to the effect that the *sanglier,* or wild boar, hunting season has commenced.

This season extends only until January when the small animal season, *le gibier,* begins, by which they mean rabbits, hares, pheasants etc. But since all these species have been hunted to extinction the only thing left to shoot are the poor thrushes, who migrate every year to France in the often vain hope of breeding.

According to a broadcast on France Culture radio station, the number of thrushes has diminished so alarmingly because of this national pass-time of shooting them out of the sky, that there is a strong possibility the breed will be declared in danger of extinction.

Since the hunting laws appear to be sacrosanct in France no one has dared to do anything about it, although there are frequent political mutterings and protestations by Animal Rights groups and environmentalists.

The first time I visited my neighbour's house I was struck by the charm of the inside, which contrasted so starkly with the chaos outside. The cement-mixer, for example, which constantly churned out cement morning, noon and night, was situated right outside the front door. The kitchen, however, was surprisingly warm and comfortable, with a bright glow from a wood-burning stove in the corner. On the other hand the salon, or living room, sprouted on its walls the most lethal collection of guns I had ever seen.

"I, hunter," my host explained and immediately assumed a posture of stalking and hunting, every now and then shouting, "Bang, bang!" in case I misunderstood his acting ability.

I smiled nervously and asked him where he hunted and what animal. Everywhere and everything, it seemed, but wild boar in particular, a very dangerous animal to all intents and purposes, especially when cornered and wounded.

"Never go walking in the woods with your dogs in November or December," he warned me solemnly, "or you could be shot in mistake for a boar."

Was my general appearance so bizarre? I wondered, and made a mental note to get my hair cut as soon as possible since I did not want my head appearing on Jean-Bertrand's trophy-wall.

I promised to think about what he had told me, but a further treat was in store when he marched me down a long hallway to his bedroom, where the door was flung open dramatically to reveal the most hideous sight I had ever seen. Two enormous stuffed boar's heads presided on top of his wardrobe and this, one assumed, was the last thing he gazed upon every night before putting the light out, and the first thing he looked at every morning when he woke up. There is, I decided, no accounting for taste, since such a room would give me nightmares!

Daily in November we could hear the sound of gunshots and see our neighbour stalking across his garden (and frequently ours) – not, I hasten to say, in pursuit of boar but of magpies which, he reckoned, were pests and should be eliminated. To our horror, much later he shot at eagles and kites, which he claimed were swooping down to attack his chickens. We were in no doubt that it was just a daily form of gun practice, and were grateful he had decided not to treat his English neighbours as some similar sort of pest to be put down!

It was well into winter when I was awoken one night by a guest who, although embarrassed at disturbing me, was anxious to know if there were such things as hippopotamus in this part of France. I must confess I burst out laughing and said, "Mrs Oakley, this is not darkest Africa!" But she insisted I follow her to the main upstairs balcony window, where she pointed to the ground below. Clearly visible by the light of the moon were four or five black tank-like shapes.

Slowly opening the French windows, we could hear the animals' snuffling and grunting noises as they vigorously and expertly churned over the soft ground so that our lawn looked more like Cardiff Arms Park after a rugby international match. *Sanglier* – wild boar – a whole family of them, and there was little one could do to stop their determined search for worms and other titbits.

We were so alarmed at the extent of their excavations by morning light that we were tempted to tell our neighbour to come and hunt *chez-nous,* but we felt we could not stomach the ensuing carnage or the worry of him missing his target. An electronic fence was to prove the eventual solution, and the 'hippos' were forced to seek pastures new.

Fortunately for our *entente cordiale,* a common denominator with the French is our Welsh love of the game of rugby football, which local people were passionate about. Even now that we are retired and living in France, international matches, especially between Wales and France, are occasions for great family reunions as relatives and friends flock to Cardiff Arms Park or to the *Parc des Princes* in Paris, to sing, cheer and chant for their respective countries and thoroughly enjoy the finer points of the game.

My brother and his French wife vividly remember attending a France/Wales match at Cardiff one year with my brother shouting for Wales and his wife for France. Half way through the match a Welshman standing behind them said amiably enough, "Make up your bloody minds, will you!"

Rugby is popular in certain parts of France, and the South has produced many famous teams such as Narbonne, Perpignan, Beziers, and Biaritz, while every village and town has its playing fields and rugby posts. In winter the local newspapers are full of pictures of broad-shouldered muscular Catalans side-stepping and out-footing their adversaries in weekend matches.

All conversations with locals, once the international season has started, are full of accounts of the merits or otherwise of their respective players. For the French, the most striking attributes are *'le flair'* and *'l'imagination'*, and whatever else it takes to win the game. There is also *'le fair-play'*, which they concede the British may have invented but which can be overlooked in the heat of the moment.

Certainly, their attitude is obsessive, especially when they themselves are playing, since they use body language all the time and you can judge the intensity of their passions from the rolling of their eyes, the throwing of the hands in the air and shoulder jerking, just to mention a few, to express amazement, frustration, anger, despair or joy.

We discovered quickly that all the locals gathered in the village *Piano Bar* on an International day, and discussions about the result fuelled conversation thereafter for weeks on end. We might just as well have been living in Llanelli or Pontypool. Indeed, our first forays down to the local bar had been to join in the viewing of matches, and we got into the habit of calling in at the shop, then strolling around the corner to the bar for a quick drink, always accompanied by a round of hand-shaking and general conversation before making for home.

Drinks always circulated freely and it struck me, not for the first time, that the vivid colours I had learned to associate with the region – deep blue azure for the sky and sea, vermillion for the rocky coast and mountains – were not only reflected in the colour of the clothes worn by people locally (such as vivid purple shirts, red and yellow blouses), but also applied to their drinks.

Every bar sported an array of tantalising bottles filled with green, blue, red, and orange syrups and liqueurs, which were related to pears, peaches, greengages and blackcurrants. To my amazement, any one of these could be added to virtually any drink ordered. Beer, for example, that sacred beverage of the British, was often adulterated with a good splash of orange, peach or apple, which must have raised the overall sugar content alarmingly. Pastis, cognac, rum, Muscat – no matter what – everything was mixed happily together and drunk in copious quantities until cross-eyed recipients fell off their bar stools and tottered home.

The bonhomie of various bars and constant talk of rugby football led inevitably to my son, Mark, being asked several times if he would be interested in playing for various local teams, such was the esteem in which Welsh rugby was held, but realising how high local standards were he declined and agreed instead to join a local football team called 'The Gentlemen'. Some doubts as to the correctness of the name of the team arose as soon as he entered the changing room, since most of the team looked like Kelly's heroes, varying from slim, supple youngsters to varicose-veined, vitamin-supplemented virtuosos.

" *The Gentlemen ... looked more like Kelly's Heroes ...* "

Added to this was the ingredient of different nation-alities: British phlegm matched with Spanish fire and Catalan or French fanaticism. All trades and professions were represented, from bank clerks and garage mechanics to accountants and farmers.

Training proved to be as little as possible, and the selection confined quite simply to one's ability to turn up or not. There was an exceptionally big squad, as cardiac arrests were not unheard of and local fête hangovers often led to multiple substitutions.

Mark's first pre-season training session revolved around an animated discussion about whether the team should wear long shorts (pre-War style) or shorter shorts (post-War style). For two hours an argument raged about the highs and lows of hem lines plus cost – always an important consideration in any French discussion.

Finally, a break-away section said they were not prepared to make a personal contribution of any kind towards the costs, as they felt this should be a charge on the club, with which the two fully paid-up Communist Party members strongly agreed. At this, tempers flared to the point where one or two punches were thrown, until the oldest and most experienced of the side stood up and said, *"Je suis la majorité et je suis pour les shorts longs* (I am the senior here and I vote for long shorts)."

Silence greeted this remark to begin with, until some wit remarked that the only reason this particular member wanted long shorts was to disguise his revoltingly spindly legs, at which the meeting broke up to reconvene at a local café, where it was soon obvious the row would continue all night.

Discussing later the ability of the French to argue about anything and everything, we came to the conclusion it related to the French wanting to be seen as *serieux* and it is true that thanks to the training in basic philosophy at school, earnest discussion rages to and fro on every subject under the sun.

Mark never did discover who won the motion since, as with all French style debate, the original problem was soon obscured by a dozen equally pressing matters. As for his contribution to matches, he failed to complete the season when a motor-bike accident in Spain caused him to cancel the rest of his fixtures.

It was several weeks later in the local *Piano Bar,* as he was leaning against the bar to take the weight off the swollen ankle he was nursing, when two large Catalan rugby-players barged their way up to the counter with the single-minded gait of those who have already had more than enough to drink. One or two of the locals slipped unobtrusively off their stools and headed for the calmer waters of the back-room, while George, sitting beside Mark, muttered warily, *"Petit Pepés",* which roughly translated to 'wide boys'.

The bar at the *Piano* stands at about elbow height, and after two large drinks one of the new arrivals suddenly lifted himself upwards and backwards to land sitting down on the bar itself. *"Pas mal* (not bad)," muttered someone, but the inevitable followed when, with a disparaging move-ment of his hands, the inebriate invited anyone there, for a fiver, to do the same thing. No one responded, and when all gazes seemed to shift to my son, he was quick to point to his strapped up ankle.

The sneer from one of the *Petit Pepés* with which this was greeted made Mark's heckles rise, which was unfor-tunate because the next moment he found himself chal-lenged to a French arm-wrestle and *'Numero Huit'* echoed like an alarm bell in his head! Seemingly unable to refuse, however, he tried mentally to psyche himself up to the occa-sion by swinging his arms to get the adrenalin pumping as furiously as possible around his body. Since the motor-bike accident he had been, as it were, 'grounded' from normal activities and the long mountain runs to which he was accustomed.

"Sur le bar?" he asked.

"Non," replied the gorilla, *"sur la table au coin* (on the table in the corner)."

By now Mark was cursing himself for having found himself in this situation, since, sizing up the Neanderthal specimen opposite him, he realised he was probably on a losing ticket. The locals, of course, began shuffling their feet for a better view, while the ape-man's side-kick was busy trotting around the bar, with his hat outstretched before him, taking bets. Needless to say, the Catalan was odds-on favourite.

A quickly appointed *arbiter* (referee) – there's always someone around somewhere – and the instructions came for the two contestants to put their left arms behind their backs and take up a hold.

A rapid count of three, and tension made veins bulge and eyes pop with the strain. Twisting his grip suddenly, Mark heard himself say, "Come on then... is that all you've got?" which, in a way, was a method of trying to motivate himself but managed instead to provoke his opponent into a slam.

A ragged cheer went up, but without wasting an instant the Frenchman settled himself down for another tournament, doubling up the betting at the same time.

Manoeuvring his grip somewhat Mark managed to hold the pressure for several minutes until he sensed a slight easing in his adversary who thought, obviously, he was on a money-spinner. Summoning up what reserves he had, Mark made a dramatic counter-attack and stretched his adversary to the horizontal, crashing the hand down hard on the table sufficiently to rock it on its unstable legs. Immediately the Frenchman was on his feet, kicking over first the table in the process, and then every empty chair he could find *en route* to the bar.

Sitting alone among the debris, Mark felt the rising apprehension of a bar room brawl and began to think in terms of a quick exit route when, to his immense surprise, due to one those abrupt and unexpected changes in French mood, the gorilla leapt back, embraced him in a bear-like hug and kissed him soundly on both cheeks. Mark recoiled and thought he would much prefer a bar room brawl!

But, all of a sudden, it was drinks all round and bonhomie returned to the *Piano Café*. Thereafter, whenever he met his opponent in the street, it was a friendly handshake and slap on the back. All something to do, Mark surmised, with 'keeping face'.

It was a few weeks later that the local bar's drinking pattern was disrupted when the mayor gave his blessing to the building of a bowls ground. As we had long been fascinated by the French game of *'boules'*, we became enthusiastic, if not competent, players. There was no shortage of tutors and much good-natured ribbing at our first efforts. *Boules* appears to be a very simple game but, once skills are acquired, the nuances and complexities reveal themselves. I decided, quite quickly, that psychologically it resembles croquet, since there are basically two main aspects to the game: *'Pointer'*, which is to pitch the bowl as near the *cochonnet* (the little red ball thrown to the end of the bowls area) as possible and thus hope to score a point, either for yourself or for your team; or *'tirer'*, which means that you can try as hard as you like to smash your adversaries out of the way. Genteel Victorian ladies were expert at demolishing their opponent's game in croquet.

Having played several games on the village pitch, which was smooth and perfect, we transferred our newly won expertise to our more hazardous home territory.

"... played several games on the village pitch ..."

This was a very different story, as the ground around the house sloped in several directions and was covered in a mixture of gravel, which successive rainfalls and storms had heaped into piles, so that the whole terrain presented something totally unknown to the normal bowls player.

Our first adversaries arrived, in the form of our neighbour and his family, plus a cousin who was visiting from Bordeaux.

The cousin, Raoul, unlike our small and stocky neighbour, was tall, thin and studious looking with a stunningly attractive daughter with light blonde hair and china blue eyes. To our amazement, this extremely pretty girl was accompanied by a boyfriend who, having decided to have a swim before our match, appeared looking like stone-age man, since most of his skin was covered in thick black hair. It was rather like having a bear-skin rug in the pool, and when later he joined us for a *boules* match I was mesmerised by the sight of his great hairy fingers encircling the ball, which he rolled with a corresponding grunt down the pitch. Naturally, it cavorted from one stony outcrop to another, finally coming to rest a yard beyond the *cochonnet*.

Not a good shot, was the general unspoken verdict, at least from the British section, now familiar with the terrain, and a rather dangerous silence ensued as the gorilla sensed our unfavourable response to his efforts and made several rude French gestures to convey his disgust – not at his performance, but rather our reaction to it.

"What a pissing awful pitch!" was his immediate and only remark, and once translated our blood was up. After all, we had designed the terrain, had practised on it and now the winning of the game was up to us. We were not to be intimidated by gorillas at any event, especially the French variety. So inspired, we smashed and wheedled our bowls over and around stones and the more the points piled up, the more sullen and resentful was the response of our opponents. When victory was in sight they conceded and disappeared next door, their tails down, while we resorted to gin and tonics and self-congratulations all round.

What we had not appreciated was that tails down or not, the occupants of the house next door had decided to hold a council of war, and long into the night, with several bottles of cognac, tactics and revenge were discussed. It all had something to do with the French conviction of individual and collective superiority over all other nations, and the upshot of this debate was a request for a 'return match', which with too many gin and tonics and overconfidence we were happy to accept.

Sadly, on the appointed day and with just one hour of difficult play, the British were routed and the French cockerels left, crowing their hearts out.

A week later, walking through the market in Prades, I bumped into the cousin from Bordeaux and asked innocently, *"Comment vont vos boules* (how are your bowls going)?"

He hesitated then, clutching hold of my sleeve urgently, he whispered in my ear, "*Madame,* never ask a Frenchman how his balls are, you might find it... inconvenient."

"Vive les boules," I murmured weakly, and have practiced restraint in my enquiries subsequently.

Chapter 18

Mice Patrol

The onset of our third winter was a sudden and dramatic one, with freezing nights and temperatures that swung crazily from -3° to +15° Celsius by midday.

It was hardly surprising, therefore, that we awoke one morning to that extraordinary silence that falls on a region when there has been a heavy fall of snow and, looking out of the window, we could hardly believe the dramatic changes in the landscape around us. There was at least six feet of solid snow and huge flakes were still whirling and twisting in the air, but one's pleasure in the wondrous nature of it all soon turned to dismay when we thought of mundane matters like our daily bread. It was with great reluctance that Ray set off eventually, muffled up and with tennis racquets strapped to his feet, to try and reach the village shop, but within half-an-hour he was back, empty-handed and suggested that someone else should 'have a go'. There were no takers and we remained breadless.

So we foraged and survived for several days on supplies already in store and, having rung the mayor to ask what help was available to clear the road, we waited expectantly for the cavalry to appear over the hill.

It was several days later when the roar of an engine alerted us to the fact that help was at hand. Unfortunately, the make-shift 'snow-plough' turned out to be nothing more than a farm tractor pushing a lethal-looking blade, which, as it proceeded up the drive, not only removed the snow and ice but half the drive as well!

As soon as I saw the quantity of stone and gravel being

hurled in the air by the 'monster' machine, I waved frantically to the council boys to stop, but mistaking my action for enthusiasm they carried on happily digging a trench right up to the front door and waving back to me at the same time. The repair bill several months later was framed and hung on the wall, as was my chagrin.

Proof of the onset of polar conditions, if proof was needed, was at the same time provided by *les souris,* field mice, who made, for the first time, a determined assault on the kitchen and cellar, obviously wishing to get installed into warmer seasonal quarters.

The first meeting, when a larger than usual specimen popped out of a half-eaten packet of cereal in the pantry, had me reeling back to the door in shock-horror, but worse was to come when, reaching for a saucepan to cook the porridge, two jumped out of the pan as I removed it from the cupboard!

Investigation of the cellar revealed a trail of half-eaten apples with mice droppings everywhere, while scratching noises from above during the night testified to their reconnaissance in the loft.

" ... les souris ... made a determined assault on the kitchen ... "

A trip to the market on Tuesday morning found us buying half a dozen mouse traps in the local *Droguerie,* much to the delight of the shopkeeper, who told us we were the third customer that morning for the very same thing. Why were the British under attack in this way? I wondered, but the French locals, it seemed, well versed in country ways, all kept cats that spent their lives stalking and keeping down the rodent population.

Discussions at the *Brasserie de la Paix* with other ex-pats revealed a surge of discontent at the mice invasion, especially Jennifer who, on her return from a week's holiday in Spain, had discovered a nest of mice in her bed, with much of her pillow having been torn to shreds to facilitate the breeding season. She did not have to wait long as, within 24 hours, all the offspring were busy suckling away. Bedding and mattress were hastily removed and, reluctant to buy replacements before the invaders had been routed, Jennifer retired for the night in a sleeping bag in the middle of her lounge floor – it was a state of siege!

On the advice of the chemist she had bought large quantities of poison and broken it up into lumps to place at strategic intervals along the beams in her loft, as well as around the perimeter of the cellar, since the roof and basement seemed the most likely points of entry. To her amazement ,when she examined the loft the following morning, all the poison had been examined scrupulously, then rejected and pushed off onto the floor. However, the remains of a baguette in her breadbasket had been devoured down to the last crumb – the newcomers had declared a state of war.

"These are not mice of the ordinary variety," was Jennifer's verdict of these strange events.

Two mornings later she discovered, for the first time, a dead mouse in one of the traps but, horrified at the thought of touching it, she had donned gloves and pushed the whole device, plus body, into a plastic bag ready for ashbin removers. As this process was repeated on a daily basis thereafter, she spent a great deal of her time driving to and from the local *Droguerie* buying half a dozen traps at a time. The owner of the shop could not believe his luck.

A likely solution to her problem came in the form of

André, the local bar owner, who arrived one morning with a delightfully knowing grey cat which, he said, had excellent hunting qualities .Not really wanting to be tied to the house with domestic animals of any kind, she was half-inclined to refuse, as graciously as possible, when to her surprise the cat suddenly leapt from André's arms to seize a mouse between its jaws which no one had noticed entering the room.

"I'll have it," said Jennifer firmly and, shutting the door, busied herself opening a tin of sardines to welcome the latest addition to the family and hunting fraternity.

That night, for the first time in weeks, she risked leaving the lounge and slept, still zipped up tightly in her sleeping bag, in the middle of the mattressless bed. She was both delighted and at the same time revolted to find in the morning, when she descended to make her morning rodent rounds, the half-eaten remains of at least four mice in the cellar. But where, she wondered, was Hercules the cat?

A plaintive mewing from a pile of sacks in the corner disclosed one Hercules, stretched out, suckling four kittens – which accounted for André's generosity in passing on the animal!

A hasty renaming ceremony from Hercules to Hermione took place and, fortunately for Jennifer, such was the mice invasion of the British colony in the Roussillon that, within no time at all, willing hands arrived to carry away the babies to do mice duty elsewhere. In fact, she was actively encouraged to make sure Hermione went on hunting and breeding at one and the same time.

While we had been engaged with our trapping problems, darker and more serious events were taking place elsewhere in France, with a plethora of strikes crippling industry and causing many French men and women to query whether their politicians were governing or not. Things came to a crisis point when we watched French police on Television News one evening using CS gas and water cannon to break up a demonstration march by doctors and nurses protesting against conditions in the French National Health Service. The fury of the British Labour Party Conference over threatened services in the

English system seemed muted in comparison.

The attack on the nurses, several of whom had been injured in the demonstrations, caused righteous indignation from the country as a whole and great play was made of the 'peaceful' nature of the march and the traditional role of 'healers' in the nursing profession.

The farming community, on the other hand, were continuing to use ugly measures to make their discontent felt by depositing lorry loads of manure on political doorsteps, and carried this still further by burning a container lorry, full of live sheep, which had us wondering whether they were Welsh sheep at that!

What was noticeable in these particular outrages was the absence of baton charges, leave alone CS or water cannon, so far as the farmers were concerned, but a turning-point came when angry representatives of the French Farmers' Union invaded a political luncheon and systematically overturned and destroyed the carefully prepared tables of food and fine wines. This sabotage of delectable food was seen as the ultimate sacrilege by the French nation and even one of the cameramen filming the incident was heard to shout when the wine came in for abuse, "For God's sake, drink the stuff, how can you waste it?"

It confirmed my belief that the French are at their most serious when it comes to food and wine, in a way in which I could not imagine the British reacting in similar circumstances. Even the President of the Republic was moved to condemn the farmers' action, while the nurses were invited to meet Prime Minister Edith Cresson, for talks to try and find solutions.

The right of assembly and demonstration is a strong feature of French life, as it is in many western democracies, but the surge of discontent brought a spate of television discussions from politicians of all parties. These culminated in an interview with Raymond Barre, who seemed in no doubt that the government of the day was not addressing itself to the real problems of the nation, in much the same way that Americans were appealing to their president, George Bush, to spend less time circling the globe on foreign affairs while domestic matters at home seemed to be running out of control.

To our own private dismay, both political parties in the United Kingdom seemed obsessed with the National Health Service to the exclusion of debate on the economy, the tragic increases in unemployment and our participation in the European Community. Politicians of all shades and hues seemed to be spending their time dodging the firing line and in their diversionary tactics looking for safe havens and quiet harbours.

We came to the reluctant conclusion that, for most of the serious questions posed, there were no answers, at least none acceptable to the electorate as a whole – but then politicians are not magicians, cannot perform miracles, and always have their eye on their re-election potential.

We decided it was far easier for us to cope with the deviousness of French mice.

"... wonderful finds of crab apples, walnuts, late figs and mushrooms ..."

Chapter 19

Take a Basket With You

As the autumn advanced it became obvious that the object of much of our walking group, not to mention our guests, was to research the area for mushrooms (especially the prized *Cèpe*), chestnuts, late figs, walnuts and whatever else was available seasonally.

Margaret and Ray would return home late on Thursday with nothing but admiration for the hawk-like qualities of their fellow walkers, who either knew the terrain from old or simply had keener eyesight for whatever delicacies the countryside contained.

Of all French mushrooms, the *Cèpe* is the most prized, the most difficult to find, and the most highly priced in the market.

One such Thursday walk had abandoned its normal Indian file style to allow individual sorties in different directions, resulting in occasional scuffles when six members descended on the same group of *Cèpes* simultaneously. My sister took a delightful photograph of six large backsides protruding from one bush where the magic mushroom had been discovered!

Imagine our delight, therefore, when a local farmer was persuaded one day to take a group of *Rozinante* guests on a *Cèpe*-hunting expedition.

Having been ordered to get up at 6 a.m., it was a rather cold and bedraggled group of people who assembled at the entrance of a thickly wooded area to the north of the village. My young nephew, Thomas, who was staying with us at the time, had been the most reluctant to join us – until we mentioned the price he could secure for the produce once we found it.

It was well after 7 a.m., however, with serious evidence of insurrection in our ranks, before the farmer concerned eventually arrived and, sliding off his tractor without a word of greeting, motioned us silently to follow him. All chatter just gradually died away in the face of his sullen behaviour, and I began to wonder if he was afraid the *Cèpes* would run away if they heard us coming.

The next forty minutes saw us pushing and clawing our way through thick brambled undergrowth, occasionally disturbing birds from their slumber, with our breath ballooning in misty swathes in front of our miserable faces. Not one single mushroom, of any kind, had presented itself and baskets and plastic bags rustled at our sides with admonitory persistence.

At no time in our journey had our beloved leader uttered a single word, and I jumped involuntarily when Thomas suddenly hissed in my ear, "We are going around in circles after this comedian."

"Quiet!" I hissed back. "We must be grateful that this man has put his expertise at our disposal."

But one hour later Thomas triumphantly showed us a handkerchief which he had tied to a branch – irrefutable evidence, he claimed, for our being hopelessly lost or just incredibly naive to think this old peasant was going to share the secret of his mushroom crop with us.

A halt was called and, with as much diplomacy as possible, I suggested that the morning mist had caused us to wander a little off course. Again, without a word, the old man shinned up a tree with incredible ease in order, as we discovered later, to see if he could take a bearing from the village clock-tower. Once down again, he put his head down and started to trot off determinedly in a totally new direction, and the pace was such that we quickly realised the mushroom hunting expedition was now officially cancelled.

Fearful of being left to rot forever in the damp and miserable entrails of the wood, we all charged after him, and it was with real relief that two hours later, just as a fitful sun was emerging from the autumnal gloom, we found ourselves free of the trees but miles from home!

When we staggered eventually up the drive of *Rozinante*, still with empty baskets, it was hard to escape the fact that we had all been conned into a military-style route march, with nothing to show for our endeavours. The old farmer, we realised, had happily led us on a wild goose chase, confident we would never attempt to hunt down *Cèpe* again.

Later, talking to a *notaire* from Isle sur Tet, it was explained to me how the farming community relied on produce they harvested from the countryside, as it provided them with a modest supplement to their often frugal income. Hence visitors from the town could be regarded as plunderers when they took day trips to the countryside armed with baskets to take what they could find.

The town, explained the *notaire*, had clearly defined rules and regulations such as where to park, speed limits, shop closing and opening times. The countryside had no such delineations and careless visitors leaving gates open or stripping trees of their harvest were violating unwritten rules and were often resented by the farming and village communities.

I was pleased to have this information, and passed it on to guests thereafter. However, our delight knew no bounds when we found a wonderful crop of mushrooms in the garden of *Rozinante*. The most luxurious patches were down at the bottom of the garden near the cess pit, a fact we kept silent about when producing weeks of mushroom recipes for our guests. Just how much encouragement the cess pit provided was debatable, we felt, and no one complained about the number of mushroom dishes on the menu.

Having lived in rural Wales for many years the use of cess-pits was familiar, although the *Rozinante* version consisted of a strange collection of manholes and pipes, with funny caps, protruding into the air, reminiscent of periscopes from some mysteriously buried submarine. Unlike the Welsh Lavender Wagon, as it was called, which emptied our cess-pit every now and again free of charge, we were forced to use a company in Perpignan who charged around £400 every time they came to blast out our underground chambers. On the whole the system worked well, but the day arrived after a winter of severe snow storms, followed by a spring of torrential rain, when the well, or *puit-perdu,* overflowed in a dirty black tidal wave.

" ... like an odd array of periscopes from a mysteriously buried submarine. "

As it was a Bank Holiday no one was prepared to come and examine the situation, leave alone correct it, and the guests were urged not to bathe and to only use the toilets in dire necessity.

Since the weather was reasonable, there were odd little sorties into bushes and behind trees in the garden all over that weekend, and there was considerable humour about it all, although attitudes hardened dramatically when the clouds gathered and it began to pour with rain. Everyone out visiting Prades made a point of finding the public lavatories before coming home, although there was some confusion on how to use the Arab-style variety in the central *Place* – did you use a frontal attack, or reverse in? – difficult to say.

Early one morning, shortly after the Bank Holiday, I realised after more futile phone calls that no help was coming from the council authorities, which forced me to use the private company in Perpignan. I rang and made a specific appointment which they ignored, arriving eventually without warning in the middle of a lunch party on the lawn, so that my guests were regaled not only with the sight of the massive pumping-out operation, but also with the noxious fumes it provoked, aggravated by a nauseating cloud of horse-flies that found the whole operation a field day for blood sucking operations.

How many of my guests would be infected with typhoid? was my agonising reflection as I paid up the hundreds demanded and enquired of the men working what the problem was in my well. Was it choked, blocked, in need of repair?

"No, Madame," they assured me, "it's the snow and the rain, all will be well in the course of time and when it overflows, just fill in the hole with earth and plant *laurier* roses, they soak up everything."

I tried to imagine what kind of monster *laurier* roses would emerge, triffid-like, from such a planting, and the general consensus of opinion was to leave the well … well alone!

Three weeks after the cleansing yet another awful surge of black water in the nether regions prompted more phone calls to friends and, one by one, plumbers, builders, sanitary salesmen appeared and gazed at the offending pit, only to give a series of macabre explanations ranging from blockage by the roots of trees to a surfeit of modern soap powders. Many suggested its abandonment and the construction of an entirely new system.

Week after week went by and visits to the bottom of the garden to lift the offending lid and peer into the murky depths became part of the daily round. Friends, when they rang, all began their conversations with a cheerful enquiry as to the state of my cess-pit problem, and this might have continued indefinitely had not one day a monstrous black toad, the like of which we had never seen before, appeared swimming vigorously around our swimming pool.

He was huge and, once fished out, opened his great jaws to let out the most indignant roar I had ever heard from a bullfrog, promptly accompanied by a defiant jump back into the pool. One friend with a wry sense of humour suggested I should try and kiss it, in the hope it would turn into a handsome prince. My reply was that it would just be my luck if such a gesture merely turned me into an equally horrid toad!

There was considerable speculation as to where this coal-black specimen came from. We were soon to find out as, when lifting up the well lid one day, a huge black object leapt out and flashed its long, inky legs over my shoulder, so that I screamed, dropped the lid and did a double somersault backwards. Not gremlins, not fairies, but toads – and masses of them – at the bottom of the garden, all breeding like mad in the turgid waters of my *fosse septique*. One learned to approach the pit cautiously, and to warn the unwary of the hidden spawn in the depths. Eventually, and much to our relief, the local farmer who had led us on the *Cèpe* hunt and who was familiar, it seemed, with the problem, arrived with a huge net and fished the well out.

Heaven knows how many he carted away, all of which he dropped, at my suggestion, in the direction of my neighbour's duck pond, where they were happy to propagate and provide a nightly chorus of such depth and quality that Jean-Bertrand actually considered moving house. We could not have been more delighted at the prospect.

As for the cess-pit, it suddenly started to work perfectly and was renamed Toad Hall, while our persistent swimmer in the pool was allowed back occasionally just to thank him and to encourage him to keep up the grand job he was doing next door.

Even more appreciable was the superb basket of *Cèpe* left behind by the farmer with the fishing net. *Come back, all is forgiven,* I breathed as I wrote a warm thank you note.

Chapter 20

Les Ronds Cuirs

One thing that unites all Frenchmen, far more than political loyalties, is their frustration and contempt for bureaucracy while, at the same time, encouraging their young to seek employment in this sector since it is 'safe' and remunerative.

Ever since the 17th Century economist Jean-Baptiste Colbert introduced central planning under the monarchy, the French have felt a special bond with the state as guarantor and protector. The facts are, however, that the French endure the highest taxes in the Western world in order to pay for their government services, and public spending consumes more than half of the country's Gross National Product – a proportion greater than any other industrial country.

The contradiction that is inherent in French life is nowhere more manifest than in their acceptance of the vast bureaucracy that governs their lives, yet their individual attempts to circumnavigate it – which is most evident in their tax evasion games, and if not paying taxes, then claiming for every benefit under the sun. This accounts for a deficit economy, provoking riots and conflict on the streets when the French decide in the face of proposed government cuts that they do not want to give up benefits of any kind, since they are seen as a natural right.

Some French will explain that the strong role played by the state helps to control the excesses of a freemarket, but President Chirac never tired of proclaiming that France must move from a culture of assistance to a culture of responsibility.

Regarding the British in France, most can produce horror stories of their first brushes with French bureaucracy in trying to secure their *Carte de Sejour,* which is a kind of permission to live in France.

The French themselves carry a *livret,* a most comprehensive document which gives not only information about yourself, but also your forebears – in fact, a kind of potted family history. It enables you, the mayor explained, to travel around the world with instant details about yourself, which is invaluable for emigration travel, banking, birth, death and other family occasions.

He then went on to detail what documentation was needed for my *Carte de Sejour,* which forced me to tear the house apart finding the essential papers: birth certificate, marriage certificate, financial statements, etc, all of which had to be translated into French by an official French translator. Once the papers had been handed over to the mayor, you may imagine my horror when, after six months, his secretary telephoned to say, with regret, that my dossier had been lost in the post so would I please start all over again? As no photocopies had been kept, the whole painful process had to be renewed!

There were similar stories from other ex-pats and one rather pompous Englishman, who went in to complain about the delay in issuing him with a *Carte,* had to watch the mayor's secretary remove his dossier from the top of the pile and place it deliberately on the bottom! It was a warning none of us ignored.

It was shortly after my brushes with officialdom over my *Carte* that I took my first long train journey in France, and was able to observe French attitudes to this plague.

In all French railway stations there is a machine at the entrance to the platforms into which all passengers must push their tickets, so that they are punched automatically and thus rendered useless for other journeys. Should the *controleur* subsequently find this function has not been completed, then the passenger is subject to an immediate fine. This deterrent serves a dual purpose, since it discourages cheating and indulges the French love of automation.

France has been passionately involved with new technology ever since the pundits agreed at the end of the last

War that the reason for their defeat at the hands of the Germans in 1940 was their lack of scientific and technical expertise. Culture, the arts, and their beloved philosophy were to take second place to *les Hautes Écoles,* great scientific institutions through which every aspiring Frenchman hopes to pass. The preoccupying use of *Minitel* in France – a precursor to the world wide web – was an obvious demonstration of the public's love of gadgetry, though this is now shut down.

Having punched my own ticket on a return trip from Marseilles to Perpignan, I felt no unease when the ticket collector arrived at our compartment door, but as the young Frenchman opposite me had failed to complete this manoeuvre, he was consequently called to account by the functionary – a solid, impassive little man of some 45 years who was quite unmoved by his protests and insisted upon the fine being paid immediately. The money was eventually handed over to the collector who, with quiet satisfaction, put it in his leather bag and left his victim fulminating in the corner.

Moving on to the next passenger, the young girl barely looked up from the page of the book she was reading but handed her ticket to him in a way that seemed to say, *I cannot understand why you are asking me for it.*

Once again the ticket was refused, this time on the grounds that it was for a single journey only and not a return. Thus she was not only liable for a fine but a double one at that. Without changing her hunched-up position over the book, the girl launched into a long and complicated explanation, which somehow involved the compliance of the ticket clerk in the Narbonne railway office. But it was soon evident that the controller was totally unimpressed, no doubt having heard thousands of versions on the same theme through a long and weary travelling life. Ignoring the flood of explanations washing over him, he took out a charge sheet and asked for a name and address which, at first, she refused to give him. Patiently, it was explained that a refusal to admit her indiscretions would only mean an increase in the amount of fine she would be responsible for ultimately.

"Do what you like, but make sure the ticket clerk in

Narbonne is sacked, do you hear? Sacked!" was the *cri de coeur* of the damsel in distress, and while most of us averted our eyes in embarrassment, the young man beside her was ardent in his support.

No sooner had the carriage door shut behind the controller than all the French passengers launched into a flood of criticism and abuse of all functionaries, especially small ones, who, they agreed, were making life intolerable for all law-abiding, honest citizens.

However, a sudden silence fell upon all our outrage when at Perpignan railway station three armed police-men entered the compartment next to us and arrested, with difficulty, three young men who had been reported by the controller for not having tickets, no money to pay for any, and no passports to prove their legal entry into the country.

The mutterings of my fellow-travellers gave way to united condemnation of illegal immigrants who were living, it seemed, in France at the expense of hard-working men and women who resented this abuse of their liberty, equal-ity and fraternity.

These were arguments that were to dominate the next week's television screens on account of the Euro-elections and, encouraged by friends, I registered for a vote and held myself in readiness for the electoral propaganda which I assumed would soon be pushed through my letter-box. When none arrived and polling day approached, I took the precaution one evening to walk down to the village *Place* to look at the posters that were plastered everywhere. Studying these, I discovered that France was not short of political parties: there were *'Travailleurs pour l'Europe de la Democratie'* along with *'Les Vrais Ecologistes'*, which presupposed the existence of false ecologists, as well as parties for Communists, 'Hunting, Shooting and Fishing', the Green Party, and finally a party for *'L'Autre Europe'* – which consisted of Philippe de Villiers, Jimmy Goldsmith and Charles de Gaulle.

I was so bemused by it all I felt quite apprehensive on the day of voting and, entering the main hall of the *Mairie,* was even more taken aback by the crowd assembled, not to mention a table at the far end of the room smothered completely in promotional material.

To my dismay the mayor, with whom I had a good relationship, was not to be seen and in his absence his deputy, M. Delville, advanced towards me, his large face creased with concern at the task of helping me to vote since, clearly, help would be required.

"Bonjour, Madame Barter," he boomed in the loud, ringing tone that he always assumed when he saw me. Knowing my imperfect knowledge of French, he had long decided that shouting at the top of his voice and articulating each word separately was the most effective way of communicating with me.

"Bonjour, M. Delville," I answered weakly, even more confused since his loud welcome had alerted all those present to my entry, so that several pairs of inquisitive eyes swivelled round to survey me. For an instant the room froze, no one moved and no one spoke, and the wretched thought crossed my troubled mind that everyone would now take time off to watch how *l'Anglais* would vote.

Feebly I asked what I should do and, anticipating the question, Mr Delville held out a much-worn hand and pulled me determinedly towards the loaded table at the end of the room. Pointing to the several piles of paper he suggested I should take one of each, study them in the seclusion of the voting box curtained off in the corner of the room, then select the one I wanted and place it in an envelope before putting it in the ballot box.

As there were 16 possibilities I exclaimed immediately that such an operation would take me all day and, again, the ever-helpful M. Delville picked up the first paper which happened to be for Jean-Marie le Pen and said, as I understood it, "Well, here you are, take the first one."

I jumped as if stung by a wasp and said loudly and determinedly, "Oh no, not le Pen."

Worried now that this really was going to be a complicated and long-winded affair, M. Delville advanced down the line of papers, picked up the one for de Villiers, Goldsmith and de Gaulle and said with a sly grin, accompanied by an exaggerated and conspiratorial wink, "Then this is the one for you, Madame." With this advice he emphasised the choice by giving me a very definite shove in the direction of the voting booth and, pulling the curtain around me, he continued to hover outside, breathing heavily, while I committed the paper he had given me to the appropriate envelope and then allowed myself to be propelled to the ballot box, into which I dropped in my contribution.

A weak smile around the room confirmed in everyone's eyes my supine and lacklustre performance and I escaped to laugh at myself, walking back up the hill to *Rozinante,* to think of the secrecy of the ballot box, which I had just violated.

When the results were announced on the media, it was to learn that de Villiers, Goldsmith and de Gaulle, a virtual new trio, had made significant inroads. Later, in the village bar, listening to the locals' post-mortem of the proceedings, I refrained from contributing any comment since keeping one's head below the parapet is a wise maxim to observe when living abroad.

Significantly, all the promotional material I had been waiting for so anxiously before the election arrived one week later. Reading through it – out of curiosity more than anything else – allowed the reflection that the one thing the French do not lack is a representative collection of political parties.

Much later, when the presidential election was held, in which as a foreigner I could not participate, I was interested to hear the differing political viewpoints of the candidates concerned. It was soon clear, listening to both Left and Right political lines, that the 20th Century was forcing France to move away from state control to the market place, but arguments continued to rage between those who spoke of a Social Conscience which is protectionist, state-managed and firmly committed to social welfare, while others sought to pursue market economies.

Some of the contradictions were manifest in the promises made to cut taxes, raise wages, increase public spending, avoid any pruning of health care, reduce unemployment, tackle the public sector deficit, and heal France's *fracture sociale.*

Somewhat cynically, a few French press comments made it clear they believed that Chirac, who won the presidential election, came to office with no clear objective other than to be popular and enjoy being president.

Talking to French friends, I came to understand that most French men and women now realise that the state sector has grown too big and too ambitious and cannot go on providing adequate succour from 'womb to tomb', as one newspaper put it, but the French are no different to any other nation when it comes to economies. They believe in them so long as they only negatively affect *other* peoples' pockets, but not their own!

As to France's future in Europe, it seemed the French were undecided, as barely 51 per cent voted for Maastricht in the referendum and not much happened subsequently to endear the Treaty to them.

As for Britain, I was nonplussed one night when, on French television, an interview was being shown of traders operating in a well-known London street market. Asked what they knew about Maastricht, they generally looked confused, wondering if it was the name of a Continental football team or a new make of sausage. Finally, one cheeky Cockney said, "If it's anything to do with the Jerries again, well, we wopped 'em once, we wopped 'em twice and if we 'ave to guv, we'll wop 'em again!"

I just prayed our French and German compatriots were not listening!

Chapter 21

Un Petit Coin du Paradis

All our guests enjoyed the excitement of the football World Cup but were disappointed to see Britain beaten in a shoot-out with Germany.

Some days passed and we gathered from the British Overseas radio service that Nicholas Ridley, a member of Mrs Thatcher's Cabinet, had resigned because of an uproar over remarks he had made about Germany's Nazi-style dominance of European affairs. On the whole the resignation did not seem to have much significance, until one evening a car drew up at the door and out stepped a tall, athletic-looking blond man, who grasped my hand firmly with a slight inclination of the head, the whisper of a heel click, and in a very determined tone announced, "Mr and Mrs Lindenberg; ve are Chermans, you know."

"Delighted," I said equally firmly, but inwardly wondered if Ridley's imprecations had had much publicity in the Fatherland.

Mrs Lindenberg, in contrast to her husband, was small and dark and very shy with no English or French, so it seemed appropriate to show them their rooms as quickly as possible, where they busied themselves settling in for a while.

Finally, Mr Lindenberg appeared and asked if it was permitted to use the lounge for reading, and when I agreed he looked around the room, appraising it slowly, and with smiling approval said, "It's good and posh!"

The expression, somewhat archaic, made me smile, and he quickly picked this up and said, "It's not good, posh?" and I hastened to reassure him that I was far from offended, and asked him if he knew the derivation of the word. Since he did not, I was happy to explain that in the days of the Empire, English passengers to India chose to travel 'port side out' and 'starboard home', in order to secure a little shade and relief from the sun on the journey. Port Out Starboard Home = POSH.

I left to make some tea and the Lindenbergs wandered around the room examining the paintings, the carpets and one or two very modest *objets d'art,* and just as I slid a tray-load of tea onto the table in front of him, he asked me abruptly what my opinion was of Mr Ridley's resignation.

I sighed and said I thought his statement had probably been taken out of context and was sorry the press had chosen to exaggerate and sensationalise, as always, certain aspects of what he had said. One could only regret the general tenure of his remarks, however, and I hoped it would have no lasting effect on the good relationship between our two countries.

I then switched the conversation to football and the World Cup, seeking less dangerous ground, but was completely taken aback when Mr Lindenberg asked me abruptly, "Vhy did Madame Tatcher go to var over ze Falklands?"

"I think it was a question of principle," I replied weakly.

"Very dangerous to go to var over a principle," he intoned solemnly.

"That depends," I parried, "on the principle in question. In this instance the somewhat unexpected but happy outcome of the war with the Falklands was the downfall of the Galtieri regime, which had been a hideous abuse of privilege in Argentinian history. People had been arrested without trial, democratic usages had been suspended and victims frequently tortured to death with no recourse to any semblance of normal law and order."

I stopped aghast in mid-flight as I realised that what I had been describing was an apt description of the very Nazis Ridley had been talking about!

But Mr Lindenberg had not finished with me.

"Vhy," he asked, "are der Breetish still vatching var films?"

I gasped a bit at that and momentarily was inclined to

say, "Because ve von ze var!" – but common sense prevailed and I found myself explaining how sad it was that so many old films were shown today, but maybe cost-effectiveness was the main cause.

At this point, mercifully, the telephone rang (*saved by the bell!* I thought), and so ended the interrogation.

Several hours after the Lindenbergs had enjoyed a leisurely meal served in the garden, where the evening sunlight shifted differing shades of light around on the summit of Canigou, it was apparent the overall beauty of the scene had engendered a wonderful relaxation in his mood.

"You are a good cooker," he announced, and I wondered if he was going to add, "but most of the British are not." But... a good supper, a lovely evening, and the faint antagonism was gone, so it seemed.

He asked for an English newspaper, which he read while his wife, having discovered our three dogs, spent the evening chasing them around the garden with Germanic thoroughness crying, *"Liebchen, liebchen, kommhier zu mir!"*

The dogs were appalled and went into hiding.

When they left the following morning I wondered if they had really enjoyed their stay, and was delighted consequently to receive a card some weeks later from Koblenz which said: *Thank you so much for your so warm welcome, we enjoyed so much your little corner of paradise.*

I breathed a sigh of relief and wondered if I should write to Mr Ridley to explain how hard I was working to counteract his influence in Europe.

It was not long after this that the Wright family arrived – six all told, mother, father, mother-in-law and three children. We had been expecting them and, as usual, as soon as the station wagon pulled up all three dogs, plus two hunting dogs from next door who had long since decided our home was more agreeable than our neighbours', charged down the drive, wild with excitement at the prospect of new arrivals.

The row was deafening, but generally I found people quite willing to pat the dogs, who sooner or later stopped barking and switched to wagging their tails and slathering over the guests. It acted as a kind of lubricating process to initiate arrivals into new and strange surroundings.

This time however the treatment did not work, as Mr Wright, instead of descending to grasp my outstretched hand, stayed cowering behind the wheel, obviously frightened to death at the canine uproar all around him.

When my brother-in-law appeared to help with the luggage I whispered quickly, "What are we going to do, here is someone that doesn't like dogs – maybe even allergic to them?"

"Tough sh*t," said my normally very conservative brother-in-law.

But it was soon obvious that if the father was reluctant, the children were absolutely thrilled, and in no time at all were racing around the garden throwing apples for the dogs to catch and screaming like Dervishes.

Poor Mr Wright; for the rest of his stay he jumped and skittered out of the dogs' way, while the rest of the family, obviously normally denied their company, relished their presence and delighted in teaching the dogs new tricks and spoiling them with titbits from the table. It was amusing to see how quickly the dogs responded to their affectionate interest and became their devoted slaves.

However, Mr Wright's lugubrious face was a constant reminder of his discomfort, and I wondered vaguely what we could do to cheer him up. Help was at hand, as it often is, in unexpected forms, and in this instance our domestic water system, which was noisy at best, attracted his attention.

When he asked where the noise came from I was happy to lead him to the garage and explain the water problems I endured as a result of the main plumbing system being underground, and not in the roof space.

As a builder, Mr Wright was not the least bit bored but, rather, enthralled with the intricacies of this very French system. He decided immediately to investigate alternatives. Ladders were produced so that the roof could be explored minutely and measurements, statistics and data were compiled. In his total absorption in his task, he forgot about the dogs and began, I sensed for the first time, to enjoy his holiday.

When the day of their departure came we were sorry to see them go, and the dogs retreated to their corners, quite subdued. But to our delight a long and welcome letter of thanks arrived a week later containing a beautifully constructed sketch for the installation of a new hot water tank system. It seemed their homecoming had been a rapturous reception from their three cats who, desolate at not being able to get back into the house in their absence, had been seen by neighbours on the roof peering mournfully down the chimneys!

Chapter 22

We'll Keep a Welcome

Having grown up in Wales where singing, like rugby, is a way of life, we often lamented the absence of a piano in the house. During the War years, when Free French, Poles, Canadians, Australians and Americans, to name a few, had accepted my mother's open-house invitations, the evening's entertainment, after a fortifying meal, had always ended in a sing-song around the piano.

Subsequent to the War years many deplored the decline in interest in piano playing and singing, due largely to the all-pervasive influence of television and people's passive acceptance of its entertainment potential. Thus nothing had been done at *Rozinante* about home entertainment except to provide guests with the usual television facilities.

It was therefore with considerable surprise one day that I saw a van driving up to the front door with the address of a South Wales Removals Company on the side. For some days previously I had heard Mark and Ray discussing a 16th Century chest in my lounge and, knowing how much my son wanted to return to the UK and take the chest with him, I had made it clear I was not willing to part with it and hinted he might have to wait for my demise before securing it.

You may imagine my dismay when, no sooner had the van stopped at the door, I could hear Mark requesting Ray's help to get the chest out of the house. Leaning out of the bedroom door in my nightdress, I shouted down to the two young men climbing out of the van, "No furniture leaves this house without my permission!"

That they were startled by this interdiction was obvious

and one of them said to my son, who had now opened the door, "Who the hell was that?"

"Just my mother," said my son by way of explanation, and shouted up the stairs for me to come down, as he had a surprise for me.

Well, surprises, I have learned through bitter experience, are rarely pleasant and my anger knew no bounds when I saw my much-prized chest being pulled out of its customary place and hauled into the hall.

At the same time a piano was being extracted from the van, while the help of several guests was being enlisted to carry it safely to the space vacated by the chest.

"It's a present, Mum!" my son kept explaining, but I was too preoccupied with the fate of my chest to appreciate the gift and, to make my position clear, I ordered those guests who were occupied with the piano to put it back in the van and replace the chest to its original position.

Back and forth the argument raged, with my son on one side urging the guests to unload against my equally determined efforts to put things back!

In the end the two young men from the van said, "Do you want the bloody piano or not?"

And finally, with assurance that the chest would not take its place, the instrument was installed and the van owner sat down to play the opening chords of the *Moonlight Sonata*.

Anger and incomprehension gave way to delight, and that is the operative word for the pleasure that playing this instrument provided the family and guests for years to come, since a good meal and excellent company somehow quite naturally leads to a happy bout of singing. Several returning guests have since brought their own musical instruments to add to the enjoyment.

Much to our amazement, the young men from the van turned out to be the owners of a piano shop in Swansea, South Wales, where the notice in the window had prompted my son's interest since it said: *We Deliver Anywhere.* He had forced the proprietors to live up to their word and deliver to the south of France, a country which neither had ever visited before. It had, they said, been quite an experience, and the notice in the window had now been removed!

There was an amusing sequel to this when some months later I arranged for an English piano tuner who, I had heard, was visiting the area, to come and service mine. He was due to arrive at 4 p.m. and when eventually, an hour later, a car drew up at the door, I went out immediately and said, "Good, glad you've arrived at last, follow me – it is in here."

The young man, quite nicely dressed, seemed oddly reluctant.

"Come on," I urged, "the piano is in here."

"But, Madame," came the reply in French, "I know nothing about pianos, all I want is a room for the night!"

I apologised profusely and had to admit we had no vacancies and, after he left, my sister said to me, "How could you mistake him for a piano-tuner when he was so obviously a tourist – and French at that!"

I let the remark pass and, half-an-hour later, was surprised to hear the roar of a powerful motor-bike coming up the drive. Looking out of the window I was dismayed to see a large, heavily built young man, unshaven, long-haired, wearing the standard bike gear of tight jeans and heavy, black leather jacket with fringes and brass studs.

"I'm sorry," I said firmly again from the bedroom window, "but we have no rooms available, there's a hotel just up the road."

"That's alright, love," came the amiable cockney reply, "I've just come to tune your pianner!"

I almost fell out of the window with surprise! But that's exactly what he had come to do and when an hour later, extremely proud of my new Broadwood addition to the house, I asked him what he thought of it, there was no hesitation in his reply.

"Alright for a knees-up, darling," he said with a cheeky grin and with that he was off with a roar down the drive, leaving me with mixed feelings. Needless to say, 'how do you spot a pianner tuner' became a new family game!

Chapter 23

Chanter, Chanter Avec Nous

One winter, when *Rozinante* was comparatively guest-free, I decided to join a choir. Distinguishing between the merits of various groups was quite a problem, but in the end St Vincent de Clos won the day and I was delighted to find an enthusiastic group of mixed nationalities meeting every Friday evening in a modern *Salle de Fête* which boasted a fully-stocked bar, along with one of the most stupendous views of the foothills of the Pyrenees.

Friday evenings from then on were consecrated to learning the alto role of varying pieces of music, mainly Catalan in origin, and enjoying a drink and chat with ex-pats at the bar.

Our first concert was a Christmas party for the aged of the village. Like other members, I sported a black ensemble with a bright red waistcoat since Catalans, I discovered, love symbols of death and fire and the 1993 Olympics at Barcelona had amply demonstrated this passion for drama and pyrotechnics.

The concert concluded with the British section singing *We Wish You a Merry Christmas*, followed by a traditional tea during which we munched our way through nuts, raisins, muscatels, nougat, mandarins, *pain d'épice* (gingerbread) and prunes. The last caused great amusement when I explained that the British only thought of these 'black-coated workers', as the War-time radio doctor called them, as a response to a chronic attack of constipation!

Prunes locally are a traditional delicacy, and never

thought of by locals for medicinal purposes. My remarks provoked a wry tale of burnt custard and soggy prunes at school meals, at which the French shuddered, since it confirmed their worst fears about British cuisine.

It was some weeks later, on my way to choir practice, that half-way across a narrow bridge my headlights failed and I had to wait until an old farmer in a ramshackle van appeared and kindly shone his lights for me to clear the rest of the bridge. Thanking him, I asked if he would call at a local garage to get help, but while I was explaining the problem, and much to his consternation, a couple of cages-full of live chickens fell off the back of the van. Before the farmer could retrieve the situation, the squawking inmates had succeeded in freeing themselves and promptly flew up the road.

There was instant confusion as the farmer threw up his arms and ran off in hot pursuit, yelling over his shoulder for me to do the same. After an ensuing vigorous chase up the road, to my dismay the white hen I was chasing hopped over a wall and disappeared down a bank to the river below. Nothing daunted, I scaled the wall, only to drop down into several feet of solid mud. But though I was thus trapped, so was the hen, and despite the slime it was with a great sense of triumph I grabbed her tail feathers and shoved her under my jacket.

Getting out of the mud and back over the wall was a tortuous business, and returning to the van I was half-mollified and half-annoyed to see the farmer concerned standing in the road making clucking noises, to the point where the remaining escaped prisoners were simply responding to his calls and clucking equally frantically back to their master!

My mud-stained offering was received gratefully, and with a good deal more squawking the van lurched away. True to his word, some thirty minutes later a break-down van arrived to solve my problem. However another difficulty which could not be solved so easily was my appearance, which caused a sensation when I finally turned up for choir practice as, quite apart from the mud, I had somehow managed to acquire several white feathers in my hair.

"Geronimo!" a close friend said as I sidled into place, and regretfully the sobriquet remains!

The drama of *les poules* soon paled into insignificance when a competition was announced to judge the best choir in the Conflent. Since some fifteen entrants had been registered there was considerable incentive to work hard, and it was with a certain measure of trepidation that we turned up at the main theatre in Perpignan on the appointed day to measure our competence against everyone else.

Our confidence quickly evaporated once we began to hear and appreciate the quality of the other contestants, so it was with definite nervousness we mounted the platform and coped with the kind of stage-fright which comes automatically once you see a sea of faces in front of you, none of which, I thought, looked particularly friendly.

For this special occasion our choir mistress had selected a lament, which was intended to inspire sympathy, but no sooner had we started to sing the opening phrases when I perceived several people smiling in the audience. Smiles soon turned to titters and then to loud guffaws, until everyone burst into wild and unrestrained laughter!

Our poor choir mistress, with her back to the audience, could not contain her fury and turned to wave her baton angrily at the now hysterical mass in front of us. It was only when several people pointed helplessly to a group of ferns and potted plants at the side of the stage that the reason for the hilarity revealed itself.

It seems that right at the beginning of our performance a very tiny Chihuahua dog had appeared, sniffing the foliage and cocking his leg to pee here, there and everywhere. To exacerbate matters, he had run quickly behind our backs to continue peeing on the foliage on the other side of the stage.

As our lament had been entitled *By the Waters of Babylon, I Sat Down and Wept,* the watering incident had been much appreciated!

It was with great relief that the dog was removed, order

restored, and we were allowed to sing, coming eventually fifth out of a total of fifteen, which under the circumstances we felt was not too bad.

The Babylon piece was, however, relegated to the bin, as we could never henceforth sing it without laughing.

Chapter 24

Entente Cordiale

O ne of the happiest days spent at *Rozinante* was the occasion of the 50th Anniversary of the D-Day Landings in World War II, when fifty friends came to share the day with us.

The occasion was celebrated even more spectacularly in northern France with a parachute drop by veterans of the 6th Airborne Division, the 2nd Ox and Bucks Light Infantry, and the 7th Battalion of the 5th Parachute Brigade, who returned to Benouville, the small Norman village on which they had descended just after midnight on June 6th, 1944.

This commemorative drop reminded the world of the 7,000 British Parachutists and the 13,400 Americans who dropped on the eve of D-Day with high casualty rates. In fact, during the Normandy campaign the 6th Airborne lost 4,400 men, killed, wounded or missing in action. Fifty years later, at least two of the forty-one U.S. veterans who took part in the air drop suffered minor injuries, and Earl Draper, 70 years of age from Florida, raised a fist in victory as he was taken by helicopter to a Cherbourg hospital, with back injuries.

For us, as a family, there were no such dramatics; just a tremendous amount of planning in order to provide food and drink for a large number of people. Blowing up red, white and blue balloons was our most exhausting effort, apart from running up British, French and American flags.

Among our guests were two British and one American who had taken part in the landings on Omaha Beach and Arramanches. They still found it difficult to remember the day's events without chagrin and sorrow for the friends who had died, some almost minutes after descending from the landing craft.

At *Rozinante*, however, the day dawned bright and clear and the sun shone down from a cloudless blue sky, so much so we were concerned with parasols to provide enough shade to stop the ice melting in the buckets that kept the wine cool.

Everyone arrived bearing gifts of food and drink, so that the two dining room tables had to have a third added in order to accommodate the delicious pies and pâtés, quiches and hams, quite apart from the desserts and cheeses. It was a sight to gladden the heart of the most inveterate gourmet, and justice was duly done to such a feast.

At a brief pause in the celebrations, and before guests started plunging into the pool, I decided to give a toast to thank my French friends for their kindness to the British who had settled and lived amongst them.

I started by reminding those present of some of my family's experiences in the early days of the War when, after the fall of France, at the age of 11, I had become concerned at the possibility of a German invasion of Britain.

"What will you do," I asked my father, "if the Germans arrive?"

"Don't worry, Gene," was the reassuring reply, "I still have my old Smith and Wesson revolver with three bullets, one for your mother, one for you and one for your sister. I shall never let you fall into the hands of the Bosche!"

I went to bed that night quite unwilling to tell my younger sister, who was only eight years old at the time, of the fate my father had in store for us, and wondering whether being ravished by the Bosche might not be a better alternative to being shot (and perhaps badly at that) by my father!

Later on, two council workmen arrived to chip out the word 'Penarth' from the lintel above the door of the Public Baths, and when I asked what that was all about I was told it was to confuse the enemy. All over the country signposts were being turned around and place names eroded, so much so that no one knew where they were, and those travelling up north found themselves south and those *en route* east ended up west. I remember my father remarking wryly one day that the only people who would know where they were if they landed would be the Germans, as with their customary efficiency they would have plenty of accurate maps to help them!

Thus D-Day was a tremendous relief for us as a family, since it lifted the fear of being shot by my father and restored the town's name to its rightful place.

At that juncture I switched into French and reminded my listeners how from 1066 the main enemy of England had been France – William the Conquerer and all that, although it was thanks to the Norman invasion that Britain enjoyed a French heritage.

Later, with the revenge raids of Henry V, Agincourt and Cressy, not to mention much later Waterloo and Napoleon... for so long the main enemy had been France, it was difficult for the British to imagine any other, but by the beginning of the 20th Century and German expansionist aims it was clear to both countries that we had found a common enemy, and hence the ensuing two World Wars.

From this moment, *entente cordiale* was born, and this had been the theme of the Queen of England and the President of France with the opening of the Channel Tunnel. Nevertheless, I felt that the real *entente cordiale* was better expressed in the friendship we were sharing on this commemorative day.

Swimming and dancing was then the order of the day, and when people drifted away finally it was with a marvellous sense of pride in one of our greatest moments in history, and a strong sense of hope for peace in the future.

The day was also memorable for the comportment of our neighbour, Jean-Bertrand, who not only turned up dressed in his best suit but also spent his time helping with the serving of drinks, and generally being amiable and just plain neighbourly.

"Anything more I can do?" he enquired as he was about to leave, and when I signalled that all that could be done had been done he smiled as he turned away and then said casually over his shoulder, "Then may I borrow your pump for a day or two?"

And now, three months later, we are still waiting for him to return it. *Plus ça change?* – don't you believe it!

Chapter 25

The Men in Blue

The highlights of the D-Day party were soon lost in the day-to-day minutiae of guests coming and leaving, while back in the UK family problems were evident to the point where we felt we must return to give a helping hand, leaving us with very little option but to put *Rozinante* up for sale.

One evening, while I was serving drinks to new arrivals on the lawn, one of them asked me if I knew of any B&B's for sale and when I said, "Yes, this one," their astonishment quickly turned to interest. Within weeks the deeds were exchanged and I was immersed in the quest for a small house to keep for holiday purposes, being unwilling to sever our links with this beautiful part of the world. I settled eventually on a much-neglected house just up the road from St Eulalie on the edge of the next village. The house presented a pitiful appearance, since it had been burgled twice in the owners' absence, leaving radiators torn off the walls, smashed windows and broken doors. Kitchen and bathrooms needed complete refurbishment and I planned to divide the house into two and let out half as a *gîte* (holiday rental), thus still providing myself with an income of sorts but without the work of an *auberge*.

Friends rallied around to take some of the work off my shoulders and the new owners of *Rozinante* persuaded a couple of English painters and decorators to come down on a working holiday to paint the house inside and out.

Fred and Ron turned up in a van piled high with paint, brushes and cleaning equipment and on their very first night made the rounds of the local bars. By the second night they had settled into a casino in Vernet les Bains for a 'spot of roulette'. I began to fear that the bulk of their wages would disappear long before they returned home!

I found myself driving up and down to the industrial estate at Perpignan to buy cupboards, refrigerators, dishwashers and all the other necessary accoutrements, and it was on one of these expeditions that I had what was to prove one of the most frightening experiences of my life in France.

Not being familiar with the industrial estate, I found myself one evening hopelessly lost, and when approaching an intersection cautiously, looking for road signs, two police officers on motorbikes came hurtling around a corner at such alarming speed that the first one hit my car nearside with such force he was propelled upwards high over the top of my car, during which his helmet came off so that he landed bareheaded on the ground the other side of me with a sickening thud. Immediately a passer-by rushed up to the officer and, dramatically clutching her hands to her breast, proclaimed to the crowd rapidly gathering around her that the man was dead!

My immediate reaction was to wonder whether prisoners were still sent to Devil's Island, but before I could gather my scattered wits a police car drew up, followed minutes later by a Black Maria, a fire-engine and an ambulance – all summoned by the other surviving officer.

Instinctively, I had turned to him to ask, "Were you not travelling rather fast?" to which he replied, *"C'était un cas d'urgence* (it was a case of urgency)," and I made a supreme effort to say to myself that I must remember the phrase when giving evidence in court!

At this point another police officer brusquely pushed me into the Black Maria and started a long and intensive interrogation, demanding my parents' names and eventually my mother's maiden name. I was so fazed by this last question that I blurted out, "Smith", since I could not think of anything else – and then sweated at the thought of the accusation in court of lying to police officers!

Hours later, or so it seemed, when the injured man (still alive apparently) had been removed to hospital, the officer told me to follow him to the main police station, but on examining my car it was obvious from the totally destroyed radiator and front headlights and bumper that the vehicle was unfit for travel of any kind. Quite how I did eventually reach the station I have very little recollection, but once arrived at the car park I was told abruptly to leave it and park on the pavement *outside* the station.

Once inside the station I was again subjected to a long and detailed interrogation of the accident, after which I asked feebly if I could phone a local Citroen garage to get my car towed away for repairs. The problem of how I was to get home without transport was never discussed!

When the breakdown lorry did arrive, I was forced to empty the car of a week's groceries including large quantities of frozen food, eggs, ice cream and butter, now melting everywhere on the pavement without surveillance and vulnerable to passing theft!

Returning to the station reluctantly, I was left alone in a bare miserable room for a further three hours until an officer returned from the hospital to say the injured man had only sustained light injuries and that I was free to leave.

Tearfully, I asked should I consult a lawyer for any impending court case only to be told that the police accepted responsibility and there would be no follow-up.

I left the station in a dream of relief, but angry at the uncaring officers, who could have told me immediately that the accident was due entirely to the excessive speed of the officers in response to an urgent call for help. The morning after this traumatic experience an English friend rang to ask how many policemen I intended to kill that day! News travels fast in an ex-pat community.

Still, my release from the threat of penal servitude was an enormous relief and I immersed myself in packing up my affairs at *Rozinante* in order to move on. The leave-taking was painful, for the years we had spent there had been full of life's richest experiences; there had been highs and lows, joys and frustrations but overall such enormous fun! We knew it was an era we would never repeat again.

Chapter 26

En Fin de Compte

At the time of writing these final words, I have to admit to certain changes in France since coming here 20 years ago. France seems worried about its future, unsettled by international instability and often scathingly contemptuous of what they see as an ineptitude, corruption and hypocrisy in some of their politicians and public figures. It was a British political journalist in a debate one night who said of European leaders, "Schroder has gone, Berlusconi is always in trouble, while the French Chirac is one foot away from helping the police with their enquiries!"

Many officials say that the main problem is one of a declining economy, with unemployment a continuous issue. New waves of immigration stoke unrest in crowded inner city areas, sparking riots and car burnings led by young, mostly naturalised, immigrants, protesting against the passive racism which, they claim, excludes them from jobs and a place in society.

French confidence had been based on the fact that France is a rich country, and many firmly believed that by hard work it would be possible to succeed in life. Even those at the bottom of the social scale seem almost equally divided on the subject of whether it is work or nepotism that brings success, and in this way hope and despair are equally balanced.

I reminded myself that the 18th and 19th Century Industrial Revolution in Great Britain had changed irrevocably the face of the countryside, with whole populations forced to move from country to town to find work and the means to live. France had not suffered this trauma in the same numbers, and certainly not in the Roussillon, where little industrialisation had ever taken place, so that the environment remained unchanged and contributed largely to the charm of living there.

It was subsequent to the Second World War that a movement from country to town had occurred in France, with the rise in technology, the computer, the software revolution and the increasing unwillingness of young people to endure the often harsh and lonely life of farming in isolated communities. In addition there were broadening opportunities of education which opened doors that had been closed hitherto for the great majority.

Writing in *Vive la France!*, Laffont, 1970, Francois Nourissier said, *"Il est vrai de dire que le bachot a été la grand maladie de la petite bourgeoisie, l'obsession des pères de famille, le symbole de l'accession à la classe moyenne. Pas de bachot? En bleu de travail et les ongles noire! Bachelier? En route pour les titres universitaires et les professions prestigieuses."*

Roughly translated, this means that access to education (hitherto denied them) became obsessional, to the point that fathers of families saw the Baccalauréat as a symbol of access to the middle class lifestyle. Without this badge of recognition it was back to blue overalls and black fingernails.

Unfortunately, as some French friends explained, this desire, via education, to move from one class to another had created many new difficulties. Far too many young people overestimated their intellectual abilities and, failing their examinations, were left looking for positions well below what they had previously entertained as their right. Instead they often found themselves in mediocre businesses or small-time bureaucracy, causing frustration and resentment.

It has to be accepted that there is a limit to the number of professional people a country may sustain, while places for technicians, engineers and other skills remain unfilled. Happy indeed the country whose educational system caters for its citizen's true requirements, and accords at the same time with the aspirations and private ambitions of its people.

Significantly, the British keep arriving to live in France in a steady stream, often to buy and renovate very old property for permanent or holiday homes. Their interest in property means that many estate agents now have notices in their windows saying "English spoken here"!

The French, on the other hand, if they do inherit an old property, prefer to keep it un-renovated as a holiday home and, if the opportunity to buy does occur, they prefer newly built flats or villas. Sometimes they even abandon the idea of owning their own property and prefer to live in rented accommodation. Surplus income is swallowed by items they consider indispensable to civilised life such as food, restaurant meals, fashionable clothes and holidays. So while the average young British couples immerse themselves in the long, often complicated process of mortgage repayments as the underlying bedrock of their lives together, the French are off to restaurants in their most fashionable clothes!

Just as their general appreciation of food and wine is different to that of the British, so French attitudes to sex and extra-marital affairs is certainly very different to the British who, according to the French, suffer from Anglo-Saxon Puritanism. The French never understood British outrage over the Profumo scandal, or the Parkinson resignation, for most French people are aware of sexual weaknesses and not only tolerate such situations but are discreet about them, laughing privately at other nations for their hypocritical outrage at what to them is *'au naturel'*.

With the emancipation of women today and the opening up of careers, women in France nowadays may have affairs but do not always consider leaving their husbands or breaking up the family unit. Divorce, once very difficult in a Catholic country, is now easier but family life, and love of children, is still very strong.

Women's Lib, on the whole, moves very slowly here because men do not like to do what they consider to be 'women's jobs' in the home, such as using the dishwasher, ironing, shopping, or taking a sick child to the doctor. Most men pay lip service to female emancipation but expect the woman basically to stay in the home and run it.

However, in weighing up the differences between my own country and France, I am struck by the fact that whatever the gulf between Left and Right political forces, which has so dominated British politics since the War, at the end of the day in France there is a natural willingness on the part of most concerned to say, "Well, what is best for France will win the day."

It is a pragmatism I have come to admire and I took happily to the oft-repeated phrase *'ce sont les affaires'* – it is business – which is always the café owner's response to his hard lifestyle but *raison d'être.*

Perhaps you had to be defeated in a war and learn through patriotism to have pride in being French again. Whatever their problems – and there are plenty of them – France's public face is splendid. The streets are clean, public buildings, parks, buses, metro, trains and motorways are all well looked after. It all has to do with the importance France attaches to 'civilisation' and their concept of the 'rightness of things'. The role of food, drink, clothes and fashion, not to mention intellectual discussion arising from the relevance in schools of the subjects of philosophy and debate. This sense of seriousness and civilisation permeates everything. It is a country essentially, quintessentially, French.

Here in the Roussillon it is the wonderful climate that dictates a lifestyle largely spent out-of-doors, and the contrast between my native Wales and my home in France is vividly present in two posters in my bedroom.

The first is of Dylan Thomas' poem *Fern Hill:*

Now as I was young and easy
Under the apple boughs
About the lilting house and
Happy as the grass was green,
The night above the dingle starry,
Time let me hail and climb
Golden in the heyday of his eyes,
And honoured among wagons
I was prince of the apple towns
And once below a time I lordly
Had the trees and leaves
Trail with daisies and barley
Down the rivers of the windfall light...
... which shows how green indeed the Welsh valleys are,

in comparison with the second poster, of Collioure on the Mediterranean coast, which is a riot of blue sky and sea with vermillion-roofed houses.

It was this explosion of colour that attracted artists to Collioure at the beginning of the 20th Century, so that it became famous for *'Une lumière blonde, dorée, qui supprime les ombres...',* 'the colour gold that subdues the shadows...'

It is on this happy note that I leave my readers, in the hope that they will take comfort from the fact that if you conclude, as Don Quixote did, that you need new adventures before it is too late to do anything at all, then you must first find your very own *Rozinante.*

Bonne chance et bonne aventure!
Banyuls-sur-Mer, France, August 2006

Recipes

From

Rozinante

INDEX OF RECIPES

✂ DRESSINGS

When we first visited the Roussillon area of the south of France looking for a suitable property to run as a guest house, we stayed in a modest little hotel in Perpignan from where, every evening, we set out to explore the centre of the city and discover new and, we hoped, interesting food for our main evening meal. Admittedly, it was January – not the height of the tourist season – so many restaurants were closed, and our choice limited.

Consequently, our first meal started badly with a dispirited looking soup, fortunately enlivened with garlic-flavoured croutons and a generous bowl of Aioli – the Catalan version of garlic mayonnaise, which is delicious. We discovered that in this part of France it may be spread on croutons and eaten with soup, or served with fish and meat and with every kind of salad, so it is fitting that our first recipe should be for Aioli, closely followed by French Dressing and Vinaigrette, which is essential for all salads.

Aioli

Makes 1–2 cups

6 cloves of garlic (or more to taste), peeled and
    minced finely
½ tsp of salt
1 whole egg
1 egg yolk
1 – 1½ cups olive oil

Put the minced garlic paste into the food processor and add egg yolk and whole egg. Process for several seconds, then pour in the oil in a slow stream until the mayonnaise emulsifies. This will keep for several days in a jam jar in the fridge if necessary. A friend of mine always adds a tablespoon of breadcrumbs with the eggs, which changes the texture a little.

You may serve aioli in a separate bowl with practically anything. It is lovely with fish and I also like it with a Chicken Liver Salad or 'Hot Salad' as the French call it.

Ordinary Mayonnaise

Not everyone likes garlic, so here is a recipe for the ordinary variety, which is quick and easy.

1 whole egg
1 egg yolk
½ tsp salt
1 tsp sugar
½ tsp mustard
White pepper
2 dessert spoons of vinegar (either white wine or
    cider vinegar)
1–1½ cups olive oil

Place all ingredients except the olive oil into your food processor and whizz until blended. With the machine still running, pour in a thin stream of olive oil (the mildest you can find, or mix some olive oil with ordinary oil) through the feed tube until the mixture thickens. The more you pour the thicker it becomes, and you stop when you feel you've reached the required consistency.

Vinaigrette

In France all salads are served with some form of vinaigrette dressing, while in Britain the nearest equivalent would be confectioned brands of salad dressings.

The vinaigrette is usually poured into the bottom of the salad bowl with the salad itself heaped on top, and only at the last minute before serving is the dressing delicately mixed in with the salad, preferably by hand to avoid bruising the leaves.

Quantities depend on your taste; experiment until you find the consistency you prefer.

1 good tsp salt
1 tsp pepper
1 good tsp mustard (smooth or grained)
2–3 tsp sugar (white or brown) or honey
4 tbsp cider or wine vinegar, or juice of 2 lemons
10 tbsp oil or olive oil, for a stronger flavour

Whisk all the ingredients except the oil together and then add the oil slowly, or use a liquidiser to blend, or put in a screw top jar and shake vigorously before use. You can store this in the fridge but the oil may thicken a little, so take it out before use to liquidise again.

Do experiment with quantities until you secure the taste you like. You may use clear honey instead of sugar, and only lemon juice instead of vinegar. I sometimes mix olive oil with ordinary oil, or experiment with others such as walnut oil. Add a little cold water if you wish to thin the texture.

French Dressing

A friend gave me this version of French Dressing, which is delicious.

Makes a full jam jar.

75ml sunflower oil and same quantity walnut oil
Juice of 1 lemon
1 clove garlic
1 tbsp tahini sauce (sesame seed paste)
1 tbsp maple syrup
1 tbsp soya sauce
1 tbsp French mustard
Season with salt and pepper

If you like more spice in your dressing you can add curry powder, bay leaf, cumin, coriander and mixed herbs to taste. Put all the ingredients in a jam jar, put the lid on and shake well.

⚘ OTHER ESSENTIAL SAUCES

I once had an opportunity to visit the kitchens of a celebrated hotel in South Wales, famous for its proximity to the then Cardiff Arms Park Stadium, the well-known venue for rugby football international matches.

The visit was instructive and my focus centred on the enormous *bain-marie* (water bath) in which all the sauces were kept warm before service in the restaurant began.

The *Saucier* (sauce-chef) was, the head chef informed me, one of the key components in the kitchen staff – for if the sauces were well-designed and, above all, ready for use then the light and quick cooking of steaks, chops, cutlets and other meats and fish could be accomplished at speed to be complemented at once by the sauces before serving. Until you have worked in a restaurant you cannot imagine the pressures involved when the dining rooms fill up and everyone wishes to be served at once!

Fresh Tomato Sauce

Makes 2 - 3 cups

¼ cup oil
1 onion, finely chopped
2 bacon rashers, diced
1 garlic clove, finely chopped
1 small carrot, finely chopped
2 tbsp flour
2 ½ cups peeled tomatoes, chopped
¼ cup tomato paste
1 cup stock or water
1 bay leaf
1 small onion studded with 2 cloves
Pinch of dried basil
2 tsp brown sugar
Salt and pepper to taste
5cm strip lemon peel with 2 tsp lemon juice

Heat the oil in a large heavy-based saucepan. Add onion, bacon, garlic and carrot. Sauté gently for 10 minutes. Stir in the flour and cook for 1 minute, then add tomatoes and tomato paste. Gradually blend in stock and water. Cook, stirring constantly until the sauce boils and thickens. Add all the remaining ingredients and simmer for 45 minutes, stirring frequently. Remove the bay leaf, clove-studded onion and lemon peel. Adjust seasoning and serve as it is, or liquidise for smoothness.

You can serve this sauce with pasta, meatballs, beef fondue, barbecued meats and stuffed cabbage leaves. I used to make large quantities and store some in the fridge and sometimes freeze what wasn't used immediately.

A quicker version uses tinned tomatoes with onion added, having first softened by frying lightly in butter. Add garlic, salt and pepper, dried herbs and sugar to taste. Simmer for 40 minutes until it thickens and check to see if anything else needs to be added. Liquidise for a smooth sauce.

Espagnole Sauce, or Brown Sauce

Makes 2 cups

60g butter
2 bacon rashers, chopped
1 carrot, chopped and sliced
1 stalk celery, chopped and sliced
1 onion, sliced
4 tbsp plain flour
3 cups bone or beef stock or vegetable stock
4 mushrooms, sliced
2 tbsp tomato paste
Bouquet garni, salt and pepper
2 – 3 tbsp sherry, or any sweet wine available

Heat the butter in a heavy saucepan and add the bacon, celery, carrot and onion. Cook gently until vegetables are golden brown, but be careful not to burn.

Add the flour, stir well and cook over gentle heat until the mixture is a deep gold brown (12–15 minutes). Add the stock and bring to the boil, stirring continuously. Add the mushrooms, tomato paste, bouquet garni, salt and pepper and simmer gently, uncovered, for at least 30 minutes, stirring frequently and skimming if necessary. Strain through a fine pointed strainer and add sherry. Taste and adjust flavour if necessary before serving. Again, do double quantities if you wish to freeze.

I often use boiled water and a stock cube if I have no original stock, and sometimes add one or two teaspoons of black treacle to enhance the flavour and the colour.

Gravy

Part of my life was spent in a small Welsh village where the only shop was run by the harassed-looking diminutive Mrs Williams, whose husband spent most of his time in the Blue Boar pub, too conveniently placed directly opposite the shop.

One day she excitedly said she had finally persuaded her husband to leave the confines of the Blue Boar to take a continental bus trip holiday to Switzerland. Never having left Wales before, she was ecstatic with anticipation.

A month later I was curious to know how she had enjoyed the trip. "Oh, Mrs Barter," she said, "it was wonderful, the scenery, the mountains, the lakes..." She paused, sighed heavily and said finally, "the only trouble was Dad missed his gravy!"

Barely concealing a smile, I probed further and she revealed that he had not been able to eat any salad because 'it was all messed up with oil'. Mr Williams was obviously happy to be back in the Blue Boar!

Catering for different nationalities at *Rozinante* I realised the importance of gravy for the British, but found the French much preferred the residue of the juices in which the meat had been cooked with a little help from stock or wine, but never thickened with flour.

You always start with the residue in the bottom of the roasting pan after cooking a joint, and I have usually mixed this with flour and water or stock to make the gravy. You may want to add red or white wine to flavour, and with beef I used to add horseradish or mustard; for lamb: garlic, redcurrant jelly or mint; and for duck: orange peel and mixed herbs. For chicken, add lemon juice and tarragon; for pork, add honey or apricots; and for veal, add sherry, brown sugar and mixed spice.

I cooked several onions and garlic around the joint, and sometimes rested the meat on a bed of chopped onions, carrots, parsnips, peppers, courgettes and apple. Occasionally I poured cider or cider and water around the joint and then covered the whole pan tightly with foil to seal it. I would remove the foil and let the joint brown for the last half hour. The vegetables, cider and steam meant the joint was always tender and the residue in the bottom of the pan made for a lovely gravy – Mr Williams would have been delighted!

For thickening gravy and sauces, I often used potato flour instead of wheat flour.

Blender Hollandaise Sauce

Excellent with fish dishes

250g butter
3 egg yolks
2 tbsp lemon juice
Salt, pepper and cayenne to taste

Melt the butter. Place the remaining ingredients in the blender, cover, and blend for at least two minutes. Pour at once the melted butter in a steady stream through the hole in the lid and stop the blender as soon as all the butter is incorporated. Place the sauce in a double saucepan to reheat if necessary. Add cream to taste, or dilute as required. The sauce can be made in advance and kept in a thermos, but remember it will curdle if it boils or gets too hot.

Green Sauce; Sauce Verte; Salsa Verde

Green Sauce is very popular on the continent, often served with fish and delicious with potato salad. Simply made, you add crushed tarragon and parsley to homemade mayonnaise – quantities depend on taste.

The Italian version, *Salsa Verde,* is made as follows:

3 spring onions, chopped
Grated zest and juice of 1 large lemon
25g gherkins, drained and rinsed
25g capers, drained and rinsed
2 tsp chopped parsley, chervil, mint and thyme leaves
150ml extra virgin olive oil
Salt and black pepper

Process all the ingredients in a food blender to a smooth consistency. If you like a nutty flavour add a little tahini (sesame seed paste).

Sweet and Sour Sauce

Excellent for barbecue cooking

4 tbsp oil
2 tbsp granulated sugar
1–2 tbsp soy sauce
1 tbsp sherry
2 tbsp malt vinegar
2 tbsp tomato sauce
2 green peppers, or one red and one green
2 carrots
1 large onion
2 slices pineapple (fresh or tinned)

Chop and finely slice all of the ingredients. Heat oil and add the vegetables. Fry quickly for two minutes, then stir in all the other ingredients.

Red Wine Sauce

For red meat

30g butter (or fat from the meat)
2 finely chopped shallots
25g plain flour
250ml meat stock
100ml red wine
½ tsp sugar
Salt and pepper to taste

Heat the butter in a saucepan and fry the shallots, scraping away any that stick to the bottom of the pan. Stir in the flour and continue stirring while pouring in the meat stock. Bring to the boil and cook for a few more minutes. Pour in the wine and season to taste with sugar, salt and pepper.

Orange and Thyme Sauce

For poultry and game

1 finely chopped shallot
15g butter
2 tbsp fresh thyme or 2 tsp dry thyme
100ml thick chicken or game stock
100ml vegetable stock
200ml orange juice
125ml *crème fraîche*
Salt and pepper

Heat the butter and fry the onions. Stir in thyme, stock and orange juice. Bring to the boil and simmer until reduced by a half. Stir in the *crème fraîche* and continue cooking for a few minutes. Season to taste with salt and pepper.

⚜ MARINADES

In my early twenties, wishing to improve my French, I had an opportunity to spend three months working in a market garden near the town of Albi, a place strongly associated with the celebrated artist, Toulouse Lautrec, whose work could be admired in the town's Gallery.

The owner of the market garden, Loetitia Nassivet, was short and stockily built, with the arms of a wrestler from years of hauling sacks of vegetables from ground to local market. Her gypsy complexion, almost black from the sun, matched her glistening dark hair which, she informed me, she never washed but oiled regularly.

At first sight the farmhouse was impressive. It faced a large courtyard with a well which, I was to discover, was central to my work load, since carrots and many other vegetables had to be washed first, then tied in bundles ready for market.

Inside, the house was shrouded in darkness from shuttered windows which initially concealed the layers of dust, unmoved for years as work outside was more vital to existence than labour inside.

The kitchen, I was relieved to see, did sport a large fridge but meat was kept mainly in a wire mesh safe in an adjoining barn, the door of which when opened allowed a swarming collection of flies to escape from unhappy captivity. So much for the safety of the meat!

My bedroom, when I flung open the shutters, proved to be the master bedroom and majestically the large double bed was crowned with red velvet and shrouded in curtains to match which, when disturbed, released clouds of dust into the room. I decided it was best to leave the shutters closed.

Work in the field was from day break to dusk. Meals were unimportant and sporadic, one large frying pan being used to fry everything from fish to meat or poultry, eggs, or whatever.

Most worrying of all was Leotitia's special drink, a homemade lemonade, consisting of fresh lemon juice, sugar, water and bicarbonate of soda! By the time I returned home I had lost a stone in weight!

Sunday, when we often had visitors for lunch, was the one day we ate well after Leotitia had killed one of the rabbits she fattened up in hatches in one of the barns. Having killed and skinned it she would make a marinade and place the rabbit in this, in a stone jar for three days, lovingly turning it before its final preparation.

The marinade was undoubtedly the secret of its success and I was happy to use this in *Rozinante* for several dishes.

Marinade

85g brown sugar
3 tbsp Worcester sauce
3 tbsp soy sauce
2 tbsp wine vinegar
5 tbsp tomato ketchup
1 tsp mustard
275ml pineapple or orange juice
275ml stock
Garlic, crushed
Chilli, or any other sharp tasting sauce
A little rum, as an option

Mix all the marinade ingredients together and pour this over the meat to be marinated (chicken, spare ribs etc). Cover with film and put in the fridge for 24 hours, turning the meat in the marinade from time to time.

To cook, place the meat in a shallow baking tin and pour in sufficient quantity of marinade to cover. Bake in a low oven, 150C/300F/gas mark 2, until the meat is tender. If the meat is done and too large a quantity of the marinade remains then remove the meat, keep warm, and boil up the marinade quickly to reduce to a thicker quality. Serve the meat with the marinade poured over.

A Milder Marinade

Good for poultry or lamb

4 tbsp olive oil
1 onion, chopped
2 cloves of garlic
Sprigs of rosemary
2 tsp clear honey
2 tbsp wine vinegar
Grated zest and juice of a large lemon
Salt and pepper

Heat the oil and fry the onion and garlic for two minutes and add the remaining ingredients. Simmer for two to three minutes and allow to cool before using as a marinade.

⚜ STARTERS

Tuesday, we had been told, was market day in our local town of Prades, and our first trip to collect supplies was a revelation for the sheer variety of fruit, vegetables, cheese, eggs, poultry, fish, jams and preserves, not to mention stalls selling second-hand clothing, pottery, flowers, plants, kitchen utensils, hunting gear... There were also stalls selling prepared foods such as paella and other rice dishes, quiches, salads, charcuterie, cooked hams, chicken, barbecued meats – we were speechless.

Some fruit and vegetables were unknown to us, so when a friend mentioned a Catalan cookery course at Vinça we set off one day a week for six weeks to learn more about Catalan cooking procedures.

To our surprise, instead of a well-rounded exponent of local cuisine, Madame Costello turned out to be diminutive beyond belief – almost skeletal, so that we wondered if she ever ate any of the recipes she so stoutly defended against all other forms of cookery regimes.

There was no doubting her authority, however, or her expertise, for scattered on the kitchen table in front of her were several of her publications on the art of local cuisine. We were, without doubt, in expert hands!

We discovered in the course of time that she was an authority on the history of food in Catalonia and had written books on medieval recipes, a time many ingredients such as tomatoes and potatoes were unknown to Europe.

Needless to say, we thoroughly enjoyed her lessons and one great surprise was her use of dark chocolate in meat dishes which, she said, not only gave colour but heightened taste.

I was particularly grateful for her help in devising starters to meals, and I happily gave guests all the chocolate they could possibly want in different guises.

Guacamole Dip

2 ripe avocadoes, halved and stoned
Pinch of chilli pepper
½ tsp salt
½ tsp paprika
Juice of ½ lemon
1 clove garlic, crushed
Olive oil

Scoop out the avocado flesh into a blender and add all the ingredients, except oil. Start blending and then slowly add just enough oil to allow the mixture to blend completely. Taste and adjust seasoning, pour into a bowl and sprinkle with paprika.

Walnut Paté

2 cloves garlic
250g walnuts
7 tbsp olive oil
½ tsp salt

Put all the ingredients in a blender and blend until the walnuts are reduced to tiny pieces.
   Serve this paté with sticks of carrot, cucumber, celery, spring onion, fennel, radish, pickled chilli peppers and bread.

Salmon Mousse

This dish can be made in advance of guests arriving.

500g cold poached salmon, flaked but not mashed
15g gelatine
125ml mayonnaise or sour cream
Lemon juice
1 tsp salt

2 tbsp finely chopped dill (optional)
300ml lightly whipped cream

Dissolve the gelatine in half a teacup of water over a gentle heat, and then pour into a mixing bowl. Whisk in the mayonnaise, lemon juice to taste, salt and dill. Fold in the finely flaked salmon, then carefully fold in the cream. Pour into a mould and chill for four hours minimum, or overnight. Unmould onto a serving plate and decorate with salad.

Chicken Liver Paté

115g butter
1 tbsp olive oil
200g chicken livers (washed with gristle removed)
2 cloves garlic, sliced
2 tbsp cooking brandy
2 tsp mustard powder
Pinch each of nutmeg, salt and pepper

Fry the chicken livers in 85g of the butter and olive oil. Add garlic over gentle heat for about 5 minutes. Pour in the brandy and remove from the heat, making sure you mop up all the juices. Place the cooked ingredients with the mustard, nutmeg, salt and pepper in a food processor and reduce to a paste. Put the paste in a container and cover with what is left of the melted butter. Leave in the fridge overnight and serve with hot toast.

Chicken Liver Mousse

This can either be made in a terrine or in individual small pots and cooked in the oven. It is often served with a fresh tomato sauce.

200g chicken livers
55g butter and a little oil
4 eggs

4 tbsp *crème fraîche* or double cream
1 tsp tomato purée
Salt and pepper
1 tbsp brandy

Fry the chicken livers in a little butter and oil mixed to prevent burning and sticking to the pan. Once cooked, crush the liver in your food processor and add the eggs, *crème fraîche*, tomato purée, salt, pepper, and brandy. Check the seasoning and put in ovenproof dishes with bases lined with greaseproof paper.

Stand the pots in a baking tin half-filled with boiling water and bake for 20 minutes in oven gas mark 4/180C/350F. Test by inserting the blade of a knife, which should come out clean.

Turn the mousse or mousses out and garnish with lettuce, gherkins, and small onions – or round each one off with a fresh tomato sauce.

Asparagus Mousse

1 tin asparagus, or freshly cooked asparagus tips
Same quantity of good mayonnaise, OR whipped cream,
    OR fromage fraîs, OR *crème fraîche*
1 packet or just under 15g gelatine

Drain a few tbsp of the juice from the tin and soak gelatine until dissolved.

Save a few asparagus tips for garnish, then tip all the ingredients into a food processor and blend. Pour into a large dish or individual pots, and put into the fridge to set. Garnish with asparagus tips, having dressed with a little vinaigrette.

This can also be served with a few spears of fresh asparagus, cooked and allowed to cool, and again, the tips dressed with vinaigrette.

Stuffed Tomatoes

6 large tomatoes
1 slice of white bread
Milk, to soak the bread
1 egg yolk
6 pork sausages
2 tbsp fresh parsley
2–3 cloves of garlic, chopped
Olive oil where necessary

Slice off the tops of the tomatoes (keeping them aside).
De-seed and take out the pulp.

Lightly salt the tomatoes and leave them upside down
for the excess juice to drain from them. Soak the dried
bread in milk, then squeeze out most of the liquid. Remove
skins from the sausages and add the meat to the egg yolk
and the moist bread. Mix together with the parsley and
chopped garlic, and fill the tomatoes with this mixture,
replacing the sliced-off caps to re-close the tomatoes. If
liked, pour a little olive oil over the tomatoes before cooking
for 1 hour in a medium oven, 180C/350F/gas mark 4.

Stuffed Peppers

6 red peppers
6 fresh tomatoes or 1 tin chopped tomatoes
2–3 tsp sugar
Salt and pepper
½ tsp dried herbs or 2 tbsp chopped fresh parsley
    and chives
12 anchovies (optional)
Olive oil as required

Wash the peppers, cut in half lengthwise and de-seed, but
leave the green stem on if possible as it looks attractive.

Dip fresh tomatoes in boiling water and peel the skin from
them, then chop them up (or use tinned chopped tomatoes,
drained). Fill the peppers with these, adding a little sugar if

they are a bit acid, along with the salt, pepper, and herbs. Drizzle olive oil over the mixture and if you like them, lay two anchovies across the top of each tomato in a cross formation. If the anchovies are very salty, amend the salt inclusion accordingly. Cook in a moderate open, 180C/350F/gas mark 4, until soft.

Summer Starter

1 cucumber
3 large tomatoes
450ml of water
Chicken stock cube
15g gelatine
1 tbsp tomato purée
2 cloves garlic
Black pepper
1 carton sour cream OR natural Greek yoghurt
175g peeled prawns

Peel and grate the cucumber. Peel the tomatoes, remove core and chop the flesh. Squeeze the garlic through a press. Combine water, stock cube and tomato purée in a saucepan and bring to the boil and simmer for 5 minutes, stirring occasionally. Remove from the heat and stir in the gelatine until melted. Allow to cool then stir in the cucumber, tomatoes, lemon juice, garlic and season with pepper. Chill until lightly set then scoop carefully into individual bowls, leaving a central space in which you put the soured cream and top with prawns. Sprinkle with a little cayenne and serve well chilled.

OTHER FIRST COURSE SUGGESTIONS

For a first course, and to save time, I frequently served shop-bought smoked fillets of fish with salad and crab sticks, with prawns mixed in mayonnaise. Served with salad it was always a firm favourite.

Another very quick and easy first course was hard-boiled eggs, covered lightly with a good homemade mayonnaise, criss-crossed with anchovies and surrounded by salad. You can also buy little pots of red or black lump fish and serve in place of anchovies with the eggs.

Slices of melon, when in season, were served with very thin slices of smoked ham.

Asparagus in season was served either very simply once cooked, with a vinaigrette sauce or with finely chopped up hard-boiled eggs in a little mayonnaise.

Avocadoes were another favourite, sliced open and stones removed, then either filled with shrimps or prawns in mayonnaise or with a simple vinaigrette dressing.

France also has an abundance of pâtés, mousses and smoked sausages to serve with salad.

If I had a surplus of green runner beans, I would cook them, then serve them cold with vinaigrette sauce topped with anchovies and slices of hard-boiled eggs.

I had a round scoop that I used for making a cocktail of fresh melon balls dressed with bottled ginger strips and moistened with the ginger syrup from the bottle.

Once we had become accustomed to the routine of running *Rozinante*, it began to worry me that as so many of our guests and friends were English, we were not making any progress in learning the French language. As I mentioned earlier, my one attempt at lessons with a local retired French school teacher had ended disastrously, so we were delighted to learn on one of our market trips of a French walking group who met every Thursday at Prades' railway station for a full day's walk. My sister and her husband were experienced walkers and were welcomed into the Caminem group, but I retreated after one strenuous session with them to what was known as the Strollers, the easier Monday group.

I was warned to wear stout shoes, carry a walking stick and bring a packed lunch in a rucksack. Two members in their seventies had been part of Alpine clubs, so were delegated leaders who carried first aid accessories or brandy in case of emergencies!

Turning up rather nervously on my first morning, I was surprised to find a group of about 40 people, mostly aged 60 plus, and as usual there was the normal French debate in full swing as to the destination for the day, the route to be taken (there was some divergence of opinion over this) and how many cars were required to get us all to our starting point, quite apart from who should lead and who should bring up the rear!

The fast and furious rattle-like fire of the French spoken caused me some initial concern, but help was at hand when another English couple, the Phillpots, came over to take me in hand. We happily all piled into cars and set off on an adventure into the unknown!

The lunchtime break came not a moment too soon for my somewhat amateurish approach to an all-day hike in the mountains, when I had imagined myself fit for anything! Squatting down in a shady clump of trees overlooking a valley shimmering in the heat, I discovered another English couple, the Middletons, and having struggled with school-learned French all morning I relapsed happily into my native tongue and ate, with quiet satisfaction, my very English sandwiches.

It was only after several such hikes that I discovered how very different the British contingent was when it came to packed lunches. The Phillpots brought Earl Grey tea in a thermos, with Marmite sandwiches; the Middletons brought Ribena fruit juice and corned beef sandwiches, while I was no more adventurous, with Nescafé instant coffee in a thermos, and Spam and pickle sandwiches.

It never varied, while all around us the French produced small bottles of wine or water, with plastic containers full of all manners of delicious looking dishes of chicken and rice, *charcuterie* and salad or largely, I discovered, their leftovers from elaborate Sunday lunches!

All manner of soups were consumed, such as Watercress, Gazpacho and Provençal Pistou. I collected as many of these soup recipes as I could and I am pleased to include them here.

⚭ SOUPS

The memory of the insipid quality of our first ever Catalan soup made me determined to return to the stock-pot base of my mother's recipes, and so all *Rozinante* soups were home-made. The stock-pot of my childhood was bubbling perma-nently at the back of the kitchen range and was 'boiled up' every day for its life cycle of 5 days to allow for 'skimming off' the froth, fat and other impurities.

Basic stock was made with bones, ham and veal for pies, beef for nourishing winter soups and casseroles, pigs' trot-ters for a glutinous stock, which formed a jelly when set, and sheep's head for mutton broth or brawn. A small bundle of dried herbs grown in our garden, such as rosemary, thyme, sage and bay leaves, would be added and later discarded. Chicken and turkey carcasses would be boiled up with plenty of root vegetables, carrots, onions, turnips, leeks, parsnips and celery. This would serve as a general stock base for many recipes. Duck and goose remains were rare and had to be well skimmed for their fat content before use.

At *Rozinante* I found the supermarkets sold large-sized turkey legs and these, boiled with herbs and root vegetables for 45 minutes, made an excellent stock, especially for the pies which became such a favourite with guests. I would use garlic freely when cooking, but the quantity is always a question of taste. If I ever ran out of my own stock I used commercial stock cubes, and there are a number of differ-ent flavours available now. But if I used a stock cube then I would start a soup by frying onions, garlic and herbs in a mixture of butter and oil, occasionally adding a lardon of raw bacon for flavour. Water added to this with a stock cube or two and later strained provided a good stock base for most dishes.

The soups I served at *Rozinante* depended on the time of year and what was in season. My brother-in-law was a keen gardener and raised a wonderful amount of fresh vegetables in our own potager and, being Welsh, we used a lot of leeks.

Leek and Potato Soup

3 large leeks
1 large potato
Knob of butter
1 litre chicken stock
Salt and pepper
2–3 tbsp single cream

Trim off the green tops of the leeks to within about one inch of the white part, and cut away the base. Slice length-wise through to the centre and wash well in cold water. Shred the leeks finely. Peel and chop up the potato into cubes. Melt the butter in a saucepan and add the leeks and potato.

Cover and cook over a low heat for about 5 minutes to allow the vegetables to soften, but don't allow them to colour. Stir in the stock and bring to the boil. Re-cover and simmer gently for about 30 minutes or until the vegetables are quite soft. Purée, return to the pan and season, if necessary, adding the cream just before serving.

Watercress Soup

3 bunches of watercress
1–2 medium onions
45g butter
1 large potato
600ml chicken stock
300ml milk
Salt and pepper

Wash the watercress well and set aside a small amount for garnish. Remove the coarse stalks, roughly chop the leaves, and then peel and finely chop the onion. Melt the butter in a saucepan and add the onion. Garlic may be added to all soups and this is a matter of taste when it comes to quantity. Fry gently for about 5 minutes, or until soft but not brown. Peel the potato and dice into large pieces. Add the potato and chopped watercress to the pan, and coat them in the onion-flavoured butter. Allow to cook for a moment, then add the stock and the milk. Bring to the boil, cover and simmer for about 30 minutes.

Purée the soup and return to the cleaned pan, season, and garnish with the remaining leaves.

French Onion Soup

This is a soup for cold days and you need three to four large onions, peeled, chopped, and cooked in butter with garlic to taste. Add stock with mixed herbs and, if you like, 1 teaspoon of yeast extract and the usual seasoning. Pulverise in your liquidiser and serve with croutons and grated cheese.

Russian Borscht Soup

This soup was always appreciated for its colour as well as its flavour.

2 onions, chopped
2 cloves of garlic, chopped
4 small potatoes, cut into pieces
450g raw beetroot, chopped
1 litre stock
3 tbsp cider vinegar
Salt, pepper, ground nutmeg to taste
Natural yoghurt to taste
Chopped parsley to garnish

Chop the vegetables and cook first in a little butter and oil, then add the stock and other ingredients and cook until the vegetables are soft. Season accordingly. Liquidise and serve garnished with a little yoghurt and the chopped parsley.

Jerusalem Artichoke Soup

These are not easy to find but make the most delicious soup. You need eight to ten artichokes. Peel as finely as possible and cut into small pieces. Use garlic and onion sparingly, with a cooked melted butter base, so as not to detract from the subtle flavour of the artichokes. Add the artichokes to the onion and the stock and once all the vegetables are cooked then pulverise, adding cream and milk to taste.

Carrot and Onion Soup

Again, use an onion and garlic base, cooked in butter, and add the chopped carrots once the onion and garlic are soft, along with the stock and orange juice to your taste. Once thoroughly soft, pulverise and adjust seasoning.

Mushroom Soup

675g mushrooms
125g butter
2 small onions, chopped
1 garlic clove, chopped
Salt and pepper
85g flour
1.75 litre stock
175ml cream

Peel and rinse the mushrooms well and pat dry with absorbent paper. Cook the onion and garlic to taste in a mixture of butter and oil. Add mushrooms, thickening with flour and added stock. Cook until soft, then pulverise and add cream.

Gazpacho

Spanish and French guests always loved gazpacho but the British, with their cold climate, were never very appreciative.

¼ cucumber
1 or 2 small green or red peppers, or 1 of each
250g tomatoes
2 onions
Garlic to taste
300ml tomato juice
Fresh parsley
1.75 litres stock
Salt and pepper
Tomato paste to taste

Roughly chop all the ingredients and blend in small quantities in the liquidiser until smooth. Chill and serve with croutons.

Provençal Pistou

3 tbsp olive oil
1 onion
1 clove of garlic, peeled and crushed
1 leek
2 celery sticks, trimmed, scraped and chopped
225g carrots, scraped and chopped
400g can chickpeas
1.2 litres vegetable stock
4 fresh tomatoes, skinned and chopped
1 medium courgette, trimmed and cut into slices
50g small pasta shapes
4 tbsp pesto sauce
Salt and pepper
Freshly grated Parmesan cheese to serve

Cook onion and garlic in the oil over a medium heat, then add all the other vegetables. Sauté the vegetables for about 10 minutes or until soft, then add the pasta, pesto, salt and pepper, and blend together. Add cheese to serve.

Pea and Pesto Soup

I always cooked peas the French way, that is only adding peas to the saucepan after I had sweated some chopped up left-over green salad with 6–8 chopped up spring onions in some butter. I would add water with a chicken stock cube and a small amount of sugar before putting in the peas for five minutes. When I had left-over peas from a meal I would add boiled water (amount depends on how much soup you are making) with another stock cube if necessary and pesto sauce to taste. Boil together to infuse flavours and liquidise.

My earliest experience of eating in France was in 1950, not long after the end of the Second World War, when my sister and I spent a week in Paris. Through an army friend who had been stationed in Paris during the War, we secured the address of an inexpensive hotel in the Rue Danou, near the Place de l'Opera and immediately opposite the famous Harry's Bar.

We arrived in the early evening of a beautiful spring day to be greeted by a decrepit concierge with two of the blackest front teeth I had ever seen. The small foyer and reception desk were as dingy and unsavoury looking as the man in front of us. To add to our dismay the main access to our room, number 21 on the third floor, was an iron-caged lift of dubious ancestry which rattled and jerked us violently upwards, to the point where we could not scramble out quickly enough when it finally shuddered to its required destination.

The bedroom, when we opened the door, proved to be as equally unwelcoming as the rest of the place and the hot water tap, when we turned it on, just emitted a long weary sigh and a short puff of steam but no water at all!

Nothing daunted, however, we set out for our first evening's exploratory stroll and, as we had only been allowed by HM Government to bring £25 spending money each, there was a long and anxious scouring of the back streets to find somewhere to eat that we could afford.

Exhausted, we eventually settled for a tiny café with a slate outside advertising the *plat du jour* (dish of the day), which proved to be *Tripes de Caen*. I was quite happy once inside to settle for that, but my sister refused categorically. This was France, home of great cuisine, and tripe was far from that standard in her opinion! So, with the waiter's help, we settled finally for an *omelette fine herbes* served with a fresh, crusty baguette, all washed down with a glass of red wine. It tasted heavenly and such was our obvious appreciation that, without warning, a door opened at the back of the restaurant and a very large, perspiring Chef appeared bearing a gift for *les Anglaises* of a large bowl of haricot verts, freshly cooked with slivers of bacon and onion. We both felt that we had never tasted anything quite so delicious and went to bed that evening feeling the French experience was proving to be everything we had hoped for.

However, that was the only restaurant experience we could afford and for the rest of the week we haunted food markets and stall sellers in the street, picking up bags of tomatoes, different cheeses (there are over four hundred varieties throughout France), together with a daily trip to the *boulangerie* for baguettes and other delicious breads of varying shape and colour.

Happily *al fresco*, we ate our picnic meals on park benches or on whatever transport we had to places like Versailles and Fontainebleau, and daily I ticked off the list I insisted we had to visit if we were to feel we had done justice to our first trip to France. Fortunately, I had taken the precaution of wearing sandals but my sister, more fashion conscientious and aware of French chic, had opted for high heels – with the result that on the fourth day she collapsed with blisters, and my list was relegated to the wastepaper basket!

ॐ OMELETTES

Long after we returned home, the memory of our one and only restaurant meal remained vivid and so it was hardly surprising that omelettes, quiches and egg dishes featured largely on the *Rozinante* menu.

I always refer to Elizabeth David's description of how to make a good omelette, in which she stresses the importance of always keeping an omelette frying pan specifically for omelettes and never used for anything else. Secondly, never beat the eggs too savagely – stirring is preferable – and thirdly, never let the filling detract too much from the flavour of the eggs.

A 25cm omelette pan should be sufficient for an omelette of three to four eggs. Beat lightly, add salt and pepper and allow about 15g butter in the pan, which should be warm but not too hot before you pour in the egg mixture. But once poured, turn the heat as high as it will go.

Add filling and, once the omelette starts to firm, tip the pan this way and that, moving the egg mixture away from the edge from time to time so that the uncooked middle can pour sideways until that too is cooked. An omelette *'fine herbes'* means to mix in freshly chopped parsley, tarragon and chives.

For a ham omelette, simply add a heaped tablespoon of cooked ham, finely chopped, and mixed with a little parsley.

My favourite is to beat in 1 tablespoon of finely grated Parmesan cheese with the raw eggs and then, when the omelette is in the pan, add 1 tablespoon of fresh Gruyère cheese, cut into small dice, and 1 tablespoon of thick fresh cream.

Just experiment!

Tortilla Espagnole

This is a Spanish style omelette which is very filling.

Serves 4-6 people.

350g of red and green peppers, finely diced
10 eggs
30g butter
200g of Chorizo (Spanish sausage), cut into small rounds
Chopped chives to taste
¼ tsp paprika
A little dried herbs
Salt and pepper

Melt the butter in a large pan. Beat the eggs with salt, pepper and paprika and pour into the pan. Add the remaining ingredients and cook for 10 minutes on a medium heat, until the egg has set. Serve with a salad.

Tarragon Eggs in Cocotte

1 small onion
225g tomatoes
Garlic to taste
25g butter
1 tsp tarragon
Salt and pepper
4 eggs
4 tbsp (60ml) fresh double cream

Finely chop the onions and tomatoes. Melt the butter in a pan and cook the onion. Add the tomatoes and tarragon and cook gently until soft and pulpy. Adjust seasoning and spoon mixture into 4 individual ovenproof dishes. Make a well in the centre and break an egg into each one. Spoon over the cream and bake in the oven at 200C/400F/Mark 6 for 10–15 minutes.

Catalan Omelette with Potatoes

This style of omelette was, I am told, taken by the local peasants in wedges to the fields for lunch when the harvest season was at its height and time was of the essence. It is extremely hearty and only for the very hungry!

6 eggs
2 potatoes
100g mushrooms
100g bacon, dice
100g peas (optional)
1 tbsp finely chopped parsley
1 tbsp chopped chives
100ml milk
Salt and pepper to taste

Dice the potatoes and slice the mushrooms. Cook the potatoes for about 10 minutes until just tender. Fry the bacon, remove, and fry the diced potato in the bacon fat for about five minutes. Add the mushrooms, peas, bacon and herbs to the potato and continue cooking.

Beat the eggs and milk in a bowl and add seasoning to taste. Pour the mixture into the pan along with the vegetables. Cover and cook over a low heat until the omelette thickens. Lift the edges of the omelette from time to time so that the uncooked mixture runs underneath and sets.

To serve, cut the omelette into wedges and wrap in foil for picnics, or serve with tomato slices and grated cheese at home.

Quiche

I have always made my own ordinary pastry in a food mixer but the readymade pastries today are also very acceptable. I used to have trouble making quiches until I came to France and discovered the wonders of crème fraîche, which I always use now instead of milk and cream – hence no troubles since!

Pastry
250g ordinary flour
125g butter
1 egg yolk
300ml water
1 pinch salt

Put all the ingredients except the water in the food mixer and blend. Gradually add sufficient water to make a firm pastry. You can use this pastry straight away or you can cool it slightly in the fridge before use. Roll out into a circle of sufficient size to cover the base and sides of your quiche dish (I always use a metal based tin), pressing the pastry firmly into the corners.

Filling
One or two onions, depending on size of quiche
3 whole eggs, plus 1 additional egg yolk
Knob of butter
Any leftovers such as salmon or other fish, courgettes
    or tomatoes, asparagus etc.
Sufficient *crème fraîche* to make a firm mixture
Grated cheese to garnish

Having placed your pastry circle on the dish, fry the onions in the butter until soft and, when cool, place on the pastry bottom. Arrange whatever filling you have on top and beat the eggs and additional yolk firmly into sufficient *crème fraîche* to cover the filling. Smooth the top and cover with grated cheese. Bake for 45 minutes in a moderate oven until firm in the centre to touch.

✿ PIES

It was the height of a very hot summer when an excited English couple returned from their house hunting to say they had found the 'house of their dreams'. As it happened a foursome from Vichy were staying with us at the time and were happy to join in a celebratory meal with champagne, at which I presented the *pièce de resistance* – a steak and kidney pie.

Immediately one of the Vichy guests pointed to the pie and asked, "What is it, Madame" and, having had a little too much champagne I regret to say I burst into song to the tune of *Sing a song of sixpence, pocket full of rye, four and twenty blackbirds baked in a pie...*

The poor man looked horrified and said, *"Les merles, Madame, we are eating les merles!"* He was evidently not happy at the prospect until, relenting, I confessed that the blackbirds were in fact good old-fashioned British steak and kidney. Once reassured he confessed he had never eaten a pie of any description and I realised that this was now a British innovation to present to French guests in the future.

After the meal was cleared away I asked him if he liked cooking and it was his wife who laughed and said, "Oh Madame, in Vichy my husband is a Master Chef with his own well-known restaurant!"

I resolved to stop drinking champagne and singing at dinner parties in future, but pies of all descriptions became standard fare at *Rozinante*.

Long before my arrival in France, I knew the French were deeply suspicious of English cooking, for which reason I tried hard to improve our tarnished reputation. So we introduced French guests to English dishes, and this pie became very popular, although we varied the traditional English version with slight Catalan overtones.

Steak and Kidney Pie

175g prunes
600ml dry cider
1kg stewing steak
500g kidney
2 tbsp flour
50g beef dripping or 4 tbsp oil
1 onion, skinned and finely chopped
300-600ml beef stock or water
350g puff pastry
1 egg, beaten
Salt and pepper

Soak the prunes in the cider overnight then stone and halve them. Put the cider aside. Cut the steak and kidney into bite-sized pieces and coat with flour seasoned with salt and pepper. (The easiest way of doing this is to mix the flour and condiments in a plastic bag. Place the steak and kidney in the bag and shake well). Heat the fat in a casserole and brown the meat, a little at a time. Keep warm in a low oven.

Sauté the onion in the oil for 5 minutes until soft and sprinkle on any remaining flour, cook for a further couple of minutes, stirring to prevent burning and then pour on the cider in which the prunes have been soaked, and the stock or water. If you think the sauce may be too thick then add more liquid.

Stir until the sauce boils, then replace the meat and the prunes. Cover the casserole with a tightly fitting lid and cook on top of the stove, just simmering for 45 minutes. Transfer the contents to a large pie dish and leave to cool. When quite cold roll out the pastry and cover the pie with it. Trim and decorate with pastry leaves and cut a few air vents in the centre. Brush with beaten egg yolk and bake in a hot oven 220C/425F/gas mark 7 for the first 20 minutes, then lower to 180C/350F/gas mark 4 until the pastry is risen and golden brown.

Turkey and Pepper Pie

Turkey Stock:
1 large turkey leg
2–3 carrots, chopped
2–3 parsnips, chopped
3 large onions, chopped
2 stalks of celery, chopped
2–3 tbsp freshly chopped parsley, chives and thyme
   (or use dried herbs)
Salt and pepper
Enough water to cover

Pie Mix:
2–3 peppers, cut in strips
2–3 carrots, cut in strips
2 sticks celery, sliced
3 onions, sliced
3 cloves garlic, chopped

For the stock:
Poach the turkey leg with the vegetables and herbs for about 45 minutes. (This stock makes excellent soup and sauces.)

Strip the turkey meat off the bone, and keep aside.

To make the pie:
Sweat the vegetables in a little butter until softened but barely cooked through. Place the vegetables with the chopped turkey pieces into a pie dish. Moisten with the stock, thickened a little if necessary, and cover with a puff pastry top.

Brush the pastry with beaten egg yolk to form a glaze. Bake in a hot oven, 200C/400F/gas mark 6, until the pastry is risen, and then reduce to 180C/350F/gas mark 4 until you are certain the contents are cooked.

Whenever we served a poultry or meat dish we would often cover 'the remains' with a pastry lid and so produce another pie! Beef and kidney was a favourite, and beef with mushrooms. Similarly, when I made Moussaka, I always did an extra quantity of the meat element and put it in the freezer for emergencies. Once defrosted I added breadcrumbs or Quaker oats and an egg yolk to the mixture, with chopped fresh parsley to give a firmer consistency. I would then use this as a filling for the pastry case described with the Meat Loaf recipe.

Hasty Shepherd's Pie

The mixture for the Pastry Parcel (next recipe), moistened with gravy or other sauce, may be very easily transformed into a quick Shepherd's Pie by placing the meat in a flame-proof dish with a generous covering of mashed potato and grated cheese. Cook in a moderate oven until heated through and nicely browned.

Pastry Parcel

750g minced beef
Cup of dry breadcrumbs or oats
1 onion, grated
3 carrots, grated
¼ cup tomato purée
1 egg
2 tbsp chopped parsley
Little mixed herbs with salt and pepper
Horseradish sauce or sweet pickle
A few cheese slices – any dry, firm cheese such as
    Cheddar, Edam or Gouda works well

Fry the beef with the onion and carrots until cooked. Then mix in the breadcrumbs or oats, the tomato purée, egg, parsley, herbs, salt and pepper, horseradish sauce or sweet pickle. Use this mixture for a pastry parcel, either using your own puff pastry or the commercial kind.

Roll out the pastry into a square, brush the edges with egg yolk and then place slices of cheese down the middle of the square. Place a sufficient quantity of the meat mixture onto the cheese and then fold the sides of the pastry into a firm pleat in the middle and further seal by pressing together the ends. Very carefully, flop the whole parcel over to the other side (bottom to top) so that no pleat exists, and cut a few strokes to let the steam escape.

Brush with beaten egg yolk to glaze, and decorate with pastry leaves. Cook in an oven 200C/400F/gas mark 6 for 25 minutes until the pastry is brown and golden and the inside cooked. Serve either hot or cold.

You can experiment with other meat or fish leftovers provided the mixture is firm and not likely to leak out of the pastry case when cooking. The addition of hot chilli sauce makes a good variation.

The same meat mixure can be shaped into meatballs and lightly fried before serving with tomato sauce and spaghetti – in other words, Spaghetti Bolognaise.

❦ FISH

Rue de Couronnement

A year after our arrival in France, my son Mark set off to find a place of his own and, after several frustrating months of trial and error, he purchased a house of character, with an attached barn, ripe for renovation, situated right in the middle of the seaside resort of Argeles-sur-Mer.

The town was happily one of those charming old-fashioned resorts with a magnificent stretch of clean sand and safe bathing, ideal for family holidays. The broad sweep of the promenade was lined with typical French villas surrounded by palm trees and oleanders that offered a profusion of white, pink, yellow and purple blossom set against a backdrop of Les Albères mountains.

Mark's house, although some distance from the sea, was set in the middle of one of those typical narrow village streets that are almost medieval in appearance, with washing, geraniums, dogs, cats and people everywhere, talking, laughing, encouraging children to play hop-scotch while the elderly drowsed in the sun, watching the world go by.

Once installed, the activity at the home of the Englishman became a source of endless fascination, especially for the older men in the street who hung around, squatting like Arabs on their doorsteps, or merely standing at vantage points on street corners. Their daily conversations were a local grape vine or, as the locals called it, *le telephone arabe,* for news spread quicker than France Telecom and Mark was constantly amazed at the amount of domestic information relayed by these unemployed squatters each and every day.

One couple, living on the corner of the street, actually had their window enlarged so that they had a panoramic view of who went by and for what purpose. It was a far more intensive surveillance than the KGB, and Mark felt he had no hope of a private life and eventually gave up worrying about it. He never once left the house without someone coming out to say, *'Salut* Mark, you're going shopping?' or 'You're going to see your mother?' or 'Your girlfriend has gone to see the doctor?'

However, other neighbours were extremely helpful with advice and one such conversation led Mark to the local fish market, so that every time he came to see us he brought a huge shopping bag of fish and so enlarged our menu considerably.

"... village streets almost medieval in appearance ..."

Fish Pie

Any leftover fish can be used up in this way. The addition of salmon pieces gives the pie a more colourful appearance.

Spinach - enough for 4 people
2–3 cloves garlic, finely chopped
2–3 cutlets of cod or other firm white fish, fresh or frozen
White wine, to taste
1 cup shrimps or prawns, shelled
1 cup crab meat, flaked, or crab sticks, chopped
1 cup mussels
2 slices lemon
1 bay leaf
White sauce (see next recipe)

Thoroughly wash the spinach and remove any tough stems. Cook the leaves lightly in butter with garlic to taste. As the spinach has been washed and strained there is already enough water on the leaves without adding more liquid for cooking. Once cooked, drain well, chop finely and place in the bottom of a large ovenproof dish.

Lightly poach the fish for 2–4 minutes in fish stock or water, with a little white wine, lemon slices and bay leaf.

Drain and flake the fish, add the rest of the seafood, and arrange on top of the spinach in the dish

Cover with white sauce. Top with a little cream and a layer of breadcrumbs, and bake in a moderate oven 180C/350F/gas mark 4, until the contents are thoroughly heated through but not over-cooked. Serve with salad.

White Sauce for Fish

60g butter, melted with 1 tbsp flour. Whisk over a gentle heat with sufficient milk to make a coating consistency. A less rich sauce may be made with half milk and half fish stock.

Fish Chowder

3 tbsp of olive oil
15g butter
1 leek
4 cloves of garlic
250ml good fish stock
1 tbsp tomato purée
225g salmon fillet
225g red snapper fillet (or other similar fish)
225g prawns
Drop of white wine
2 large ripe tomatoes, chopped
Handful of chopped fresh basil
Salt, freshly ground pepper and a pinch of sugar

Put olive oil and butter together into a pan, and heat. Thinly slice the leek and garlic and fry gently till softened. Add fish stock, white wine, chopped tomatoes and the tomato purée, and simmer for a few minutes. Add the fish and seasoning and cook for about 2 minutes. Serve with chopped basil and garlic bread.

Sea Bream with Thyme, Cream and Parsley Sauce

4 fillets of Sea Bream (or other fish) weighing
    about 180g, with skin, scales and bones removed
1 tbsp thyme leaves, picked off the stem

Cream and Parsley Sauce:
100ml dry white wine
300ml fish stock
20g shallots, finely chopped
300ml double cream
4 tbsp parsley, stalks removed
Salt and pepper

2 tbsp olive oil
20g butter

Season the fish with salt and pepper and divide the thyme leaves between the four fillets, rubbing them into the side with the skin. Heat the olive oil and butter in a frying pan and sauté the fillets on each side for about 3 minutes, continually basting them with the oil and butter. Remove from the pan and drain well on kitchen paper.

To make the sauce, reduce the white wine, the fish stock and shallots to a quarter of their original volume. Add cream and parsley. Bring to the boil quickly and briefly, then purée in a blender. Season and keep warm.

Serve the fish with the sauce ladled over.

Fish Parcels

Fish needs very little cooking, and I found these fish parcels an excellent way of cooking fish and keeping it moist. I like to use cod, skinned, boned and rinsed.

4 thick pieces of white fish, about 150g each
1 green and 1 red pepper, thinly sliced
1 large onion, thinly sliced
4 sprigs of fresh thyme, or 4 pinches dried thyme
Knob of margarine or butter
2 small tomatoes, diced (optional)

Heat oven to 200C/400F/gas mark 6. Tear off four strips of extra wide, heavy-duty aluminium foil to make squares of approximately 35cm each. Place one piece of fish in the centre of each square and heap a quarter of the pile of sliced vegetables on top, finishing with a large piece of margarine or butter, thyme, salt and pepper.

Fold up the corners and edges as best you can to make a sealed parcel and prevent juices from escaping. Place on a baking sheet in a hot oven and cook for 30 minutes. Serve in or out of the foil in large soup bowls.

The French always add the merest drop of white wine to each parcel and it helps to keep the fish moist. I always used fish stock instead of wine, and it's so easily made by simmering the bones and trimmings of fish with onion, white of leek, celeriac, fennel leaves and mushroom trimmings. If you wish, you can sweat the vegetables in a little butter before adding just under a litre of water. Simmer for 20 minutes and strain carefully before poaching fish in this stock.

Fresh Sardines

These small fish are easy to gut and clean and once tossed in a plastic bag of flour, salt and pepper, are quickly fried, dried on kitchen paper and served with a fresh salad and lemon slices.

Whole Poached Salmon

In my experience a salmon weighing about 1.4–1.8kg will serve 12 people. Of course, the larger the fish the longer the time to cook. The advantage of a fish kettle is that it has a strainer device on which the fish sits, so that at any time you can easily draw out the salmon and check how well it is cooking.

The quickest and easiest way of cooking a whole salmon is to clean the fish (or ask the fishmonger to do this for you) and place it in a fish kettle. Boil sufficient water to cover the salmon, add slices of lemon, a little white wine, stalks of parsley and two bay leaves, then carefully pour the boiling water *around* the fish – not directly over it – until it is completely covered. Put the lid on the kettle (no further cooking required!) and after 30 minutes remove the salmon and leave it to cool. When it is completely cold, split the skin along the back and gently peel the skin and brown layer away. Garnish and serve with salad.

If you do not have a fish kettle, put the fish in a thoroughly cleaned and rinsed steel sink and cover with boiled water in the same way as described above.

Whilst we welcomed the addition of sea fish, we were able to get a fairly continuous supply of fresh trout and one favourite recipe was:

Trout with Apricots and Pine Kernels

50g butter
Plain white flour – about a tbsp or as needed
Salt and pepper
6 Rainbow Trout
100g ready to eat dried apricots, sliced
50g pine kernels
100ml sherry
Fresh chervil leaves to garnish

Set the oven at 200C/400F/gas mark 6. Melt the butter in a large frying pan. Mix a little flour with salt and pepper and use to coat the fish lightly. Shallow-fry the trout on both sides to a golden brown.

Remove the fish from the pan and arrange in an oven-proof dish. Place the apricots and pine kernels in the pan and fry these for two minutes. Add the sherry and, as it sizzles, pour the mixture over the fish. Garnish with the fresh chervil leaves or flat-leaved parsley.

On the rare occasions when we had no fresh fish, we improvised with tins of tuna fish for the following two favourites:

Pain de Thon

Boiled potatoes, roughly chopped
Hard-boiled eggs, roughly chopped
Tin of tuna fish, flaked
A little chopped onion
Good mayonnaise, preferably mixed with a little mustard
Anchovies, capers and green olives, to decorate

Mix together, in almost equal quantities, the potatoes, eggs and tuna. Then mix, also in roughly equal quantities, a little chopped onion and a very small amount of mayonnaise, and add to the main ingredients to combine.

Press lightly into a serving dish and leave in the fridge until needed. Serve with a layer of mayonnaise on top (not too thick) and decorate with a lattice of anchovies, capers and green olives.

Potato and Tuna Fish Gratin

450g old potatoes, thinly sliced
225g can tuna fish, well drained and flaked
1 onion, sliced
2 garlic cloves, crushed
Salt and pepper
2 eggs
450ml milk
75g cheese, grated
Chopped parsley to garnish

Put an even layer of the potatoes on the bottom of an oven-proof dish. Cover with half the tuna fish and half the onion. Add half the garlic and plenty of salt and pepper. Layer again with the potatoes, then the remaining tuna, onions and garlic. Finish with a final layer of potatoes. Mix the milk and the eggs together, then pour over so that it drains down through the layers. Sprinkle cheese on top and bake for one hour in the oven at 220C/425F/gas mark 7.

Poor Man's Kulebiaka

This makes a striking centrepiece for a buffet party and either fresh or tinned tuna can be used.

Serves 6-8 people.

2 x 375g packets of puff pastry
1 large bunch of fresh spinach, or
1 large packet of frozen spinach
60g butter, cut into small pieces
Freshly ground nutmeg
4 hard-boiled eggs, chopped
2 tbsp chopped fresh dill, or 1 tsp dried dill
2 x 440g tuna packed in oil, or 880g fresh tuna
1 cup thick double cream
1 egg, beaten

Roll out the two packets of pastry and then cut two fish shapes out with a sharp knife. I have a fish mould I use for fish mousse and this gives me a perfect outline. Trim stalks from spinach, wash thoroughly, then cook in butter with a little garlic until tender. Drain thoroughly and chop finely.

Spread spinach on the one fish shape, leaving a 2.5cm border of pastry all around. Season with salt, pepper and nutmeg, and dot with butter. Sprinkle chopped eggs and dill over the spinach, then the tuna broken into flakes. Spoon thickened cream evenly over the fish mixture.

Cover with your second pastry fish shape, having first brushed the edges of the bottom piece with beaten egg to make a seal. Press the top pastry firmly into place and using a sharp knife, mark gills, fins and tail and make a couple of slits for steam to escape. Brush with beaten egg to give a good glazed appearance.

Bake in a preheated oven 200C/400F/gas mark 6 for 10 minutes, then reduce heat to moderate and bake for a further 20 minutes or until golden. Serve hot or cold with mayonnaise and a green salad.

✿ SALADS

We always served salads with our meals and were fortunate that our potager in the garden supplied most of our needs.

The French contingent of the Caminem group of walkers were constantly on the lookout for things to pick, and the Brits were astonished one Thursday to find them armed with penknives and stopping now and then to dig up early dandelions – the leaves, they informed us, being excellent in salads. Mushrooms, berries of all kinds, nuts, miniature wild strawberries, nothing escaped their scrutiny.

In time we learned to be equally discriminating, although with mushrooms we were not confident about we always checked with the local pharmacy to ensure we were not likely to poison our guests.

The usual salad consisted of different kinds of lettuce, washed and leaves separated, with finely chopped chives, parsley, spring onions or finely sliced onion rings and cucumber. For large numbers, I served the vinaigrette or homemade mayonnaise separately, although the French like to pour the vinaigrette into the bottom of the salad bowl, layer in the ingredients and then turn it all over gently with their hands just before serving as this prevents bruising the leaves.

Tomato Salad

There are certain times of the year when tomatoes are so sweet and delicious that the very best salad is to layer finely sliced tomato and onion rings. Top with chopped chives or parsley and add vinaigrette just before serving.

Waldorf Salad

This salad consists of sliced apples, celery and walnuts in a mayonnaise and yoghurt dressing, sprinkled with parsley and chives on top.

Rice Salad

Simply mix cooked rice with peas, sweetcorn, diced cucumber and chopped parsley. You can experiment endlessly with different additions.

Warm Potato Salad

Most potato salads are served cold, with too much mayonnaise. I prefer to use warm cooked new potatoes, whole if small but in halves if big, and stir around gently in a pan in which you have just cooked some good fatty bacon. Crumble the bacon into pieces and sprinkle over the potatoes before serving. You can add chopped spring onions, parsley or just dried herbs – but serve it warm. A little warmed up cider vinegar and chilli sauce or mustard sauce is another little refinement and adds to the taste.

Couscous Salad

125g couscous
Juice of 1 lime
2 tbsp water
3 tbsp good olive oil
2 tbsp chopped mint and chopped parsley
½ green pepper, seeded and diced
1 tomato, seeded and diced
1 shallot, chopped finely
1 green chilli (optional), finely chopped
Salt and pepper

Place the couscous in a bowl and add the lime juice, water and olive oil. Leave for one hour. Break up the lumps with a fork and add a little more water if very dry. Add all the remaining ingredients (taking care with the chilli; don't overdo it!) and mix in gently. Chill until required. You may also serve this with marinated fish or prawns.

Cucumber, Tomato and Onion Relish

1–2 tomatoes, chopped into pieces
1 cucumber, cut into pieces
1 onion, chopped
2 green chillies, sliced
Salt to taste
1 tsp maple syrup
1 tbsp lemon juice
2 tsp coriander leaves, chopped

Mix all the ingredients together in a bowl. Cover and set aside to chill before serving.

The following are two salads we served as a main course when guests only wanted a light meal:

Chicken Liver Salad

Put a small quantity of vinaigrette in the bottom of a salad bowl. The salad itself may consist of different varieties of lettuce, spring onions, cucumber and fresh herbs.

Cut the chicken livers into bite-sized pieces, douse with flour, pepper and salt shaken together with the pieces in a plastic bag, before frying lightly in a mixture of butter and oil.

When brown (and they take very little cooking) remove and mop up excess grease on kitchen paper. Toss the salad in the dressing and pile the liver pieces on top. You may like to add tiny pieces of cooked bacon as well. Serve immediately, with croutons either mixed in with the liver or served separately.

A French refinement is to heat 1 tablespoon of brandy and, when it lights, pour it over the cooked chicken livers and add a little garlic and dried herbs. Then you do not need to drain on paper but just serve immediately on top of the tossed salad.

Salad Niçoise

350g flaked tuna fish
700g green beans
Mixed chopped herbs
1 cucumber
1kg tomatoes, peeled and thinly sliced
Anchovy fillets
Black olives
6 hard-boiled eggs

Place the cooked green beans at the bottom of a shallow dish, then cover with a layer of tuna fish and herbs before adding a layer of sliced cucumber. Arrange the tomatoes on top and then add anchovy fillets and black olives, together with the halved or quartered hard-boiled eggs. Arrange in a pattern as attractively as possible, and spoon a well-seasoned French dressing over it all. Serve with fresh brown bread and butter.

THE HUNTING SEASON

The first time I was invited into my immediate neighbour's house I was astonished to find his salon walls covered in the most lethal collection of guns I had ever seen.

"I, hunter," my host exclaimed, immediately assuming a posture of stalking and hunting, every now and then shouting: "Bang! Bang!" in case I misunderstood his theatrical ability.

I was curious to know what he hunted, and where?

Everything and everywhere, apparently, but wild boar in particular – a very dangerous animal to all intents and purposes, especially when cornered and wounded.

"Never go walking in the woods with your dogs in November or December," he warned me solemnly, "or you could be mistaken for a boar."

I made a mental note to get my hair cut, since I did not want my head to appear as a trophy on his salon wall!

" ... you could be shot in mistake for a wild boar. "

To confirm his warning, we were astounded to see in Prades market the large number of stalls devoted entirely to the sale of hunting gear – that is surplus army jackets, boots, stalking hats, camouflage of all shapes and colours. It seemed that dressing up was a large part of the hunting ritual. One could be forgiven for thinking World War Three was imminent, but in reality it was all associated with the *Notices* posted on the door of every *Mairie* in the land announcing *le debut* – the commencement – of the hunting season, whether for boar or *le gibier* (small animals, by which they meant rabbits, hares, pheasants etc).

However, we were very happy to introduce game into our menu and wild boar was very much appreciated for its rich and succulent flavour. All the farmers in the region are involved in hunting the wild boar in winter, so *sanglier* figures largely on home and restaurant menus, and is delicious.

Casserole of Wild Boar

Prepare the meat to marinade at least a week ahead of cooking.

900g boar meat, cut in pieces
2 onions, chopped and 2 carrots, sliced
2 cloves garlic, chopped
8 peppercorns
2 bay leaves
Sprigs of thyme and rosemary
8 juniper berries, crushed
2 tbsp wine vinegar
300ml red wine
3–4 tbsp olive oil
100g unsmoked streaky bacon, chopped
2 tbsp brandy
6 cloves garlic, whole
Salt, black pepper and *beurre manie* (flour rubbed into butter, for thickening)

Put the meat into a china or glass bowl with the onions, carrots, chopped garlic, peppercorns, bay leaves, thyme, rosemary, juniper berries, vinegar and wine. Cover and leave in a cool place **for at least a week**, turning the meat over once or twice each day. When ready to cook, remove the meat, onions and carrots from the marinade, strain and reserve the liquid. Dry the meat with kitchen paper.

Heat the oil in a heavy-based casserole and brown the meat in several batches, and remove from casserole when done. Add the bacon pieces to the pan together with the onion and carrot from the marinade and cook for a few minutes. Return the meat to the pan. Heat the brandy in a metal ladle or small pan, set it alight and pour while still flaming over the contents of the casserole. Shake the pan well and when the flames die down pour in the marinade liquid. Bring to the boil, add fresh herbs, whole garlic cloves, salt and pepper. Cover and simmer for 2–3 hours until the meat is tender. Thicken the sauce by stirring in small pieces of the *beurre manie*.

After cooking boar in the traditional French way I later discovered a Chinese method, which I liked just as well:

Chinese-Style Wild Boar Casserole

1.5kg wild boar (or pork)
6 tbsp soy sauce
300ml sunflower oil
2 tsp sugar
4 tbsp Chinese rice wine or dry sherry
25g fresh ginger, peeled and finely grated
2 medium onions, thinly sliced
4 garlic cloves, finely chopped
Several pieces of orange peel
2 star anise
Cinnamon powder, salt and pepper

In a large oven-proof dish, steep the meat in the soy sauce for an hour, then take out and pat dry. Fry in oil until nicely browned. Add all the remaining ingredients and cook in the oven at 200C/400F/gas mark 6, for 1½–2 hours. Check now and then to see if more liquid is required, to prevent the dish from drying out. If you think the boar is cooking too quickly, lower the temperature to 180C/350F/gas mark 4. Serve with rice.

Jugged Hare

1 hare, cut into joints
some of the blood from the hare, kept aside
75g butter
1 tbsp sunflower oil
2 onions, peeled and stuck with 4 or 5 cloves
2 carrots, peeled and roughly chopped
2 sticks of celery, peeled and roughly chopped
1 *bouquet garni*
1 clove of garlic, peeled and chopped
2 strips each of lemon rind and orange rind
Salt and pepper
150ml port or Banyuls wine
1 tbsp redcurrant jelly

Heat the butter and oil in a large, heavy, flameproof casserole with a tight-fitting lid. Brown the pieces of hare thoroughly all over in the hot fat, then remove from the pan and keep warm.

Add the prepared vegetables to the pan and cook over a gentle heat for 5 minutes. Replace the hare in the pan with the vegetables. Add the *bouquet garni*, the garlic, lemon, orange, salt and pepper. Cover the contents of the pan with water, put a piece of foil over the top of the casserole and cover with the lid.

Cook in a slow oven, 300F/150C/gas mark 2, for 2–3 hours or more, until the meat is tender and just beginning to come away from the bones. Remove from the oven.

When the meat is cool, remove from the stock (set this aside for the sauce), strip from the bones if wished, and put in an ovenproof serving dish while you make the sauce, as follows:

Sauce for Jugged Hare

Measure 850ml of the hare stock and put in a saucepan over a gentle heat. Mix 50g butter, softened, with the same amount of plain flour. Stir some of the hot stock into the paste and, when blended, stir the mixture into the rest of the stock in the saucepan. Add 1 tablespoon of redcurrant jelly and stir until the sauce boils. Stir in 150ml port wine and seasoning.

Remove the pan from the heat and pour a little of the hot sauce into a bowl into which you have saved the blood of the hare. Mix together well and then pour into the pan and mix with the rest of the sauce. Reheat gently, adding extra stock if the sauce is too thick, but do not let it boil. Pour this sauce over the hare meat in the serving dish and return to a low oven until the meat is reheated. Serve with a separate bowl of redcurrant jelly.

Quail with Sage

Quail are tiny but quick and easy to prepare and, strangely enough, quite meaty!

4–8 quail
16 sage leaves
16 rashes of streaky bacon
35g butter
2 tbsp olive oil
8 cloves garlic
3 tbsp dry white wine
Salt and pepper

Put a sage leaf inside and another on the breast of each quail and wrap securely in strips of bacon, stretching to fit tightly. Secure with string or wooden toothpicks. Melt the butter with the oil in a heavy-based pan and brown the birds all over. Add the garlic, salt and pepper and white wine and cook gently with the lid on for about 30 minutes. Remove the string and serve with the juices. Mushrooms may also be added for a different texture and flavour.

Pheasant

Pheasant may be cooked the same way as quail but should be quartered. After browning all over in a pan, add 4 chopped shallots, 4 halved tomatoes, and 1 tablespoon tomato purée and cook for 10 minutes. Then add 225g mushrooms and cook for another 5 minutes. Add 150ml wine, thyme, salt and pepper. Simmer for 20–30 minutes, then add pheasant livers and cook for 5 minutes more.

Rabbit

At one time in Britain rabbit disappeared from the menu because of myxomatosis, a fatal viral disease affecting only rabbits. But in France, as well as hunting them, domestic rabbits have traditionally been reared for consumption and every smallholding has its array of rabbits in cages, being fattened up for the pot. I once worked on a farm on the outskirts of Albi and a prized dish was rabbit placed in a stone jar for three days in a rich wine marinade before being casseroled. Absolutely delicious!

I enjoy cooking rabbit in several ways but my favourite is the Catalan recipe with prunes, although I often failed to tell British guests about the prunes since so many of them had bitter memories of rice pudding with soggy prunes for school meals!

Ask the butcher to cut up the rabbit for you and cook the heart, liver and kidneys for the dog!

Rabbit and Prunes

1 rabbit, chopped into pieces
Lardons (small bacon pieces), quantity depends on taste
Butter and oil (small amount)
2 onions, chopped
2 cloves of garlic, chopped
Stoned chopped prunes (again, quantity to taste)
Dried or fresh herbs
Stock and cider mix, sufficient to cover the rabbit

Put some plain flour, salt and pepper in a plastic bag and, having washed the rabbit pieces and patted them dry with kitchen paper, place them in the bag and toss thoroughly, then shake off the surplus.

In a large pan, melt sufficient butter and oil mixed to cover the bottom and add chopped bacon pieces and onions with garlic to cook until soft. Take out with a slotted spoon and fry the rabbit pieces in the fat until nicely browned, then replace the bacon, onion and garlic in with the rabbit and add enough stock and cider to reach the level of the meat. Add stoned chopped prunes, salt and pepper, and dried or fresh herbs.

Cover with lid and cook gently for about 45 minutes until rabbit is just done – but never overcook it, as rabbit is very dry meat.

℘ AN INTERNATIONAL CELEBRATION

Each month, apart from welcoming Mark back to *Rozinante* with his invaluable supply of fish, we were fascinated to hear the latest development in his building programme.

Unable to afford a professional builder, Mark had to rely on itinerants – people of all nationalities who drifted along the coast in search of seasonal work to finance their haphazard lifestyle. The main recruitment spot was a local café known as Harry's Bar, where a rag-tag collection of miscellaneous travellers gathered together, having run out of funds and so looking for part-time work. These included English, American, German, Spanish and some Eastern Europeans.

Mark's first stroke of luck was meeting August, a refugee from East Germany, who, reared in the Protestant work ethic, was markedly ill at ease with the more laissez-faire Catalan approach to life. He agreed to work for Mark with the proviso of having lunch provided every day. Mark was delighted, since other local workers had spent so much of their lunchtime in the bar that he was constantly running after them, begging them to come back and finish where they had left off! However, as time ran on and Christmas loomed, it became obvious that August was playing the old soldier's game of trying to prolong the job as long as possible – one good meal a day did not come easy, after all!

In desperation Mark returned to the bar and fell upon a Catalan mason, Georges, with a much-weathered face, the colour of a ripe tomato. Georges soon flew into dramatic action and cement started flying in all directions, having first stuck a stone in the wall on which a bottle of wine balanced and to which he had frequent recourse.

"What's all that for?" asked Mark suspiciously.

"Hah-hah!" chirped Georges, *"très Catalan, non?"*

He then explained the local custom of masons enjoying a drop of wine *'pour la santé'* (for one's health) when it was cold, to warm themselves or, likewise, when hot to slake their thirst. The bottle was placed upon a stone in the wall to enable Georges to carry on working without having to scramble up and down the scaffolding.

After a week Georges was as industrious as ever, although his face had become puce and mottled, and the crunch point came one morning when Mark noticed cement being flacked over and over into the same cavity, to the point where an enormous bulge loomed ominously from the wall like a great boil! Urgent calls to stop went unheeded, until the robotic and very inebriated Georges was removed forcibly from his perch.

" ... a drop of wine 'pour la santé' ... "

Happily Harry's Bar went on producing recruits until, by Christmas, my son announced *La Grange* was now ready for letting. We were all invited down to a celebratory party for his workers and the rest of the Rue de Couronnement, and our supper on the terrace was memorable for the feast produced and the capacity of those present to demolish it!

This is a description of the supper table, still talked about to this day...

Leek and Ham

Our Welsh contribution

6–8 slices of cooked ham
Same quantity of young leeks
Cheese sauce made with 350ml milk
Salt and pepper to taste
Grated cheese to taste
Butter and flour

Quickly cook the young leeks, but do not overcook, using the white only and putting the green tops aside for soup. Make a traditional cheese sauce by melting the butter, adding the flour and then gradually stirring in the milk. Once thickened, add the cheese, pepper and salt but be careful with the salt as the ham may be salty already.

Take a slice of ham, place a leek inside, and roll up. When all are done, put the rolled up slices of ham in an ovenproof dish and pour the sauce over them, sprinkling more grated cheese on top, before putting them in the oven at 180C/350F/gas mark 4, until thoroughly warmed through, bubbling, and the top is nicely browned.

An alternative to this recipe is to stuff the slices of ham with lightly cooked chicory.

Bobotie

A recipe given to me by a South African friend. Additions may include ginger, apricot jam (replacing sugar), 1 tsp turmeric, and a little vinegar.

500g minced meat – preferfably lamb
12 chopped almonds
6 drops almond essence
2 medium onions, chopped and fried in a little butter
1 thick slice of brown bread, soaked in stock or gravy
1 dessert spoon good curry powder
1 dessert spoon of ground cumin seed
1 lemon
3 eggs
1 tsp sugar
1 cup milk

Mix the curry powder and ground cumin seed with the lemon juice. Beat in one egg and the sugar. Gently fry the chopped onions. Mix the meat, onions, soaked bread, chopped almonds and almond essence together and then add the curry powder mix. Stir and blend very thoroughly. Season to taste and put in a pie dish. Beat the other two eggs with a cup of milk. Season and pour over the meat, putting two bay leaves on top for decoration. Bake in the centre of the oven until the top is set and golden brown. This should take about 40 minutes at 350F/180C/gas mark 4.

Paella

This is a very well-known Spanish dish but also figures largely on the Catalan horizon and includes both fish and chicken, among other ingredients.

Makes 3-4 servings

1 tbsp olive oil
1 onion, sliced

1 red pepper, sliced
200g long-grain rice
8 shreds of saffron, soaked in hot water
4 chicken joints, skinned, boned and cut up into bite-sized pieces
3 tbsp peas
200g squid, cleaned and cut into rings
600ml chicken stock
50g shelled mussels
275ml unshelled prawns
Chopped parsley

Heat the oil in a Paella dish or large frying pan. Add the rice and onion and cook until the rice begins to whiten. Add the soaked saffron plus its liquid and mix well. Arrange the chicken, squid, pepper and peas on top of the rice. Season well and pour over the stock. Cover with greaseproof paper and simmer for 35 minutes. Add prawns and mussels and cook for a further 5 minutes. Serve with chopped parsley.

Ratatouille

1 medium sized onion, chopped
1 large red or green pepper, chopped
1 large aubergine, diced
2 courgettes, sliced
2 tbsp oil
6 tomatoes
2 – 3 garlic cloves, crushed
½ tsp oregano
½ tsp basil
450ml tomato juice
Salt and pepper to taste

Heat the oil in a large pan. Add the onion and aubergine and sauté until the onion is transparent. Add the courgettes and pepper and sauté for a further 5 minutes, stirring occasionally. Add the remaining ingredients and simmer, covered, for 15–20 minutes. Serve hot or cold in individual bowls. Croutons go well with this.

Potato Dauphinoise

Probably our most popular potato dish and served extensively throughout the whole of France.

The amount of potatoes used depends on the quantity you are serving, but for 4 people take 6 large potatoes, peel and slice very thinly. Layer in a buttered ovenproof dish. In between each layer season well and sprinkle with grated cheese, and garlic slivers. Finish with a layer of cheese, and/or salt and pepper and nutmeg. Pour on sufficient quantity of cream or a mixture of cream and milk until it can just be seen at the top layer. It helps the cooking process if the cream/milk mixture has been heated beforehand. Dot with small pieces of butter and bake in a medium oven for 1 hour, or until the potato is cooked through.

The dessert section of the luncheon party was extremely simple and consisted of one humungous bowl of soft fruit compôte and a trifle:

Soft Fruit Compôte

In our part of the Roussillon there were large areas of territory given over to the production of plums, peaches, nectarines, greengages, apricots, and others. At the height of the fresh fruit season we had a wonderful choice, and after washing I would put them all together in a pot, cover with sugar and add sufficient water to just reach the top layer, and stew gently. The apricots were always the first to soften and could be removed gently with a slotted spoon, until all the fruit was gently cooked through. It could be served hot or very cold with fresh cream.

For the Catalans, the pièce de resistance on this day was my chocolate trifle:

Chocolate Trifle

110g butter
110g sugar
1 egg yolk
220g chocolate
1 teacup of milk
12–16 macaroons
1 tin chestnut purée (optional)

Cream the butter and sugar. Scald the milk and let it cool, then mix it with the yolk of the egg. Melt the chocolate with a little water, stir in the milk and egg mixture, and then the butter and sugar, until smooth.

In a dish, arrange a layer of macaroons soaked in a little rum or brandy, and over these pour a layer of the chestnut purée (to taste), a layer of chocolate cream, then another layer of macaroons and so on until the dish is full. Top it all with a layer of whipped cream and grate some chocolate over for decoration.

The crowning moment of this celebratory party came when Mark presented Jerome, his French neighbour and reputable builder who had given much welcomed advice throughout the conversion programme, with a Golden Trowel award (a trowel sprayed in gold paint) and some Welsh rugby shirts. The cheer that went up was as heartfelt as any ever heard at Cardiff Arms Park with a rugby international win by Wales!

Much to everyone's delight, *le patron* of Harry's Bar joined us with an enormous bowl of chips which, although rather soggy in my opinion, were received rapturously, thereby testifying to the universal popularity of 'the chip'.

Chips

Georges Pestourie was the chef at a summer cookery school I had once attended in Sarlat in the Dordogne. He had served part of his training at the Ritz hotel in London and his main memories of English fare was a love of English tea, Cooper's marmalade, and fish and chips from a local chippy not far from his digs in a much less known part of London than the prestigious Ritz!

Wherever we went to eat in France chips were ever-present, and we were constantly preparing them at *Rozinante,* but I have a cautionary tale to tell when it comes to cooking them.

It was the last day of my honeymoon in 1954, when we were packing up to leave Cornwall and return to Wales, when my husband said suddenly, "Hadn't you better make a list?"

"List of what?" I asked.

"Well, what about starting with bread and potatoes?" he replied.

Food, I thought apprehensively, *he's talking about food!* – and I gave a fleeting but regretful thought to the menu-filled days of the past week in a delightful hotel.

I am not going to dwell on my culinary efforts that followed our return home, since one burnt offering followed another, but one day, having decided to cook chips, I read in the recipe book that I should wait for a 'blue haze' to rise from the fat in the pan before adding the chips.

Whilst I was waiting cross-eyed for the attendant haze the phone rang in the hall, so I left the pan to answer the call and was deep in conversation when I smelt something burning. Running to the kitchen, I found the tea towel on the rack above the pan burning briskly from the flames arising from the oil beneath!

It was several agonised moments before I had the wits to grab a towel and soak it in cold water. Wrapping it around my hand, I grabbed the handle of the pan and, standing in the doorway, flung the whole thing out of the door onto a trellis covered in my husband's favourite Alexander Roses. The trellis responded by bursting into flames!

Even more terrified, I rushed back to fill a bucket with water and hurled it at the stricken trellis, which promptly exploded into a thousand pieces, spreading shattered woodwork and roses all over the remains of the garden.

Returning at that precise moment, my very new husband discovered that his carefully manicured back lawn now looked more like the aftermath of the battle of the Somme, while his new wife lay prostrate on the kitchen floor, with very little hair, singed eyebrows and lashes, and a very black face underneath!

"Thank God," was his first remark, "I've just renewed the insurance!" and I knew quite positively then that the 'honeymoon period' of my life was definitely over.

The lessons I learned so painfully that day were: never leave hot fat unattended, and always smother any blaze with a lid, but never water.

With experience I learned to partially cook potatoes before cutting them into chips, then cook them until nearly crisp before taking them out of the fat and only reheating them just before serving, to crisp them to perfection.

My sister, who had lived in Belgium, said she had never eaten better chips anywhere else; apparently the Belgians grew special potatoes which accounted for their excellence. It pays, therefore, to experiment with different types of potato, but be careful!

ꙩ VEGETABLES

The joy of *Rozinante* was that, until we arrived, no one had ever had a potager (a vegetable garden), and so the soil was ripe for procreation. My sister and her husband were keen gardeners, and within no time we had substantial crops of leeks, onions, courgettes, spinach, carrots, and salads of all kinds, and once a friend had given us raspberry canes we had a substantial soft fruit bed.

At the lower end of the garden mushrooms grew wild, and all around us, extending to the far horizon, were the local apple orchards offering this wonderful fruit in every variety and colour imaginable. Further up on the perimeter were cherry trees – some the deep black cherry – with fig and walnut trees, and endless blackberries.

We rarely went out without a basket, and all our guests enjoyed our fruit and vegetables. Many remarked how rare it was to find vegetables in French restaurants which, mainly concerned with *nouvelle cuisine,* only presented blobs of puréed frozen peas with a scrap of lettuce on the side of the plate.

We, on the other hand, never gave guests plated service but put the whole dish of meat or fish on the table, with accompanying dishes of vegetables and sauces, so that they could help themselves.

Pepper and Potatoes

1kg floury potatoes
1 large green pepper, seeded and finely chopped
1 large onion, finely chopped
150ml flour
60ml finely chopped parsley
100g Gruyère cheese, grated
Pinch of cayenne pepper
Salt
Black pepper

251

25g butter
150ml hot milk
150ml cream

Heat the oven to 200C/400F/gas mark 6. Peel the potatoes, cut into 5ml dice and place in a bowl. Add the chopped green pepper and onion to the potatoes and toss lightly together. Sprinkle in the flour, finely chopped parsley and grated Gruyère cheese, and toss again. Season with a pinch of cayenne pepper, salt and a little freshly ground black pepper, to taste. Use some of the butter to grease a 1.7l ovenproof dish. Turn the potato mixture into the dish and spread it evenly. Pour the hot milk and the cream over, and dot the remaining butter on top. Bake the dish in the oven for about 1 hour, or until the surface is crisp and golden brown and the potatoes feel tender when pierced with a skewer.

Tomatoes Niçoises

3 tbsp olive oil
1 large onion, peeled and thinly sliced
10 large tomatoes, skinned and thinly sliced
2 tsp sugar
1 tbsp freshly chopped parsley
2 tsp chopped basil or 1 tsp dried basil
Salt, and freshly ground pepper
250ml double cream
85g fresh white breadcrumbs
30g butter

Heat the oil in a frying pan and fry the onion slices until soft. Brush a baking dish with the remaining oil. Put one third of the tomato slices in the bottom of the dish, sprinkle with a little sugar, parsley and basil, and salt and pepper to taste. Top with a few onion slices, then pour in about one third of the cream. Repeat these layers twice more, then sprinkle over the breadcrumbs to cover the cream completely. Dot with butter and then bake, uncovered, for about 35–40 minutes at 180C/350F/gas mark 4.

Leeks with Raisins

12 young leeks
75g raisins
150ml white wine
150ml olive oil
2 tbsp white wine vinegar
75g soft light brown sugar
Salt and pepper
Chopped parsley

Trim any tough outer leaves from the leeks and blanch in boiling water for 2 minutes, then drain and chill in cold water. Arrange the leeks in a shallow dish and scatter the raisins on top. Heat the wine, oil, vinegar and sugar with salt and pepper until the sugar is completely dissolved. Pour over the leeks and sprinkle parsley on top. Leave for at least two hours to cool and marinade.

Red Cabbage, Cinnamon and Raisins

1 onion, peeled and finely chopped
2 apples, peeled, cored and finely chopped
50g butter
800g red cabbage, finely sliced
150ml orange juice
2 tbsp soft brown sugar
1 tbsp cinnamon
2 cloves
2 bay leaves
100g raisins

Melt half the butter in a large casserole dish and fry the onions and apples for about 4 minutes until soft. Add the cabbage, orange juice, sugar, cinnamon, cloves, bay leaves and raisins. Cover and cook over a low heat for 30 minutes, occasionally stirring the cabbage. To serve, remove the cloves and bay leaves and stir in the remaining butter.

Stir Fry Vegetables

1½ tsp peanut oil
4 spring onions, chopped
1 large clove garlic, crushed
125g celery, diced
75g mange-tout
50g red pepper, diced
50g green pepper, diced
75ml water
75ml soy sauce
1 tsp cornflour
Pinch of ginger
Salt and pepper

Heat the oil and add the onion and garlic. Stir fry for 1 minute. Add all the other vegetables and cook quickly for 2 minutes. Mix water, soy sauce, cornflour and ginger together and pour over the vegetables. Add salt and pepper, and stir constantly until vegetables are tender and the sauce thickens.

🎗 CATALAN RECIPES

Whenever the weather was very hot and we felt like a break from cooking, I was never afraid to recommend guests to the local village restaurant, which specialised in the Catalan dishes we had experienced at Madame Costello's. Guests who particularly enjoyed the wines of the region were relieved to find the restaurant no more than twenty minutes' walk away from us.

Estofat de Bou

(Beef Stew)

50g thick cut *lardons* (bacon), diced
750g stewing beef cut into chunks
1 cup dry sherry
2 onions, chopped
4 cloves garlic, minced
Bunch of fresh or dried herbs
1 bay leaf
1 tbsp flour
Salt and pepper
25g cooking chocolate, finely grated
½ tsp cinnamon
500g new potatoes
1 *botifarra* sausage, or other herby spiced sausage

In a casserole dish sauté the lardons until golden, then remove and drain. In their fat sauté the beef chunks until browned, then return the lardons to the casserole and deglaze with the sherry. Add the onions, garlic and herbs to the casserole, stir in the flour, then add about 500 ml water, and salt and pepper to taste. Simmer, covered, for just over 2 hours, stirring occasionally. Stir in the chocolate and the cinnamon and add the potatoes. Continue simmering, still covered, until the potatoes are soft but not collapsed. Add more stock or water if necessary, and serve with croutons.

Mar i Muntanya

(Chicken and Prawn Ragout)

1 chicken, cut into 8 pieces
Olive oil
12 prawns or scampi with heads and shells
2 chopped onions
4 tomatoes, seeded and grated (or 1 tin chopped tomatoes)
½ cup dry white wine
Small amount of Pernod
4 cloves of garlic, minced with parsley to taste
1 slice fried bread
25g chocolate, grated
6 blanched and roasted almonds
Salt and pepper

Sauté the chicken pieces in a small amount of oil in a casserole until brown, remove, drain and set aside. In the same pan, sauté the prawns in their shells until bright red. Remove and drain.

Pour off the excess fat and cook the onions and tomatoes until soft, then return the chicken pieces to the casserole and add 2 cups of water. Bring to the boil, then simmer uncovered for about 20 minutes.

Add the wine and Pernod to taste, return to the boil but then reduce heat and simmer for 10 minutes. Add the prawns and simmer for another 15 minutes or until the chicken is tender, adding more water if necessary. Mix together the garlic, parsley, bread, chocolate and almonds, moistened with a little of the cooking liquid until a fluid mixture. Just before the cooking is completed add this to the dish, along with the salt and pepper to taste.

✿ CHICKEN

Chicken dishes were very popular with guests, and these were my favourites.

Coronation Chicken

Serves 8

2.3kg chicken, cooked with flesh removed, cut into pieces
1 tblsp vegetable oil
1 small onion, skinned and finely chopped
1 level tblsp curry paste
1 level tblsp tomato purée
100ml red wine
1 bay leaf
Juice of half a lemon
4 canned apricot halves, drained and finely chopped
100ml whipping cream
Salt and pepper
Watercress to garnish
300ml mayonnaise, preferably homemade

Heat the oil in a saucepan, add the onion, and cook for about 3 minutes, until softened. Add the curry paste, tomato purée, wine, bay leaf and lemon juice. Simmer uncovered for about 10 minutes, until well reduced. Strain and leave to cool.

Purée the chopped apricot halves in a food processor. Beat the cooled sauce into the mayonnaise with the apricot purée. Whip the cream to stiff peaks and fold into the mixture. Season, adding a little extra lemon juice if necessary.

Fold the chicken pieces into the sauce and garnish with watercress.

Ginger Chicken

To serve 4

4 chicken breasts
2 finely chopped peppers (preferably yellow)
8 finely chopped mushrooms
4 pieces of ginger (fresh or preserved), chopped finely
400g thick natural yoghurt
1 tbsp olive oil
Juice of 1 fresh orange

Brush the chicken breasts with olive oil and orange juice. Place in foil in an oven dish and scatter the sliced mushrooms, pepper and chopped ginger over all.

Wrap the foil around the ingredients and place in a hot oven, 200C/400F/gas mark 6, for 40 minutes until cooked. Remove the chicken and keep warm.

Cook the juices until they are reduced, then stir in the yoghurt and mix well.

Arrange all on a dish and serve.

Chicken in a Bag

It was a friend who brought me some plastic cooking bags and introduced me to the idea of placing a whole chicken with herbs and a little white wine into a bag, sealing it, cutting a small vent for the steam to escape and then putting it in the oven to cook for about 1 hour. Carefully remove the bag and place the now-uncovered chicken back in the oven to brown, having put a little melted butter on the chicken breasts.

The chickens cooked this way were always unbelievably tender and could be served simply with juices, for the French, or with gravy, for the British.

Quick Chicken or Turkey Meals

There were many easy meals to be prepared with chicken or turkey pieces. Supermarkets today stock an unlimited number of good sauces and when you are in a hurry, you can lightly fry chicken or turkey pieces, then add them to lightly fried onions and garlic, peppers, finely sliced carrots, celery, courgettes, or whatever other vegetables are to hand. Mix the meat and vegetables with the shop-bought sauce and add home cooked stock if too dry, then serve with rice or pasta.

✿ OTHER FAVOURITES

Fillet Steak with Green Peppercorns

Put a large knob of butter with a little oil in a frying pan and lightly fry the steak on both sides. Remove the steak and pour sufficient brandy into the pan, which you then ignite to burn off excess fat, just leaving the residue for the sauce. Add green peppercorns to taste and sufficient fresh cream to form a sauce. Mix quickly and, once bubbling, remove immediately from the heat, pour over the steaks and serve.

Catalan Style Lancashire Hot Pot

8 thick lamb chops, best end of neck
A handful of flour, seasoned with salt and pepper
4 lambs' kidneys, skinned and sliced
4 onions, chopped
250–375g mushrooms (optional)
8 oysters (optional)
700g potatoes, peeled and finely sliced
Bunch of dried herbs, or fresh if possible
Salt and pepper, and 600ml water or stock

Trim the fat and skin from the chops, then finely dice the fat and melt it down in a frying pan. Dust the chops with seasoned flour and brown lightly in the fat you have just secured. Now layer the chops in a suitable casserole dish, with first the meat and then all the other ingredients, seasoning lightly as you go and tucking in the herbs. Finish with a thick layer of potatoes to cover the stew entirely. Add the water or stock. Cover and bake at 300F/150C/gas mark 2 for 1½–2 hours. Remove lid and continue cooking until potatoes are crisp and browned.

Pork Tenderloin with Stuffing

You cannot get pork with the crackling on in France, so I used to settle for tenderloin, which I would split down the middle (but not through to the base) and then fill the gap with a sage and onion stuffing (see below), often with the addition of chopped dried apricots to taste.

Close the sides of the meat with toothpicks before baking in a moderate oven, 180C/350F/gas mark 4, for 45–60 minutes, depending on the thickness of the meat.

Remove the toothpicks. Cut pork into slices and serve with sauté potatoes and a good gravy made from the drippings in the pan.

Sage and Onion Stuffing

Parboil a large onion, chop finely and mix with breadcrumbs and melted butter to bind. Add dried or freshly chopped sage, and season to taste. *(Parboiling makes the onion easier to chop finely.)*

Stews and casseroles were left for the winter months, and consisted mainly of one quick beef stew, and another of lamb with spices.

Quick Beef Stew

1kg good stewing beef, cut into bite-sized chunks
250g lardons (bacon pieces)
1 pig's trotter, cut in half, or, if not available, 2 slices
    of belly pork
1–2 cups of red wine
1–2 cups of water
Chopped root vegetables such as carrots, onions, celery, according to taste
Juice of 1–2 oranges with some orange peel

Fry the bacon pieces in a heavy casserole and lift out with a slotted spoon once cooked. If you use slices of belly pork instead of trotters, fry them with the lardons to release some of the fat.

In the bacon fat, lightly fry the onions, with the garlic to taste, and the other vegetables, and lift out. Lightly fry the beef, and remove from the pan.

Place the bacon and vegetables back in the casserole and add the pig's trotter, cut in two, on top of which you add the beef. If you are using belly pork, cut into pieces before adding to the stew.

Cover with a mixture of red wine and water, the orange juice and the orange peel. Cook in a slow oven, 150C/300F/gas mark 2, until the beef is tender. Remove the orange peel before serving, adjust the seasoning if necessary (remember the bacon does add salt to the dish already). Sprinkle with chopped parsley before serving.

Spiced Casserole of Lamb with Apricots

2 rounded tsp coriander seeds
2 rounded tsp cumin seeds
2 rounded tsp ground cinnamon
50g lamb dripping, or butter and oil mixed
900g boneless leg of lamb or lamb neck fillets,
    trimmed and cut into pieces
4 large onions, peeled and thinly sliced
1 clove garlic, peeled and finely chopped
1 rounded tbsp plain flour
250g dried apricots soaked in 600ml water for
    at least 6 hours
Salt and pepper

Put the coriander, cumin and cinnamon together in a grinder or pestle and mortar, to reduce (or crush with a rolling pin on a flat surface).

Melt the dripping or fat in a flameproof casserole dish and brown the pieces of lamb all over – a few pieces at a time, so as not to bring the temperature down in the pan. Remove when cooked and keep warm. When all the meat is cooked, lower the heat under the casserole and add the onions and the garlic to the fat. Cook gently for 10 minutes or so, stirring all the time, until the onions are soft.

Stir in the flour and the spices and cook, stirring from time to time, for about 5 minutes. Then add the apricots and the water in which they were soaked, and stir until the sauce boils. Replace the meat in the casserole and if necessary season with salt and pepper, cover with a lid and cook in a moderate oven, 350F/180C/gas mark 4, for 1 hour, or longer if required.

With 300 days of sunshine a year all houses in the Roussillon had barbecues. Ours was exceptionally large and built into the side of our kitchen patio, where meals were usually served. My sister and her husband had lived and worked for an American company for fifteen years in the Middle East, so barbecues were a normal way of life and I happily left the cooking of all meats and fish in their capable hands, while I supplied the sauces.

Guests liked to sit and have aperitifs and watch their meal being prepared – well done, medium rare, it was theirs to command and, with the sun slowly sinking behind Canigou, the sacred mountain of the Catalans, and a fresh breeze whispering through the orchard trees, these were the moments when we felt all was well with the world!

Duck Breasts

Duck breasts are always available in France, often at reasonable prices. I experimented with different ways of cooking them and finally decided that to score the fat and sear the breasts over a high heat until a good brown colour, then place the breasts in a preheated oven, 200C/400F/gas mark 7, for about 15 minutes, produced the best results. You can slice the breast on the diagonal and serve on a mixed salad dressed with vinaigrette, or serve with a sauce.

Blackcurrant Sauce for Duck

My favourite sauce was a blackcurrant one, which you can make with 150ml dry red wine, 2 crushed garlic cloves, a few sprigs of thyme, 150ml chicken stock, 3 tbsp blackcurrant jam or conserve, and 25g butter cut into cubes. Put the wine in a pan with the garlic and thyme and boil for 8 minutes, until reduced by half. Pour in the stock and reduce again by half. Stir in the jam and add a little butter to give it a shine. Taste and adjust seasoning, then strain through a sieve and discard the solids. Pour sauce over duck and serve.

♋ HOMESICK

It has to be said there was a certain amount of English food we missed in France, notably English-style bacon, gammon and ham joints, Marmite, Bovril, English tea, marmalade, Heinz beans and pickles, to name but a few.

I missed pickles, since I had grown up in a household where every kind of fruit and vegetable pickle was made, and many a night as a child I 'cried' while helping to peel onions for pickling, and later shredding cabbage for red cabbage pickle. These pickles and chutneys were eaten with the cold remains of a Sunday joint on Monday, while anything left over was minced for a cottage pie on Tuesday. No party in my memory was complete without these additions to platters of cold ham and beef, the mainstay ingredients.

My brother-in-law was devastated to find himself deprived of bacon and eggs, and nothing would compensate for his lifelong addiction to the 'English Breakfast'.

It did not surprise me therefore to hear one day that an enterprising English couple had opened a restaurant on the motorway to Paris from the south with a huge sign that said simply 'English Breakfast served all day'. It proved a stunning success for both the English and the French, and for other tourists who had always maintained our breakfast was the only British meal worth eating!

The absence of bacon from our lives meant that, with our compatriots, we searched the meat stalls at markets to find substitutes. The *charcuterie* stalls were astonishing for their displays of smoked meats and French sausages, which were totally different from our own, being much coarser in texture, all highly seasoned with red peppery substances. They were often quite fatty but, sliced thinly and spread across a wide dish, half a dozen different varieties were often buffet party centrepieces, accompanied by bowls of olives, gherkins, pickled cucumbers, and other relishes. As time went on I used more and more of these highly spiced sausages in my cooking. My favourite, however, was *boudin noir*, or black pudding, which I cooked with apples.

"... on the hunt for a substitute for English bacon."

Black Pudding and Apples

450g *boudin noir* (black pudding), skin removed,
    and cut into portions
900g sweet apples, peeled, cored and quartered
25g butter
25g caster sugar
Pinch of cinnamon
Salt and pepper
2 tbsp oil
2 onions, chopped

Cook the apples with the butter and sugar over a low heat
until soft, then add salt, pepper and cinnamon. Heat the
oil in a frying pan and fry the chopped onion until golden.
Add the black pudding for a few minutes, turning over for
10 minutes more. Serve on a bed of apple.

Catalan Assiette

(Catalonian Platter)

We had a plentiful supply of figs in the garden, so an easy meal was to put a large dish of figs on the table and serve with a homemade paté and a plate full of *charcuterie – sauçisson de montagne,* chorizo, pepperoni and all kinds of salamis. Add plenty of bread and butter and it made an attractive meal.

Chorizo and Spaghetti

I used to cook spaghetti frequently, in plenty of rapidly boiling water, until *al dente,* and then drain and toss in 1 tablespoon of olive oil and set it aside whilst mixing other ingredients in a bowl to accompany it. These might be olives, anchovies and parsley in a little vinaigrette, but I often used bite-sized pieces of chorizo or other salamis with a chilli sauce.

✥ BUFFET PARTIES

Large buffet parties were frequent, and as we enjoyed 300 days of sunshine a year, most of them were outdoors. Our biggest and most successful was the day we celebrated the 50th anniversary of the Second World War; three of our guests had taken part in the Normandy landings and survived the terrible ordeal when so many of their comrades had not.

On the big day, everyone arrived bearing gifts of food. *Rozinante* had never seen anything quite like it! Three large tables covered with delicious concoctions, while the centre-piece was our famous whole salmon *en croute*. This meal had become something of a signature dish whenever we had large parties, but on one memorable occasion it nearly caused my sister and I heart attacks.

The occasion was a party celebrating the diamond wedding anniversary of an American couple who had long lived in the beautiful medieval village of Villefranche de Conflent.

Some weeks prior to this event, my son had arrived from Argeles with a small half-starved specimen of a cat which he had found abandoned in his yard one day. As he had no time to care for it we took on the responsibility, and were much encouraged by the friendly acceptance of this pathetic little bundle of moth-eaten fur by our three dogs, especially Buster, our very large golden retriever, who had been so sympathetic that Mozart, the cat, slept between his paws each night.

Daytime saw Mozart vainly trying to catch butterflies in our cabbage patch; otherwise, he never seemed to stop eating, and everything we presented was swallowed without reflection or hesitation. We all rejoiced in his progress and accepted his presence without too much examination, which was to prove fatal.

On the day of the party, having completed the setting out of the food on the table, we covered it with a cloth and disappeared to change into party clothes.

Guests arrived, drinks flowed, conversation became animated and eventually I flipped off the cloth from the food – only to find a completely unconscious Mozart lying amidst the demolished remains of our centre piece, the salmon *en croute*!

My immediate response was shock-horror but my sister, whose affection for cats has never been in doubt, said "Don't be cross, have you ever seen a cat so blissful?"

Blissful! The word choked in my throat and Mozart, replete with stolen salmon, was angrily disengaged from his demolition site and locked in the cellar – far too mild a punishment in my view!

Other parties, especially in the winter, were much quieter and to inject a little variety we devised games with 'trivial knowledge' questions, where guests were divided into teams – nothing stimulates a party of mixed nationalities like a little competitiveness.

Easter one year we gave an egg party. Soon after arrival, and before too many drinks had circulated, we gave everyone a list of clues to find the twenty-odd Easter eggs we had hidden in the garden. It took a good hour for all the eggs to be found and the winner, an elderly Welsh friend of ours, was duly applauded and given the largest Easter egg he had ever received as a prize. The occasion was remembered by everyone for the delightful impromptu speech of thanks he gave, starting with, "What an eggstraordinary day it has been, in such eggcellent company with an eggceptional lunch, following an eggciting egg eggcercise. It was," he concluded, "an eggsemplary eggsample of eggcentric, eggstravagant English behaviour, but an eggsperience I shall never eggstinguish from my memory."

We loved every minute of it!

✿ DESSERTS

It is customary, when invited out, to take a bottle of wine or a dessert with you as a gift to your host, or, failing that, an exquisite box of Belgian or Swiss chocolates, or a bouquet of flowers.

Growing up in Wales during the Second World War, with food rationing and severe shortages, our desserts were essentially puddings of a very solid nature to fill the gaps left by the absence of almost everything.

Rice pudding, semolina, macaroni, bread and butter, boiled treacle pudding, and boiled jam sponge, for example, with endless tarts – apple and rhubarb being the most obvious.

Stewed prunes and thick, tasteless custard was standard fare, and in direct and stark contrast to the wonderful *pâtisserie* shops we found in France that offered the passer-by a tantalising array of beautifully arranged open tarts – apple, plum, and apricot, to name but a few, not to mention the exotic meringue creations and spun sugar confections of dazzling and imaginative presentation.

In the face of such competition you had to work hard at *Rozinante* to produce desserts that passed muster, but since I enjoyed the 'pudding' aspect of catering I was happy to oblige.

I often served a cake, since this could be made and frozen before guests arrived and used up afterwards for tea-time sessions. The most useful was a crusty sponge, without fat, which stored well and could be cut in half to serve two occasions.

Crusty Top Sponge

150g plain flour
Pinch of salt
4 eggs, separated
250g caster sugar
1 dessertspoon orange flower-water
20cm diameter cake tin

Preheat the oven at 180C/350F/gas mark 4. Prepare the tin with butter and a dusting of flour to prevent sticking.

Sift the flour and salt well. Place the yolks, with half the sugar and the orange flower water, in a bowl and beat with a heavy whisk or wooden spatula until thick and mousse-like.

Whip the egg whites until stiff and add the remaining sugar, one tablespoon at a time, and continue whisking until the mixture stands in peaks. Then, using a metal spoon, fold the egg whites into the yolk mixture with the flour. Pour the batter into the prepared tin and bake in the oven for about 45 minutes. Turn out and cool on a rack.

I used to split this cake in half (cutting sideways to make two). Without any fat in it, the sponge was so firm and porous it lent itself to having any syrup mixture poured carefully and gently into it. (Make it more porous by piercing with a metal skewer). I would then cover the top with whipped cream and whatever fruit was to hand – peach, apricot, pear, strawberries and raspberries. As for the syrup mixture, either use the juice from a tin of fruit or make your own by boiling sugar with water to the consistency required, and flavour as you wish.

Nut Cake – 'Le Creusoise'

150g butter
6 egg whites
100g flour
125g nuts, ground to a powder
200g sugar
½ tsp salt
1 tsp vanilla essence

Preheat the oven to 200C/400F/gas mark 6, and while it's heating soften the butter in the oven. Beat the egg whites until stiff and then mix into the whites the flour, nut powder, sugar, and salt. Lastly, add the softened butter plus a teaspoon of vanilla essence. When well mixed (but not beaten), turn into a good-sized baking tin and bake in the oven for 45 minutes, until the top is lightly browned and the centre is not too soft to the touch of a finger. The egg yolks can be used for such things as mayonnaise, *crème anglaise* or *paté sable*.

Pineapple Upside Down Cake

150g butter or block margarine
50g soft dark brown sugar
225g can pineapple rings, drained
Glacé cherries, halved
100g caster sugar
2 eggs, beaten
175g self-raising flour
30–45ml pineapple juice or milk

Preheat the oven to 180C/350F/gas mark 4. Grease and base-line an 18cm round cake tin. Cream together 50g of the butter and all of the brown sugar, and spread it over the bottom of the tin. Arrange the pineapple rings, each with a cherry in the middle (cut side up), on this layer on the bottom of the tin.

Cream together the remaining butter and the caster sugar until pale and fluffy. Add the beaten eggs, a little at a time, beating well after each addition. Fold in the flour, adding enough pineapple juice or milk to give a dropping consistency, then spread the mixture on top of the pineapple rings.

Bake in the oven for about 45 minutes. Turn out onto a warmed serving dish, pineapple-side up, and serve with cream if wished.

Other fruit such as tinned apricots or pears or fresh greengages may be used instead of pineapple.

Chocolate Cake

In time I acquired quite a reputation for my chocolate cakes, but this was the favourite. The liquid glucose can be bought at the local chemist shop.

5 tbsp liquid glucose
450g plain dessert chocolate
5 tblsp rum (optional)
570ml double cream
75g sweet biscuits, crushed with a rolling pin
Cocoa powder for dusting

Line a 23cm cake tin with a circle of greaseproof or silicon paper and brush the base and sides with oil. Sprinkle the crushed biscuits over the base of the tin.

Break up the chocolate and put in a heatproof bowl together with the glucose and, if you wish, the rum for added flavouring. Fit the bowl over a pan of slowly simmering water and leave until the chocolate has melted and become smooth. Take off the heat and cool for 5 minutes.

In a separate bowl, beat the cream until only slightly thickened and fold it into the chocolate mixture. When blended, spoon into the tin. Cover with cling film and chill Just before serving run a palette knife around the edge to loosen and turn out onto a dish. Sift cocoa powder over the top before serving. If this is not all eaten at one session you can freeze it.

Chocolate Brandy Cake

225g butter
225g dark chocolate
3 tbsp brandy
225g digestive biscuits, crushed into crumbs
75g walnuts, broken into bits
75g glacé cherries, roughly chopped
2 large eggs
75g caster sugar

Melt the butter and chocolate together in a saucepan over a gentle heat. Stir until well mixed, then cool. Add the brandy, crushed biscuits, broken walnuts and chopped cherries.

Whisk the eggs and sugar until really thick and pale and fold into the chocolate brandy mixture. Line a 1 litre loaf tin with silicon paper and pour the chocolate brandy mixture into the tin, cover with cling film and put in the refrigerator to set. When it is really hard, run a palette knife down the sides between the paper and the tin, turn the cake onto a plate and peel off the paper. You can then lay walnut halves and halves of glacé cherries in rows on the top, if you wish.

Mille Feuille

1 packet of puff pastry
Raspberry jam
Stiffly whipped cream

Roll out the pastry as thin as possible and cut into three strips matching in shape and size. Place on a baking sheet and bake at 200C/400F/gas mark 6, for 10–15 minutes until puffed up and golden. Remove and cool completely.

Cover two of the strips with a layer of melted jam and then a layer of stiffly beaten cream. Put one of these strips on top of the other in layers, and use the last strip as a lid. Dust with icing sugar and serve.

Tarte Tatin

250g puff pastry
75g softened butter
175g caster sugar
750g (about 5) large firm dessert apples, preferably Cox's
Vanilla ice cream or *crème fraîche* to serve

Preheat the oven to 190C/375F/gas mark 5. Roll out the pastry on a lightly floured surface and cut out a 26cm disc (slightly larger than the top of a 20cm *tarte tatin* dish, or a reliably non-stick cast iron frying pan). Transfer to a baking sheet and chill for at least 20 minutes.

Spread the butter over the base of the *tarte tatin* dish, or frying pan, and sprinkle over the sugar in a thick even layer.

Peel, core and halve the apples, trimming them very slightly if necessary to fit but keeping their nicely rounded shape, and then tightly pack them, rounded-side down, on top of the sugar. Place the *tarte tatin* dish over a medium heat and cook for 20–25 minutes, gently shaking the pan now and then until the butter and sugar have been amalgamated with the apple juices to produce a rich toffee-coloured sauce and the apples are just tender.

(Remember that as you cook it the caramel becomes darker, so you must watch that the butter and sugar do not burn.)

Lift the pastry to lie on top of the apples and tuck the edges down the side of the pan. Prick the pastry several times with the tip of a small, sharp knife or a fork, transfer to the oven and bake for 25 minutes until the pastry is puffed up and cooked.

Remove the tart from the oven and leave it to rest for 5 minutes. Then run a knife around the edge of the tart and invert it onto a round, flat serving plate. Serve warm, cut into wedges with whipped cream, *crème fraîche* or vanilla ice cream. Perfect!

Pear and Almond Tart

Sufficient pears to fill a quiche dish
230g short crust pastry
85g ground almonds, same amount of caster sugar
280ml full cream milk
2 eggs

Peel, halve and core the pears (or use tinned ones). Roll out the pastry and line a 25cm flan ring or quiche dish with it. Cover with greaseproof paper, put in a handful of baking beans and bake blind in a hot oven, 200C/400F/gas mark 6, for 10 minutes. Remove from the oven and allow to cool slightly.

Mix the ground almonds with two-thirds of the sugar and spread over the base of the pastry. Arrange the pears on top. Beat the milk, eggs and remaining sugar together and pour this custard over the fruit before baking for about 30 minutes at 180C/350F/gas mark 4.

This tart is best served warm, but may also be served cold.

Catalan Almond Cake

4 medium eggs, separated
175g golden caster sugar
Pinch of ground cinnamon
200g ground almonds
Pinch of salt
Strawberry or orange slices, dusted with
    caster sugar to serve

Preheat the oven to 180C/350F/gas mark 4. Butter the sides and base of a 22cm diameter deep spring-form cake tin. Line with baking parchment.

Beat the egg whites in a bowl with the pinch of salt until soft peaks form. Whisk in half the sugar, a tablespoon at a time.

Whisk the yolks in a separate bowl with the rest of the sugar and cinnamon until thick. Mix in the almonds and then gently fold in the whites.

Put in the tin and bake for 50 minutes until the cake is firm to touch. Remove from the oven and cool, then turn onto a wire rack, dust with icing sugar and serve with the fruit.

Occasionally I would find myself collecting egg whites, and then a very easy pudding was to put stewed apples in an ovenproof dish, whip up meringues in the mixer, add sugar and pour this over the apple. When nicely browned in the oven it is ready to serve.

Speaking of meringue, I did have one disaster when, one evening, I made a Baked Alaska for a party of newly arrived guests.

This pudding has a sponge base topped with ice cream and then coated with meringue. It has to be put in a fairly hot oven at the very last minute before serving in order to set the meringue but NOT to melt the ice cream! Having reached the point of just putting the pudding in the oven I was surprised to hear angry voices coming from the dining room and, by opening the door a crack, I realised that a political debate between the guests was getting out of hand! So, preoccupied with the shouting, I completely forgot the Baked Alaska until a strong smell of burning joined a loud swishing sound, making me turn in horror to find the meringue and ice cream oozing angrily out of the oven door all over the kitchen floor!

Rushing to cope with the situation I slipped on the mess and fell flat on my face in the pudding I had so lovingly prepared. My only recompense was that my scream had alerted my guests to the crisis and, rushing to my aid, one or two of them ended up as sticky as I was and laughing our heads off! It was one of the guests who solved the dessert situation by opening a tin of pineapple, which we all sat down and enjoyed, thus bringing what might have been an unpleasant evening to a harmonious close!

✿ *FRUIT PUDDINGS*

With an abundance of fruit in the area and apples all around us, we were able to serve many delicious fruit-based desserts.

For most baked apple desserts, you can soften the apples in a microwave beforehand if you are worried about them not being well enough cooked when you take the cake out of the oven.

Apple Strudel

This is a very easy pudding, especially if you use shop bought puff pastry instead of making your own.

225g puff pastry
6 eating apples, peeled, cored and finely diced
Sultanas
Cinnamon and brown sugar to taste
Almond slivers

Place the apples in a bowl and cover with brown sugar and cinnamon, with sufficient sultanas to make a good mix.

Roll out the pastry as thinly as possible and place the apple mixture all over, leaving a gap of about 2.5cm around the sides. Starting at one end, roll the pastry into a sausage shape, then curve the ends in and press together. Place on a greased baking sheet. Spread the pastry with a little melted butter and sprinkle on some almond slivers. Bake in a hot oven 200C/400F/gas mark 6, for 30 minutes until puffed up and golden. Dust with icing sugar and serve with whipped cream.

Apple Dessert Cake

225g self-raising flour
1 level tsp baking powder
225g caster sugar
2 large eggs
½ tsp almond extract
150g butter, melted
250g cooking apples, peeled and cored
25g flaked almonds

Preheat the oven to 140C/280F/gas mark 3, and lightly grease a deep 20cm loose-bottomed cake tin.

Put the flour, baking powder, sugar, eggs, almond extract and melted butter into a bowl and mix well until blended. Spread half this mixture in the prepared tin.

Thickly slice the apples and lay on top of the cake mixture in the tin. Pile the apples mostly towards the centre, then spoon the rest of the cake mixture over the apples, covering it well in the centre. Sprinkle with the flaked almonds and bake in the oven for well over an hour, until golden and coming away from the sides of the tin.

Devil Peaches

Another very easy sweet. Serves 6.

6 firm peaches or nectarines
175g almond ratafia biscuits
100ml brandy
3 tbsp soft brown sugar

Set the oven at 220C/425F/gas mark 7. Cut each peach or nectarine in half and remove the stones. Place on an ovenproof dish or tray, cut-side uppermost, and cover with ratafia biscuits in the centre of each half. Spoon brandy on top of each half, cover with brown sugar, and bake for about 5 minutes. Serve with whipped cream.

Baked Figs with Crème Fraîche

In this recipe, the sugar slightly caramelises and the figs are surrounded with a lovely red juice.

2–3 figs per head
2–3 tblsp caster sugar
1–2 tblsp water
Crème fraîche, or *fromage frais,* or whipped cream

Heat the oven to 190C/375F/gas mark 5. Put the figs in an oven dish, sprinkle with caster sugar and water. Bake for 10 minutes. Allow to cool and eat with *crème fraîche* or *fromage frais.*

Fresh figs are often served with Parma ham, instead of slices of melon, as a first course. Black figs are generally considered superior to the green variety and may be served just as they are, on a bed of green leaves for dessert.

Fromage Blanc Pudding

500g *fromage blanc* (i.e. *fromage frais)*
130g sugar
4 eggs
1 soupspoon cornflour

Mix the egg yolks with the sugar, cornflour and *fromage blanc.* Beat the egg whites until stiff and then fold into the rest of the mixture. Turn into a well-buttered mould and bake at medium heat 180C/350F/gas mark 4, for 40 minutes. When the pudding is cold turn it out onto a plate and decorate it with whipped cream and a coulis of raspberries.

Lemon Tart

This is the quickest and easiest tart I have ever made.

Serves 6

225g frozen short-crust pastry, thawed
350g lemon curd (bought or homemade variety)
2 eggs, lightly beaten
Oil for greasing
Icing sugar
1–2 lemons, thinly sliced

Oil an 18cm flan tin lightly and set oven at 180C/350F/gas mark 4. Roll out pastry evenly to fit the flan tin. Prick the base with a fork.

Mix the lemon curd with the eggs and pour the mixture into the pastry case. Bake for 25 minutes. When the tart comes out of the oven dust it immediately with icing sugar and place under a hot grill to caramelise. Decorate the top with very thin slices of fresh lemon.

✿ CHEESE

It was General de Gaulle who once remarked in sheer frustration that it was impossible to govern a country that had at least 300 varieties of cheese!

The Pyrenean varieties are superb, especially the ewe's cheese made high up in the mountains where the shepherds still keep their flocks of sheep. So I often served *Brebis*, the ewe's cheese, which was much appreciated for its different flavour.

As a starter I often made one of the following:

Roquefort Turnovers

225g puff pastry
50g Roquefort or other Blue Cheese such as Blue Auvergne
1 tbsp *crème fraîche*
1 egg yolk, beaten

Heat the oven to 220C/425F/gas mark 7. Roll out the puff pastry very thinly and cut out 4 strips measuring approximately 20 x 10cm.

Mash the cheese and mix it with the *crème fraîche*. Put a spoonful on one half of the strip. Dampen the edges of the strips with water, fold in half over the cheese mixture and press the two layers of pastry together, making sure they are completely sealed.

Mark the edges with the prongs of a fork, cut a small slit on top of each and brush all over with egg yolk. Put turnovers onto a baking sheet and bake in the oven for 15 minutes until they are piping hot and golden.

Warm Goat's Cheese on Toast

12–16 slices of baguette-style French bread,
    each slice 1.25cm to 2cm thick
12–16 slices round or log-shaped goat's cheese,
    roughly 1.25cm thick and 6.25cm in diameter
Olive oil and black pepper

Toast bread under a grill, on one side only, then remove and set aside. Dip each slice of cheese in oil, then place it on the untoasted side of each slice of bread. Season with freshly ground black pepper and return it to the broiler, grilling until warm. Do not allow the cheese to brown.

✆ PILGRIM WALK TO COMPOSTELA

Most of our guests were keen walkers, and those with even more stamina left to undertake the 500 mile walk from St Jean de Pied de Port in France to Santiago de Compostela in Spain. The history of the walk is fascinating; it began as a pilgrimage to the relics of the Apostle James, buried in the Cathedral of Santiago. His grave was discovered in AD800 and since then thousands of pilgrims, many christened James, have made this trip in homage to him.

We were always interested, if our guests returned to us, to hear their stories. Some had only survived a weekend, others a fortnight, but many, to our surprise, had completed the 500 mile journey and told us it had been the experience of a lifetime. Not necessarily spiritual in the sense of the original pilgrims perhaps, but a wonderful enjoyment of stunning countryside, mountains and plains, orchards and vineyards, with an amusing and varied amount of accommodation *en route,* ranging from small hostels, *pensions* like ours, *auberges* or even rough bunk-houses. Some had even slept on wooden planks and had been too exhausted to notice!

The great benefit, they all agreed, had been the people they had met – their fellow travellers – all united in their stories of hardships to overcome, blistered feet and hands, aching limbs. One guest, aged about 70, said it was due to the kindness of other walkers who had had the foresight to pack first aid kits in their haversacks and consequently had been able to treat his loudly complaining feet, thereby enabling him to reach the Cathedral eventually and thank God, James and fellow pilgrims for his survival!

I always asked about the food and with one voice they all shouted 'Tapas!'. Those delicious Spanish bowls of food, sometimes a dozen at a time, placed on bars so that you could help yourself, and from what these happy but weary travellers told me, I gathered up the following...

Escalivada Gitana

(Mixed Vegetables with Anchovies)

4 tomatoes
2 onions
2 courgettes
2 aubergines
2 red peppers
6 garlic cloves
Olive oil
Salt and pepper
Anchovies

Cut all the vegetables into large pieces and put them in an ovenproof casserole. Dress with olive oil, salt and pepper and cook for one hour in a hot oven, 220C/425F/gas mark 7, then lower the temperature for one more hour. Leave to go cold and serve with anchovies – preferably from Collioure!

Fèves à la Menthe et au Jambon

(Broad Beans with Mint and Ham)

50g of broad beans
6 slices of Serrano ham, cut into small pieces
Olive oil
Salt and pepper
Mint

Cook the broad beans, then leave to grow cold. Dress the beans with olive oil, salt, pepper, and the mint, and cover with small pieces of Serrano ham.

Patatas Aioli

(Garlic Potatoes)

50g potatoes
6–8 cloves garlic, depending on taste
250ml sunflower oil
Bunch of chives
Salt and pepper

Peel the potatoes and boil until cooked, then mash. Crush the garlic and gradually mix in the oil to a paste-like consistency, then fold into the potatoes with the salt and pepper. Chop the chives finely and mix into the potatoes, spreading more on top as decoration. (You can mix the potatoes with your own aioli mayonnaise if you wish a quicker method of preparation.)

Pollo al Ajillo

(Chicken with Garlic)

1.5kg chicken, cut into very small pieces
2 soupspoons of flour
1 tsp paprika flakes
125ml olive oil
6–10 cloves of garlic, depending on taste
150ml sherry
1 soupspoon chopped parsley
Salt and pepper

Mix the flour, salt, pepper and paprika together. Cover the chicken pieces with this mixture. In a heavy pan, heat the oil and cook the crushed garlic for a few minutes, then remove and put aside. Add the chicken to the oil and cook for 5 minutes. Replace the garlic in the pan and cook for a further 5 minutes until the chicken is golden in colour. Add sherry, parsley, pepper and salt (as necessary) and cook for a further 30 minutes.

Gambas al Ajillo

(Prawns with Garlic)

250g large prawns
2 soupspoons olive oil
2 cloves garlic, crushed
2 small chillies, sliced and deseeded
Salt and pepper

Heat the oil in a pan and, when hot, put in garlic and salt. When the garlic starts to colour, add the chilli and the prawns. Stir gently together and serve quickly with plenty of bread to mop up the juices.

Lapin au Rancio

(Rabbit with Chilli)

1 rabbit, cut into very small pieces
500g tomatoes, peeled and crushed
2 onions, cut into small pieces
1 red pepper, cubed
1 green pepper, cubed
2 soupspoons chopped parsley and garlic
Olive oil
Salt and pepper
1 bottle of dry white wine
1 tsp chilli or paprika

In a deep pan cook the onion in the olive oil, then add the peppers and cook for 5 minutes. Add the small pieces of rabbit to the casserole and brown gently. Add the tomatoes, chilli (or paprika) and wine. Cook gently for 1 hour on a low flame, then add the parsley, garlic and seasoning. Serve with bread.

Sardines à l'Escabeche

(Sardines in a Red Wine Vinegar Sauce)

1kg fresh sardines
250ml olive oil
500ml red wine vinegar (or preferably Banyuls)
A little flour
4 cloves, whole
Paprika powder or flakes, to taste
½ tsp black pepper in grains
6 garlic cloves

Clean the sardines, cutting off and discarding the heads, and rinse in cold water. Roll the sardines in the flour to cover completely. Fry the sardines in the oil and, when cooked, remove and dry on kitchen paper and put aside. Cook the garlic and then pour in the wine vinegar slowly and carefully, finally adding the other ingredients. Cook for 20 minutes on a low flame in order to evaporate the alcohol content of the vinegar. Pour this sauce over the sardines and marinade for a day before serving.

Oranges with Cinnamon

1kg oranges
1 soupspoon brown sugar
½ tsp cinnamon

Cut the oranges into pieces without skin or pith. Sprinkle on the brown sugar and cinnamon and leave for 2 hours in the fridge before serving.

Crème au Touron

Touron is similar to nougat

500ml cream
100g *touron* Catalan with almonds
50g sugar
5 egg yolks

Warm the cream gently with the touron. Do not boil and, as soon as the touron has melted, remove from the heat and leave to cool. Beat the egg yolks with the sugar until creamy. Mix the eggs with the cream and touron and pour into small individual earthenware pots. Bake in a *bain-marie* for 20 minutes in a hot oven, 220C/425F/gas mark 7. Serve as they are, in the pots.

One of the Compostela walkers, before leaving for the walk, told me he was allergic to garlic, so I did my best to exclude this from my cooking during his stay.

When he returned from Spain I asked him how he had enjoyed Spanish food and, like so many of his fellow travellers, he enthused about Tapas and said it had been some of the most delicious dishes he had ever tasted. Knowing the garlic content of practically all these dishes, I had a quiet smile to myself and happily returned to peeling my much loved garlic cloves again!

It was also interesting to see how much more readily the British were to mop up sauces with bread after the Spanish experience!

Plus ça change!

❧ FÊTE DE POMMES

It is a fitting end to this brief account of Catalan and other recipes we served to guests at *Rozinante* to describe the enthusiastic celebrations all over the country once the annual harvest was completed.

In St Eulalie every year there was the traditional *Fête de Pommes* (Apple Festival) and on one memorable occasion my sister was allowed to have a stall at this very French gathering in order to sell her dried flower arrangements, all the flowers having been grown at *Rozinante*.

Thousands of people came from all over the Roussillon to buy the apples grown in the valley. Bands played, choirs sang, there was a hotly contested *boules* competition and special events for the children. Flags, predominantly Catalan, flew everywhere and the atmosphere was explosive with the kind of excitement that only the French can engender when they really are *'en fête'*.

We scarcely recognised the local farmers and their families, they were so dressed up for the occasion, and bonhomie reigned supreme – except for this particular occasion when local politicians extravagantly delayed lunch with their canvassing speeches! An unforgivable sin for the French to cope with!

Angrily, hundreds of farming families descended on the catering tent in a ravenous body, so that the stewards inside could not cope with the numbers, and inevitably the scuffles unearthed the guy ropes and the huge canvas marquee crashed to the ground.

Luckily no one was hurt and later, talking to the mayor, he blamed the emotions aroused when rugby feelings ran high at village matches, thus causing unnecessary rivalry. The politicians, however, were to be banned in the future!

Happily for us, my sister sold all her flowers and we returned home in triumph. We celebrated that evening with Margaret's favourite chicken recipe and pear dessert:

" ... the whole tent capsized ... "

Chicken with Cider and Apple

4 chicken breasts
300ml dry cider
1 large leek, cut into slivers
50g butter
1 large cooking apple, peeled, cored and chopped
50ml single cream
Salt and freshly ground black pepper

Marinade the chicken breasts in the cider for a couple of hours. Drain and dry on kitchen paper and reserve the cider for the sauce. Barely cook the strips of leek, and then plunge and keep in cold water to preserve the green colour Melt the butter in a heavy based frying pan and fry the chicken breasts for 5 minutes on each side. Add the chopped apple and the cider and cook for another 10 minutes until the apple is soft and you are certain the chicken is cooked. Pour in the cream, season, and add the leek before serving with a rice accompaniment.

Pears in Red Wine

300ml red wine
300ml water
175g caster sugar
1 small stick cinnamon
Lemon rind
6 pears
2 level tbsp cornflour

Put the wine and water in a large saucepan and add the sugar, cinnamon stick, and several pieces of thinly pared lemon rind. On a low heat stir until dissolved. Peel the pears, cut in half and add to the pan, then simmer for 10 minutes or more until they are tender. Remove and place in a serving dish. Simmer the juice until it has thickened but blend in the cornflour to reach the right consistency. Serve with sauce and cream.

Down on the coast Mark and his girlfriend, Suzie, had spent a month picking grapes at M. Armand Barreaux's *domain*. He was so impressed they had survived the whole period (apparently very few English had done so before) that they were invited to attend the final winding-up party. However, they had to submit to the indignity of having a bucket of soggy grapes thrown over them once the fruit from the last vine had been picked!

The party night proved to be an explosion of good humour and tremendous hospitality, with a *grillade* of *escargots* (snails stuffed with garlic), *sauçisse,* salad, *sanglier* (wild boar), fromage, dessert, café and cognac. Two of the team turned out to be excellent guitarists à la gitane, and others dressed up in mock flamenco costume to put on a hilarious exhibitionist display of Spanish dancing.

It is true that very few people taking part in the grape harvest actually enjoy the work process. The back-breaking slow picking of the fruit, the heat, the flies, leave alone the low wages! But everyone loves the ambience, and the sheer hardship helps to weld a group of disparate people together who feel at the end of the harvest a tremendous sense of achievement, working in harmony with one another.

One of Mark's abiding memories of this period was looking down a long line of buttocks of various shapes and sizes, all dappled with gold sunlight as it filtered through the vines! Aching limbs were massaged at the end of the hot, dry days and the first drink in the café had to be experienced to be understood by the non-aficionados.

Armand Barreaux was happy to reminisce about the days when groups of migrants, and often very poor workers in family and tribal groups, would descend on the farms for the *vendange* (grape harvest) and all were quite content to sleep and eat in rough barns. Nowadays pickers come from all over the world in Jeeps and other transport, sleeping in local *gîtes* and campsites. Patrons, on the other hand, cannot afford to take on too many people because of governmental tax restrictions. All this against a background of fluctuating prices and uncertain markets, not to mention foreign competition!

Mark had found it difficult to persuade Suzie to eat the snails at the *vendange* celebration, and I well remember the first time I ever ate them.

My husband and I were on our way back from a continental holiday in 1955 when, driving up the main motorway to Paris, I noticed on the map one of the few five star restaurants in France at a place called Avallon. Not wishing to miss this gastronomic opportunity, we left the motorway and finally arrived at a Moulin (mill) in a deep valley of the same name where, on arrival, a lady came down to greet us. She seemed to have stepped out of an 18th Century novel – tall, imposing, regal in appearance, she wore a long, black dress with a lace blouse and a black velvet ribbon at her throat decorated with a small cameo brooch.

Graciously she welcomed us to the Mill, and suggested we wait in the garden while our meal was being prepared.

I have never forgotten the sense of peace and serenity that surrounded us in a garden dominated by a mill wheel, with the soft sound of running water, while butterflies flew in and out of the lavender bushes and the air was full of the scent of roses.

Lunch, when it was served, was of an extreme simplicity.

Snails in garlic, followed by baby *poussins* (chicken) with lemon stuffing, and a dessert of wild strawberries and cream. After eating we made our way languidly to a bank by the mill stream and gratefully sank down in the lush grass, unwilling to trace our way to the car park and face the remainder of the noise and pressure of the *autoroute* and the hazardous *périphérique* of Paris. With the gentle persuasion of the ripple of water over stones, and the intoxicating scents of the garden, not to mention the after-effects of the wine we had drunk, we slipped effortlessly into sleep, which seemed to set a seal on this memorable occasion.

When we eventually awoke, oblivious to the smiles of other passing clients, we rose to say goodbye to our hostess who, with a faint smile on her lips asked, *"Vous vous êtes bien amusés?* (Have you enjoyed yourselves?)"

My husband, in a gallant mood, responded by raising her hand to his lips, replying *"C'était inoubliable, Madame* (It was unforgettable, Madame)," and her smile deepened with pleasure as she wished us a safe return home.

We knew it was a day we would never forget. As for the snails, I had been reluctant to eat them but my husband insisted and the more I ate, the more I enjoyed them!

A fitting sequel to this memory is that on a very dull and cloudy day, shortly after we had moved into *Rozinante*, our neighbour's wife, Rosanne, appeared at the back door with a very large bucket in her hand and asked, rather diffidently, that as it had just rained would we mind if she went around the garden looking for snails. Since my sister had a particular grudge against snails for eating far too much of our garden produce she replied immediately, "Please do, the more the merrier!"

Later, her bucket full, Rosanne came to thank us and out of curiosity we asked what she intended to do with them. The secret of the cleansing process before cooking apparently lay in a good dose of oatmeal which, once consumed, allowed the snails to get rid of any impurities. Two to three washings in salt water followed before cooking them in a mixture of white wine, water, chopped up parsley and garlic. She asked with a smile whether we were tempted, knowing we hadn't the stomach for it! Time would tell...

Catalan Snails

500g snails
500g tomatoes, peeled and crushed
100g Serrano ham, cut into small pieces
200g sausage meat
1 onion
1 soupspoon parsley
3 bay leaves
300ml red wine
Olive oil
Handful of salt
Pepper

Mix the snails with a handful of salt, then wash in water several times. Boil in a casserole dish of water for 10 minutes.

Cook the onion in the olive oil with the ham and, when it colours, add the sausage meat. Then add tomatoes, wine, bay leaves and parsley.

Cook on a low heat for 45 minutes, then add the snails and cook for a further 15 minutes. Remove the bay leaves before serving.

Snail Butter

Cream 115g soft butter with 2–3 tablespoons of finely chopped shallots and 2 or 3 finely chopped garlic cloves. Add a quarter of a cup of chopped parsley, and then season to taste.

Cover the cleaned snails with the butter mixture and leave in the fridge to amalgamate for several hours. Put in an oven dish with white wine and bake in a moderate oven, 180C/350F/gas mark 4, for 10 minutes, until the butter and wine have mingled.

Serve with plenty of bread to mop up the juices.

✿ VENDANGE

As a family, we were all united finally for the *vendange* on the coast at Banyuls-sur-Mer, where our English hosts had originally arrived in a sailing boat from England to settle and eventually establish a business, which flourishes to this day.

Whereas the fête at St Eulalie had concentrated on our apples, the *vendange* at Banyuls was to celebrate its very distinguished port-like Banyuls wine. In my cooking I had always preferred sweet wines for different recipes, such as Muscat from Rivesaltes and the red of Banyuls.

I am always pleased, when I return to the UK, to see Roussillon wines on sale everywhere. This part of France used not to produce wines that could match Bordeaux or Burgundy, but now the quality locally has improved and I always stock Fitou, Jean D'Estavel, Père Puig, Caramany, Rassiguères and Château de Jau among many others.

So it was with considerable pleasure we joined thousands of people on a brilliant Sunday morning in October on the beach, all busily engaged in setting up chairs and tables, lighting fires and preparing barbecues. Bands played, bottles were unpacked, along with every kind of food for rapid consumption.

All the months of hard work now dissolved in a weekend of joyous recognition that the harvest was well and truly gathered in. Symbolic Catalan sailing boats, reminiscent of Arab dhows, tacked to and fro across the sparkling waters of the bay, reminding us that, at the height of the Empire, the Romans had sailed into these waters in search of the rich, red, port-like wine of Banyuls.

We cooked some of our favourite recipes for the occasion:

Jacqueline's Fish Cake

600g fillets of fish
1kg very ripe tomatoes
6 eggs
4 garlic cloves, peeled and crushed
Basil to taste
4 dessertspoons olive oil
Salt, pepper and Tabasco sauce to taste

Peel the tomatoes and remove the pips. Crush and cook in oil until mushy and no juice is left. Take the bones out of the fish and mix the fish in with the garlic and tomatoes. Beat in eggs, basil, salt and pepper and Tabasco to taste. Place in a heatproof dish in a bain-marie and cook at 180C/350F/gas mark 4, for 40 minutes. Leave to go cold, decorate with mayonnaise, and serve.

Pork Spare Ribs and Chicken

12 pork spare ribs
12 chicken thighs
250ml cider
4 tbsp maple syrup
2 tbsp oil
2 tbsp soy sauce
2 star anise
6 cloves of garlic
Cinnamon powder

Put the ribs and chicken pieces in a dish. Mix together all the remaining ingredients and pour over the meat, making sure everything is well covered. Marinade for a day or two in the fridge and then put in an oven 200C/400F/gas mark 6, and cook for about 1 hour. Can be served hot or cold.

Catalan Meatballs

450g minced pork
40g parmesan cheese, grated
125g fresh breadcrumbs
4 tbsp finely chopped flat-leafed parsley
Zest and juice of ½ lemon
2 medium eggs
½ tsp salt
50g plain flour
1–2 tbsp sunflower oil
1–2 glasses white wine (or white grape juice)
4 bay leaves

Put the pork, cheese, breadcrumbs, parsley, lemon juice and zest, eggs and salt into a large bowl. Mix the ingredients and shape into about 20 medium sized balls. Roll in the flour.

Heat the oil in a large frying pan and brown the meatballs gently. Add the wine and cook for 2–3 minutes. Add bay leaves and pour in enough hot water to cover the meatballs. Simmer, uncovered, for about 30 minutes until the liquid has reduced, the meatballs are cooked and the juices syrupy. Serve hot or cold.

Bakewell Tart

212g packet puff pastry
2 whole eggs
2 egg yolks
100g butter, melted
100g caster sugar
50g ground almonds
2 tbsp raspberry jam
Sliced almonds to decorate

Roll out the pastry on a floured surface and use to line an 18cm pie plate or flan ring. Beat the eggs and extra egg yolks together, add the butter, sugar and almonds and mix well. Spread the jam over the bottom of the pastry case, and pour on the egg mixture.

Bake in the oven at 200C/400F/gas mark 6, for 30 minutes or until the filling is firm to the touch. Decorate with sliced almonds.

The merry-making continued until dusk when many, over-heated from dancing, were quite happy to cool off in the sea instead!

My attention, however, was centred on the Banyuls wine, and the thought that it would make a delicious addition to the port content of the sauce to accompany our traditional Christmas goose.

✆ CHRISTMAS GOOSE

What more appropriate end to a cookery book than to say bon appétit and a merry Christmas to our readers!

Roast Goose, with Apricot, Chestnut, Lemon and Thyme Stuffing

Goose was always our choice of Christmas Dinner, whether in the UK or France. Admittedly there is not a great deal of meat on a goose, but what there is is very rich. A fruity stuffing helps offset the richness, and you can make the stuffing in advance and freeze it. Two or three times during cooking, take off the fat collecting in the roasting tin and keep for other dishes, eg roast potatoes.

Goose Stuffing
For a goose weighing about 5.5 Kg (12 lb) you need:
250g dried apricots, soaked in water ovenight,
    drained, cut into small pieces
2 tbsp oil
2 onions, chopped
1 x 450g tin of whole chestnuts, drained of their juice
500g cooked brown rice
Grated rind of two lemons
½ tsp dried thyme
Salt and pepper

For the gravy you need:
A small amount of goose fat
2 rounded tbsp flour
600ml chicken stock
150ml port wine
2 tsp redcurrant jelly
Salt and pepper

To make the stuffing:

Heat the oil and sauté the onions until soft. Mix the onions with the apricots, chestnuts, brown rice, lemon rind, thyme, salt and pepper.

Stuff the goose with this mixture and roast the bird in a deep pan in a hot oven, 220C/425F/gas mark 7, for 1½ hours. Take off the fat occasionally, as suggested above. Lower the temperature to 180C/350F/gas mark 4 and cook for a further 1½ hours. Rest the goose, keeping warm, for half an hour before serving.

To make the gravy:

Tip the required goose fat into a saucepan, stir in the flour and cook for a couple of minutes. Gradually add chicken stock and wine, stirring all the time, and bring to the boil. If too thick, add more stock or wine. Add the redcurrant jelly and season with salt and pepper. Strain and keep warm until ready to serve.

Mr Williams, I feel sure, would be ready and waiting!

Cookery Conversion Tables

Measures for Pans and Dishes

Inches	Centimeters
9-by-13-inch baking dish	22-by-33-cm baking dish
8-by-8-inch baking dish	20-by-20-cm baking dish
9-by-5-inch loaf pan (8 cups)	23-by-12-cm loaf pan (2 litres)
10-inch tart or cake pan	25-cm tart or cake pan
9-inch cake pan	22-cm cake pan

Oven temperatures

°C	Fan°C	°F	Gas	Description
110	90	225	¼	Very cool
120	100	250	½	Very cool
140	120	275	1	Cool
150	130	300	2	Cool
160	140	325	3	Warm
180	160	350	4	Moderate
190	170	375	5	Moderately hot
200	180	400	6	Fairly hot
220	200	425	7	Hot
230	210	450	8	Very hot
240	220	475	8	Very hot

Liquid measures

Metric	Imperial	Aus	US
25ml	1fl oz		
50ml	2fl oz	¼ cup	¼ cup
75ml	3fl oz		
100ml	3½ fl oz		
120ml	4fl oz	½ cup	½ cup
150ml	5fl oz		
175ml	6fl oz	¾ cup	¾ cup
200ml	7fl oz		
250ml	8fl oz	1 cup	1 cup
300ml	10fl oz/ ½ pint	½ pint	1¼ cups
360ml	12fl oz		
400ml	14fl oz		
450ml	15fl oz	2 cups	2 cups/ 1 pint
600ml	1 pint	1 pint	2½ cups
750ml	1¼ pints		
900ml	1½ pints		
1 litre	1¾ pints	1¾ pints	1 quart
1.2 litres	2 pints		
1.4 litres	2½ pints		
1.5 litres	2¾ pints		
1.7 litres	3 pints		
2 litres	3½ pints		
3 litres	5¼ pints		

Weights for dry ingredients

Metric	Imperial	Metric	Imperial
7g	¼ oz	550g	1¼ lb
15g	½ oz	600g	1lb 5 oz
20g	¾ oz	650g	1lb 7 oz
25g	1 oz	675g	1½ lb
40g	1½ oz	700g	1lb 9 oz
50g	2 oz	750g	1lb 11 oz
60g	2½ oz	800g	1¾ lb
75g	3 oz	900g	2 lb
100g	3½ oz	1kg	2¼ lb
125g	4 oz	1.1kg	2½ lb
140g	4½ oz	1.25kg	2¾ lb
150g	5 oz	1.35kg	3 lb
165g	5½ oz	1.5kg	3 lb 6 oz
175g	6 oz	1.8kg	4 lb
200g	7 oz	2kg	4½ lb
225g	8 oz	2.25kg	5 lb
250g	9 oz	2.5kg	5½ lb
275g	10 oz	2.75kg	6 lb
300g	11 oz	3 kg	6¾ lb
350g	12 oz		
375g	13 oz		
400g	14 oz		
425g	15 oz		
450g	1 lb		
500g	1 lb 2 oz		

The Author

Sir Edward Heath's Private Secretary didn't take retirement sitting down ...

Born in Penarth, South Wales, Eugene Barter left school at 16 to work as a trainee journalist on two local newspapers, in the days when discrimination against women in the workplace made the job twice the challenge it was for male colleagues. Moving on to an assignment in Holland at a Unesco conference, she stayed on for two years, learning the language and working with companies in Amsterdam struggling to get back on their feet after the horrors of the Second World War. After studying with the Open University in her late forties, she became a Tutor/Counsellor after graduating, before moving briefly back into journalism, then working in the House of Commons – eventually becoming Senior Secretary to Sir Edward Heath. In her sixties she took on the running of an *auberge* in France, and this book, *Blackbirds Baked in a Pie,* is a lively and affectionate account of her time there. Now 85, Eugene's love affair with France continues, undiminished.

The Illustrator

Mary Jose is English, but she and her husband have travelled the world extensively. She was one of the first and most regular guests at *Rozinante*. She is a self-taught artist, now very happily settled near Prades, where her paintings are widely praised. There are frequent exhibitions of her work in both France and the UK. It was, in fact, the evening meal with champagne to celebrate the purchase of their house there, that the "blackbirds baked in a pie" incident took place. Visit Mary's web site at: *www.maryjose.fr*

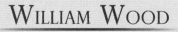

WILLIAM WOOD

A LITTLE
BOOK OF
PLEASURES

SAMPLE CHAPTERS:

A Little Book of Pleasures

by

William Woood

ISBN# 978-1-907984-07-5

About "A LITTLE BOOK OF PLEASURES"

This delightful anecdotal collection, told with wry humour and a gentle, sometimes quirky style slightly reminiscent of a bygone era, contains a mixture of description and observation, with a smattering of autobiographical incident. William Wood has lived in many places of the world, is well travelled and well written, with a keen sense of enjoyment of what he sees and experiences, and a talent for bringing that visually to the mind of his reader. The short, usually self-contained pieces make wonderful cameos both for those who do their reading in snatches, and those who will want to devour his stories in one sitting.

William Wood has led a nomadic life and his friends and relatives are far flung. He now lives and writes in Sussex where he is a full time carer for his 91-year-old parents. When he can get away he likes visiting his children in France, Rutland and Cumbria, or his in-laws in Norway and Slovakia. The diaries he keeps on these visits occasionally give him local colour and ideas for his stories. If he ever makes money from his writing he intends visiting old haunts in Africa, India and Australia – or even pastures new. For the moment, every caged day is both an adventure and incredibly frustrating.

In addition to his 'Little Book of Pleasures', William writes journalistic articles. He has had stories on the BBC World Service, and contributed to a variety of magazines and anthologies. He has also always written poems; they are, he says, "something that has to be squeezed out like a boil to give me relief". At university William wrote and directed his own plays, and later worked with amateur groups in Norway. Most often he writes short stories and novels; his first remains unpublished (as, he says, all first novels should be). His first published book was 'No Time' (Babash/Ryan, 2003). Set in South Sudan, it predicted the independence of the south nearly two decades in advance. His next novel, 'Passing Wind', was shortlisted for an Amazon prize.

Prologue

S tephen Fry – entertainer, wit and self-professed geek – was explaining on the radio the other day that blog is short for 'web log', which is just like an on-line diary. You cried: *No, Stephen, it is not!*

In a fundamental way a diary is the very opposite of a blog. A handwritten diary is something private and personal, a secret friend in whom you may confide. Some may lock it, some hide it away. Samuel Pepys wrote his in code.

There are of course some diaries that were intended for posthumous publication, but the diaries of ordinary people are for their eyes only, a record, a therapy, a way of enjoying the moment – or enjoying it again, as they write it up.

A blog, on the other hand, is public the instant it is written. It is intended to be read by strangers as well as fans. It may well have its uses: publicity, information, sales, the logging of a voyage or a project... More often than not it is an expression of pure exhibitionism by the writer, though perhaps not so obviously egotistical and self-delusional as some of the social networking sites – and Twitter is that affliction taken to extremes. Anyone who wrote in a blog or on Facebook, say, what they would write in a diary, their intimate thoughts and observations perhaps on loved ones, even a record of their more shameful actions, must at the very least be an attention seeker, at worst very sick indeed.

The pleasure in writing a diary, however, is that you can be entirely free; you have no image to project, be it true, false or imaginary. You can be honest. You can be yourself. This does not exclude description, narrative, record, but you can also give vent to your emotions; you can confess your weaknesses, explore your doubts, investigate your failings and give yourself a pat on the back for a deed or job well done. You can say what you like as long as it is true.

If you were intending these same words for the blogging public or for posterity you might lie, omit or embellish. In a diary the incident is stripped bare, as is your soul. Your diary is the shell without which you would be utterly vulnerable.

You had your first diary when you were quite small, and you were determined to fill every page. Many days have one word, "school", written across them. Others: "play with Mice", which is how you spelled Mike, your friend's name. Often in those days of post-war rationing you recorded the meals you ate.

Then, when you were nine, a family friend who passed as an aunt gave you a five year diary with the challenge that she "bet you cannot keep this going for five years". Five years seemed a life time then, though now it rushes by as quickly as five weeks. You kept the diary going though, and when you had finished the aunt had disappeared or died. She never knew she had lost her bet.

You still have all your diaries in a chest. You will never re-read them and you suppose you will destroy them before you die. You do not want to experience again, let alone have anyone else read those pages of adolescent introspection, of fumbling encounters with the opposite sex, of moral and ethical dilemmas which would now seem laughable in our more enlightened times.

You squirm even to think what you wrote as a student, night after night, though no doubt your views would throw light on the social attitudes of the time towards race, religion and behaviour, politics and the arts. You have long ceased to believe that we are individually capable of original thought, so probably just as much could be gleaned from contemporary newspapers. You are but the product of your times.

As a writer it is tempting, however, to mine the diaries of a particular year for such local or period colour, but you never want to discover what kind of person you were. It is bad enough living with the person you have become.

There is one constant. You always have kept, and always will keep, a diary.

1.

On Keeping A Holiday Diary

Your parents used a box brownie to take black and white photographs of their two weeks a year at the seaside. Your own first camera was a Bakelite development of this, the Kodak Brownie 127. A roll of film stretched at most to a dozen photos. Later you took up 35mm photography and built a cumbersome library of transparencies, but this was expensive. A film took only 36 pictures. Prints were more expensive still and so early holiday photos are limited and precious, stored in bulky photo albums. Then came digital photography, and mobile phones that functioned as cameras. The value of the permanent image was devalued, if not lost for good, among such a promiscuous abundance of photos – if that is still the correct term for disposable e-snaps.

But you also have better pictures, better than any taken by traditional or digital cameras; pictures that cannot fade or get deleted – for you have always kept a holiday diary.

Looking at an old-fashioned, two-dimensional snapshot you might laugh at the clothes and the hair styles, wonder at how young your parents looked, admire the old cars or struggle to remember the time and place of a pose. Names of beaches, villages, whole cities are lost to your memory. Years later you do not easily recall the names of other people either, hosts, friends or lovers, who occupy the frame.

In your diaries you may not often have described appearances, fashion per se has never been important to you, but occasionally you did try to capture the likeness of a person or describe a scene particularly significant in that moment. These sketches you now treasure. Your diary evokes, better than a physical picture, the feel of a place: the sound of the sheep's bells in the Norwegian mountains; the scent of a French bakery with that mix of distinctive disinfectant from the floor and the chocolaty aroma coming from the jar of *Caram'bars* when the heavy glass lid is lifted; the oppressive humidity you first encounter in the tropics as you step out of the dehydration of the aircraft and swim across the tarmac like a fish in a tank – an almost liquid envelope in which you will live and work until you reboard the plane, but an ambiance that appears in none of the photos except perhaps for a dampening darkness of clothes around the waist, across the chest and beneath the armpits. Still in the tropics, in the remotest depths of an African forest that looks pristine in the photo, your diary records the awful, tearing scream of the illegal chainsaw felling another distant tree.

Your diary will also have captured other sounds, perhaps in that same forest at night, or perhaps the total lack of sound: the silence of the Norwegian *vidda* broken only by the regular sliding of your cross-country skis uphill, or the uninterrupted scraping on the downhill slopes. Occasionally you have recorded meals, or attempted to capture the taste of a particular mango after a thirsty drive; the pleasure of that first swig of cold beer on returning from a trek.

But a diary is not simply a record of the five senses. It records also the hundred moods of the traveller, the dejection and the elation, the occasional boredom, the irritation with a spouse or a child. Anticipation, excitement; the misery of four days of migraine or an incapacitating bout of Delhi belly.

These diaries are certainly not literary works. They tell no story, merely note down scenes that take your fancy – mostly fleeting moments or incidents, the occasional anecdote perhaps. Sometimes you are as elaborate as a painter trying to fix a particularly striking scene, sometimes you simply list the places visited that day, that month, that year; or the things you might have bought on Tuesday, the cost of a meal on Wednesday night, or a tank of petrol on the way home.

Sometimes this is useful as a reference tool months or years later, to settle an argument about whether you saw minke or finn whales, or – wasn't it humpback that you watched blowing bubbles and breaching through a shoal of fish?

Sometimes, as a writer, you refer to your dairies for conversations recorded to capture the speech habits of East

Coast waitresses, Australian farmers or African politicians. Some incidents you might take as written, fresh in their emotion and immediacy, and incorporate them into a story.

On the other hand, you still have a vivid three page account of a near shipwreck of the coast of Lanzarote written the same day, and for which years later you still have to invent a tale that would do it justice. Like so many other episodes, this one has remained buried. Only by browsing through the diary years later do you chance upon it with pleasure, having forgotten, if not the event, certainly the details.

The fundamental difference, however, between the holiday photos and the diary is that the albums show how much you have changed, and the diaries how little. Re-reading them is a pleasure tinged perhaps with shame and guilt; and very, very secret.

2.

The Morning Post

A striking feature of Wilkie Collins' 1860 novel *The Woman in White* is the absolute reliability of the Royal Mail, depending as it did on a fast and regular rail service. Overnight letters fly back and forth between Cumberland and London without anyone doubting they would arrive by first post the next day. On one occasion Laura is at Blackwater Park in the north and requires an immediate response from her London solicitor. She writes to him on Day One beseeching him to send his reply on the 11 o'clock train the next morning. By 2 pm on Day Two she has received her reply, delivered to her home. The Victorians hardly needed email.

Today few of us still write letters by hand. Email is cheaper, easier and informal. Even so, however immediate, there is no guarantee anyone will open your message, or if they do they may not look at it the same day. For domestic purposes within these shores a First Class letter, though an expensive luxury, will probably be just as quickly read and, being more personal, better appreciated.

Although less and less correspondence arrives by "snail mail", you still await the sound of the red Post van in the lane, the click of the latch on your garden gate and the thump of letters on the mat. Much of the delivery comprises junk mail: catalogues, holiday brochures, and whole forests of offers from the ever optimistic *Readers' Digest*, but there is enough of a personal nature most mornings to give you a pleasurable sense of anticipation that your less charismatic electronic mail box fails to rouse.

It may be the memories of letters past, letters from the days of first post, second post – and in the village where you lived there was also an afternoon post that came at tea time. Now that there is only one daily delivery it seems unpredictably to fill all or any of these time slots, carrying with it past associations.

One quality of real mail is that it is more individual and therefore more personal. For a start, the envelopes come in all shapes and sizes and are easy to sort at a glance. Not all are welcome, but even some of the business ones are informative: utilities bills, credit and bank accounts, invoices... some of these formal envelopes might even contain a pleasant surprise: a £50 win on the premium bonds, a rebate from the Inland Revenue, or a windfall from an insurance company.

Most welcome of all are those written and addressed by hand. In some cases this is handwriting you have known all your life. Like a voice, the writing of a relative, a lover or a friend is instantly recognisable. Like a voice, too, the handwriting may become quivery and shaky with age, but the character is not lost. You have sometimes noticed that children and grandchildren inherit the handwriting of their parents as they do their looks, their voices and other mannerisms.

Seasoning the pleasurable anticipation of the morning post is a certain clinging dread. Bad news usually travels fast and will have arrived by telephone or by a policeman at the door. Sometimes, though, you tear open a daughter's or a parent's letter to be sure that everything is all right.

Your real dread stems from the vestiges of a fifteen year barrage of threats and admonitions from a neurotic ex-wife. Her letters have long stopped, but the poison hangs in the otherwise pleasantly scented miasma wafted in on the post. In your mind's eye you still see your address on the envelope, big and brazen, written in whatever the demented woman had to hand: pen, biro, pencil, crayon, felt tip, lipstick. And on the reverse, every second word underlined three times, her afterthoughts or second thoughts or third thoughts scrawled across the paper for all to see.

Inside it was always worse, saccharine sweet but sprinkled with accusation, menace and demands. The woman who stole your children continued for twenty years to steal what little peace of mind she had left you.

But the bitter increases the sweet, and over the years you have received many more pleasant than unpleasant letters, and still expect to do so: your Godmother, who for half a century has never forgotten you on your birthday or at Christmas; birthdays and Christmases themselves, when old friends and far flung family still send cards written and addressed in their own hand, often with unintentionally hilarious accounts of their doings over the year. Then there is the daughter who is predictably early, and the son who is always a week late. The joy is that they remember you at all.

Fairly often it is your own handwriting you recognise on the A5 envelopes that drop onto the mat. Though most of your literary correspondence takes place now by email, there are still those small journals and publishers, those competitions, that require one or more printed copies of your manuscripts. Ninety percent of these are returned; your working life is one long and regular rejection, but it is just this that adds spice, because once in a while a contract, a cheque or an acknowledgement arrives. Three lines of appreciation, one or more noughts on a cheque or a letter forwarded from someone who has enjoyed something you have written; any of these communications wipes out a score of rejections, if not the cost of your initial postage.

The clatter of the flap, the tumble of falling mail, carry resonances also of other acceptances and rejections – of exam results and university acceptance, of job interviews and ensuing results, of hospital admissions and of medical reports condemning you to life.

Despite technological change, the volume of mail and with it the promise of some life-changing decision, event or visit still fills your morning with a familiar *frisson*. You cannot go out until the morning post has arrived, with all of life's disappointments... and sometimes with a few of its rewards.

3.

Hello, It's Me...

A nd you know it is. You know *who* it is. Probably the 'hello' alone, whether spoken in the next street or from the furthest continent, clear or down a crackling phone line, is enough to reveal the identity of the caller.

Hello, it's me. Wherein lies the clue?

We all have an accent, particularly in England; an accent that betrays our social class or aspirations, our regional origins, even sometimes the countries or counties we have resided in for long periods – a different mother tongue even... but in the landscape of the voice these traces form only the background scenery; we all, too, have an idiolect, our individual manner of speaking. After all other features have been taken into account, this is the recipe that makes our speech our own, gives it a special flavour.

Yes, it contains accent, vocabulary, syntax, our unique way of expressing ourselves; but when you hear *Hello, it's me*, it is the tone and timbre of the voice that you recognise. Your voice is your oral fingerprint, your iris, your spectrum of sound. It is just as possible to be turned off by a voice as it is to fall in love with one.

Hello, it's me offers the briefest of pleasures. The rest of the call is far less important. What matters is that your lover, your child, your friend or your colleague has called and that you have immediately recognised him or her.

Hello, it's me. What follows may not be a pleasure. It may be a call for help, a distress signal; it may be disappointing news or simply a time-wasting chat. On the other hand it may be a huge relief. The missing child that has finally made contact; your mother to say that everything is all right now; a colleague to say your project has been accepted.

Hello, it's me may be practical information. *I'm on the train and am arriving at Etchingham at 19:11.*

It may be good news. *I've passed my exams, I'm getting married, Julia has had twins and mother and babies are all doing well.*

It may be a welcome inquiry. *Are you free to come to the theatre next Thursday? Stay for the weekend? Would you like to come on holiday with us?*

Hello, it's me may be something more intimate. *Hello it's me. I just wanted to tell you I love you.*

Except sadly nowadays, more often than not, such messages are texted; and a printed or digital text is devoid of just those qualities that make the spoken voice so special.

END OF SAMPLE CHAPTERS

A LITTLE BOOK OF PLEASURES *is available from all good online stores, or better still, support your local brick-and-mortar bookshop by ordering through them!*

SUNPENNY PUBLISHING GROUP

ROSE & CROWN, BLUE JEANS, BOATHOOKS, SUNBERRY, CHRISTLIGHT, and EPTA Books

BOOKS FROM the SUNPENNY GROUP
www.sunpenny.com

SUNPENNY PUBLISHING GROUP

ROSE & CROWN, BLUE JEANS, BOATHOOKS, SUNBERRY, CHRISTLIGHT, and EPTA Books

COMING SOON FROM the SUNPENNY GROUP:
www.sunpenny.com

30 Days to Take-Off, by KC Lemmer
A Devil's Ransom, by Adele Jones
A Whisper on the Mediterranean, by Tonia Parronchi
Brandy Butter on Christmas Canal, by Shae O'Brien
Bridge to Xanadu, by Stephanie Parker McKean
Don't Pass Me By, by Julie McGowan
Greater than Gold, by Julianne Alcott
Heart of the Hobo, by Shae O'Brien
Hunter's Moon, by Karen Saayman
Moving On, by Jenny Piper
Redemption on the Red River, by Cheryl R Cain
Shadow of a Parasol, by Beth Holland
Summer Love, Winter Tears, by Carol Collins
The Harry Stories, by Stephen Nuttall
The Rose Flowered Cup, by Wendy Schonfeldt
There's a Chicken in my Doek, by Jacqueline Dowling
There's an Elephant in my Sink, by Stephen Nuttall

and 32 books by Bishop Dag Heward-Mills!